The Legislative Process in the European Community

AF710488

EUROPEAN MONOGRAPHS

Editor-in-Chief Prof. Dr. K.J.M. Mortelmans

1. Lammy Betten (ed.), *The Future of European Social Policy* (second and revised edition, 1991).

2. J.M.E. Loman, K.J.M. Mortelmans, H.H.G. Post, J.S. Watson, *Culture and Community Law: Before and after Maastricht* (1992).

3. Prof. Dr. J.A.E. Vervaele, *Fraud Against the Community: The Need for European Fraud Legislation* (1992).

The Legislative Process in the European Community

by Philip Raworth
Associate Professor in International Business and International Business Law, University of Alberta, Edmonton, Alberta, Canada

Kluwer Law and Taxation Publishers
Deventer – Boston – 1993

Kluwer Law and Taxation Publishers
P.O. Box 23 Tel. 31-5700-47261
7400 GA Deventer Telex. 49295
The Netherlands Fax. 31-5700-22244

Distribution in the USA and Canada
6 Bigelow Street Tel. 617-354-0140
Cambridge, MA 02139 Fax. 617-354-8595
USA

Library of Congress Cataloging-in-Publication Data

Raworth, Philip Marc, 1943-
The legislative process in the European Community / by Philip Raworth.
p. cm. (European monographs ; 4)
ISBN 9065446907
1. Legislation—European Economic Community countries.
2. Legislative power—European EconomicCommunity countries.
I. Title. II. Series.
KJE5349.R39
342.4'052—dc20
[344.0252] 93-7393
CIP

KJE
5349
.R39
1993

Cover design: Bert Arts

ISBN 90-6544-690-7

© 1993, Kluwer Law and Taxation Publishers
Deventer, The Netherlands

All rights reserved. No part of this publication may be reproduced, stored in a retrieval system, or transmitted in any form or by any means – electronic, mechanical, photocopying, recording or otherwise – without the prior written permission of the publisher.

Table of Contents

Acknowledgments

First and foremost, I should like to thank the Royal Bank of Canada for its generous fellowship that enabled me to spend sufficient time in Europe to complete the research for this book.

My thanks go as well to the English law firm of Linklaters and Paines, in whose Brussels office I worked and where this book was first started. I am much indebted to their patience and indulgence in granting me office facilities on my frequent visits to Brussels.

Lastly, but not least, I would like to thank my wife, Marie-Gabrielle, my children, Kristin, James and Pierre-Alexandre, and my step-children, Emilie and François for creating a home environment in which I was able and happy to work.

Chapter I. Introduction

1. THE EUROPEAN COMMUNITY AND EUROPEAN UNION

1.1. The European Community

The European Community comprises in fact three separate Communities, namely the European Coal and Steel Community (ECSC), the European Atomic Energy Community (EAEC) and the European Economic Community (EEC). The first two are restricted to the sectors to which they refer and are overshadowed in importance by the EEC. Nevertheless, the ECSC has the distinction of being the first Community, as it was founded in 1951 by the Treaty of Paris.[1] The other two were set up in 1957 by the Treaties of Rome.[2]

The European Community was initially given competence, on either an exclusive or partial basis, over the internal free market (free movement of goods, persons, services and capital), foreign trade relations, the common agricultural, fisheries and transport policies, competition policy, corporate law, social policy, taxation, economic and monetary policy, employment and vocational training, coal and steel and nuclear energy. This competence has greatly expanded over the years to embrace additional areas such as consumer protection, public health, education, intellectual property, energy, the environment, research and development, regional policy, telecommunications, and industrial policy. The authority for this considerable increase in the scope of the Community's legislative activity was found variously in the provisions on the free movement of goods,[3] the competition rules[4] the harmonization power[5] and, perhaps most significantly, in the residual power to act in order to attain the objectives of the three Communities.[6]

---

1. Treaty establishing the European Coal and Steel Community, (ECSC), 261 U.N.T.S. 140. Future references to treaties are designated by the abbreviations appearing in brackets in the initial citation.
2. Treaty establishing the European Economic Community, (EEC), 298 U.N.T.S. 11; Treaty establishing the European Atomic Energy Community, (EAEC), 298 U.N.T.S. 167.
3. Arts. 30-37 (EEC).
4. Arts. 85-94 (EEC).
5. Art. 100 (EEC).
6. Arts. 235 (EEC); 203 (EAEC); 95 (ECSC). At its meeting in Edinburgh on December 11-12, 1992, the European Council, while upholding this residual power, nevertheless indicated that the principle of subsidiarity requires that it no longer be used to circumvent express restrictions placed on Community action by specific Articles of the Treaties — *see* Annex 1 to Part A of the Conclusions of the Presidency, (*Edinburgh Summit Conclusions*), SN 456/92, footnote 1 on p. 5. *See also infra* at p. 5-6.

1.2. The Single European Act

The Single European Act (SEA), which was signed at Luxembourg and The Hague in 1986,[7] inaugurated the 1992 process aimed at completing the internal market by January 1, 1993[8] and established European Cooperation in the sphere of foreign policy.[9] It also introduced the Cooperation Procedure, which gave the European Parliament a greater role in the legislative process,[10] and expanded the use of qualified majority voting.[11] The SEA gave official recognition for the first time to the European Council.[12]

As far the legislative competence of the European Community was concerned, the SEA did not make radical changes. It set the stage for the evolution of the EEC towards an Economic and Monetary Union,[13] but otherwise it merely legitimized and clarified the Community's hitherto implicit authority in areas such as health and safety,[14] regional policy,[15] the environment,[16] consumer protection[17] and research and development.[18] Even the provision in the SEA on foreign policy cooperation reflects what had already become informal practice.

1.3. The Treaty on European Union

The Treaty on European Union (TEU),[19] which was signed at Maastricht on February 7, 1992, creates a European Union out of the three separate European Communities and changes the name of the European Economic Community to the European Community (EC).[20] It mirrors in some way the SEA in that it further reinforces the role of the European Parliament within the EC,[21] primarily through the Co-decision Procedure,[22] and confirms and clarifies the Community's assumption of competence over industrial policy, education, energy, public health and consumer protection.[23] Unlike the SEA, however, the TEU also significantly increases the jurisdiction of the

7. Single European Act, (SEA), OJ L 169/1987.
8. Arts. 8a (EEC); 13 (SEA).
9. Art. 30 (SEA).
10. Arts. 149 (EEC); 6, 7 (SEA). *See infra* at pp. 17-18 and pp. 39-40.
11. Arts. 28, 59, 84(2), 100a (EEC); 16, 18 (SEA).
12. Art. 2 (SEA).
13. Arts 102a (EEC); 20 (SEA).
14. Arts 118a (EEC); 21 (SEA).
15. Arts. 130a-130e (EEC); 23 (SEA).
16. Arts. 130r-130t (EEC); 25 (SEA).
17. Arts. 100a(3) (EEC); 18 (SEA).
18. Arts. 130f-130q (EEC); 24 (SEA).
19. [1992] 1 C.M.L.R. 573. The Treaty is published jointly by the Council and the Commission of the European Communities as ISBN 92-824-0959-7. It is popularly known as the Treaty of Maastricht.
20. **Art. G.A(1) (TEU)**. In future, references to the EEC Treaty as amended by the TEU are designated by the abbreviation (EC) and are in bold type. Corresponding references to the EAEC and ECSC Treaties will contain the word "Revised" before the normal designation and also be in bold type.
21. *See infra* in the text at p. 18 and p. 40-41.
22. **Art. 189b (EC).**
23. **Arts 3(l),(o),(p),(s),(t), 126, 129, 129a, 130l (EC).**

Union. It adds the issuing of visas to non-EC nationals, culture, civil protection, tourism and trans-European networks to the activities of the EC[24] and provides for the establishment of an Economic and Monetary Union by January 1, 1999,[25] which will include the adoption of a single European currency. Foreign policy cooperation under the SEA is replaced by a common foreign and security policy for the Union, and there are also provisions for cooperation in the fields of justice and home affairs.[26] Another important addition is a Union citizenship that gives EC nationals the right to live in any of the twelve Member States and to vote and stand there as candidates in both municipal and European elections.[27] All the Union's activities are to be conducted within the context of a single institutional framework.[28]

The TEU envisages further developments in the form of detailed provisions on energy, civil protection and tourism as well as a revision of the number of Commissioners and Members of the European Parliament (MEPs).[29] It also contemplates giving the EC competence over some justice and home affairs[30] and raises the possibility of a common defence policy.[31] In addition, the provisions contained in the Agreement on Social Policy will probably be incorporated into the EC Treaty, should the United Kingdom ever decide to adhere to the Agreement.[32] Considerable changes will also occur as the EC proceeds towards Economic and Monetary Union.

These changes are, however, likely to be the only ones in the foreseeable future. Judging from the national debates on its ratification, the TEU represents as far as the Member States are prepared or able to go at present along the road of European integration. The arrival of new members — first the applicants from the European Free Trade Association and then those from Eastern Europe — will pose enormous problems of adaptation that are likely to foreclose any other major changes. Thus, it is probable that, apart from the possibilities outlined above and some institutional streamlining, the European Union, if it comes into being, will remain in its Maastricht form well into the next century.

24. **Arts. 3(n),(p),(t), 100c, 128, 129b-129d (EC).**

25. This date is set out in **Article 109j(4) (EC)** and the **10th Protocol (TEU)**.

26. **Arts. J, K (TEU).**

27. **Arts. 8-8e (EC).** This is, however, all that Union citizenship bestows at present. As the Danish Government is at pains to point out in its Unilateral Declaration that is appended to the *Edinburgh Summit Conclusions* (Part B, p. 9b), "[n]othing in the Treaty on European Union implies or foresees an undertaking to create a citizenship of the Union in the sense of citizenship of a nation-state."

28. **Art. C (TEU).**

29. **1st, 15th Declarations (TEU)**, respectively. The European Council has now agreed to revise the number of MEPs and the seats allotted to Member States — *see* Part A, *Edinburgh Summit Conclusions*, p. 10a and *infra* at pp. 42-43.

30. **Art. K(9) (TEU).**

31. **Art. B (TEU).**

32. The Agreement on Social Policy is contained in the **14th Protocol (TEU)**. Originally, these provisions were intended to replace Articles 117 to 122 of the EEC Treaty, but the United Kingdom would not accept them. As a result, they are annexed to the EC Treaty in the form of an agreement binding the other eleven Member States.

1.4. The Legislative Activity of the European Union

The scope of the activities in which the European Union will be involved is very wide. Most of them, including those emanating from the Agreement on Social Policy, fall within the competence of the EC, whose already broad sphere of action is further increased by the TEU. The ECSC and the EAEC, on the other hand, remain restricted to coal and steel and nuclear energy, respectively. Responsibility for the common foreign and security policy as well as cooperation on justice and home affairs would be assigned directly to the Union.

It is important to note, however, that, like the Community before it, the Union will only have exclusive jurisdiction over certain matters. These are the internal free market, anti-competitive practices with a Community dimension, the common agricultural, fisheries, and transport policies, foreign trade relations and visas for third country nationals. Monetary policy will become an exclusive Union matter once the third stage of Economic and Monetary Union is reached. The Union will share responsibility with the Member States for social, regional, economic, industrial, environmental and foreign and security policies as well for coal and steel, nuclear energy, vocational training, consumer protection, trans-European networks and research and development. The Union will only play a very minor role in education, culture, public health and justice and home affairs.

Nevertheless, the Union, like the Community at present, will still be responsible for enacting a large and varied amount of legislation. Most of this will emanate as now from the EC[33] and the remainder from the ECSC and the EAEC, as the Union's direct responsibility for foreign, security, justice and home affairs does not really encompass a legislative role. This Union legislation, like the actual Community legislation, will either replace or supplement national laws in a wide array of areas and occupy a central place in the legal order of Europe. The manner in which it is enacted is thus an important issue as a constitutional phenomenon in its own right and as a means of understanding the forces at work in the European Union and, if necessary, how to influence them.

1.5. The Concept of Subsidiarity (Article 3b of the EC Treaty)

Despite the increase in the legislative competence of the Union that it brings about, the TEU nevertheless, by way of **Article 3b**, re-affirms existing limitations and introduces a new restriction on the Union's legislative activity. Even the Commission has its wings clipped and will be required to ensure that its proposals for legislation can be financed within the limits of the Community's own resources.[34] These provisions should ensure that, contrary to popular supposition, the TEU will actually reduce the legislative role of Brussels.

33. This includes legislation enacted pursuant to the Social Agreement, which does not, however, apply to the United Kingdom.

34 **Arts. 201a (EC); 173a (Revised EAEC).**

In the first place, **Article 3b** takes up two long-standing legal principles enunciated by the Court of Justice of the Communities, namely that the Community must act within the limits of the powers and objectives assigned to it by the Treaties[35] (the principle of "attribution of powers") and that its action must not go beyond what is needed to attain the objective pursued[36] (the principle of "proportionality"). These two principles are now enshrined in Treaty form and applied to all the legislative activities of the Union,[37] including those where it exercises an exclusive jurisdiction.[38] In addition, the European Council has set out certain guidelines for the application of the proportionality principle:[39]

— financial and administrative burdens in Member States should be minimized;
— as much scope as possible should be left for national action, and well-established national arrangements and legal procedures should be respected wherever possible;
— when setting standards, the Community should preferably establish minimum standards and leave Member States with the option of setting their own higher national standards;[40]
— other things being equal, directives should be preferred to regulations, and framework directives should be used instead of detailed measures;
— where appropriate and sufficient, the Community should content itself with encouraging cooperation between Member States, coordinating national action or complementing such action;[41]
— necessary Community action should not be extended to other Member States that are not affected by the problems that it addresses.

Although these principles of the attribution of powers and of proportionality are considered part of the overall concept of "subsidiarity", the principle of subsidiarity in its strict legal sense is set out separately in **Article 3b**. It requires that the Union, in areas that do not fall within its exclusive competence, only take action "if and in so far as the objectives of the proposed action cannot be sufficiently achieved by the Member States *and* can...be better achieved by the Community."[42] In its guidelines

35 **Art. 3b, 1st. paragraph (EC)** reads: "The Community shall act within the limits of the powers conferred upon it by this Treaty and of the objectives assigned to it therein". This principle was established by the Court of Justice, *inter alia*, in *Balkan-Import-Export GmbH* v. *Hauptzollamt Berlin-Packhof*, 5/73, [1973] E.C.R. 1091 at 1107-1109.

36 **Art. 3b, 3rd. paragraph (EC)** reads: "Any action by the Community shall not go beyond what is necessary to achieve the objectives of this Treaty." This principle was established by the Court of Justice, *inter alia*, in *Balkan-Import-Export GmbH* v. *Hauptzollamt Berlin-Packhof*, 5/73, [1973] E.C.R. 1091 at 1110-1112.

37 **Art. B (TEU)**.

38 *See Edinburgh Summit Conclusions*, Annex 1 to Part A, pp. 6-8.

39 *Edinburgh Summit Conclusions*, Annex 1 to Part A, pp. 8-9.

40 This is the approach adopted in Article 118a(3) (EEC) with respect to health and safety measures and in Article 130t (EEC) and **Articles 129a(3)** and **130t (EC)** with respect to consumer protection and environmental measures.

41 This is the approach that is mandated in the European Union for education, vocational training, culture, public health and industry — *see* **arts. 126, 127, 128, 129, 130 (EC)**.

42 **Art. 3b, 2nd. paragraph (EC)**. Emphasis added.

on the application of the principle of subsidiarity, the European Council stresses that both aspects of this principle must be met and sets out additional criteria for determining whether Community action is justified:[43]

— the issue being addressed must have transnational aspects and cannot be satisfactorily regulated by national action; and/or
— action by Member States alone or lack of Community action would impair the proper functioning of the Community or damage the interests of Member States; and/or
— the Council is satisfied that Community action will provide clear benefits by reason of its scale or effects compared with national action.

The principle of subsidiarity existed prior to the TEU, albeit merely in embryonic or implicit form,[44] but the TEU imposes it for the first time as a comprehensive limitation on the legislative activity of the Union.[45] In addition, the principle is reflected in certain individual Articles of the EC Treaty and the TEU.[46] The European Council has indicated furthermore that the residual power under the various treaties cannot be used to circumvent such specific limitations on Community action.[47]

The limitations placed by **Article 3b** on the Community's legislative competence are quite considerable, and they have led to the withdrawal or revision by the Commission of a number of existing proposals and pieces of legislation as well as the abandonment of certain planned initiatives.[48] A final report on its review of the compatibility of existing legislation with **Article 3b** is due from the Commission in December 1993.

However, the European Council was also careful at Edinburgh to circumscribe the scope of application of **Article 3b**.[49] It does not call into question the Commission's right of initiative or any of the powers that are conferred on the Union by the Treaties. It does not affect the primacy of Community law or the scope of the *acquis communautaire,* nor does it prevent the use of the residual powers that are granted to the three Communities as well as to the Union itself[50] as long as they are exercised in accordance with overall concept of subsidiarity. Member States cannot avail themselves of **Article 3b** in order to avoid fulfilling their obligations under the Treaties. Where the Community is under an obligation to act, for example in order to enforce Community law or to apply its competition rules, the Article does not apply.

With respect to the principle of subsidiarity in its strict sense, the European Council also stresses that, under **Article 3b**, it only applies where the issue in ques-

43 *Edinburgh Summit Conclusions*, Annex 1 to Part A, pp. 6-7.

44 *See e.g.* art. 130t(4) (EEC) with respect to environmental measures.

45 By virtue of **Article B (TEU)**, **Article 3b (EC)** applies to all the activities of the Union.

46 *See* **arts 126, 127, 128, 129, 129a, 129b, 130, 130g (EC); K.3(2)(b) (TEU)**; **2 (Social Agreement)**. *See* Tables 1-3 for the subject matter covered by these Articles.

47 *See* fnn. 6, 50.

48 *Edinburgh Summit Conclusions*, Annex 2 to Part A.

49 *Edinburgh Summit Conclusions*, Annex 1 to Part A, pp. 3-5, 10.

50 These residual powers are set out in Articles 235 (EEC); 203 (EAEC); 95 (ECSC); **F(3) (TEU)**. But *see* fn. 6.

tion does not fall within the exclusive competence of the Union. It is not clear how this restriction fits in with the requirement in **Article A (TEU)** that decisions ought to be taken in all matters "as closely as possible to the citizen," which provision would seem to echo the subsidiarity principle and apply it without any limitation of scope similar to that contained in **Article 3b**. However, **Article A** may well just anticipate the concept of subsidiarity and have itself no substantive effect.

1.6. The Ratification of the Treaty on European Union

The TEU was supposed to go into effect on January 1, 1993,[51] but this needed all Member States to ratify it,[52] which did not happen as Denmark and the United Kingdom failed to do so. The Edinburgh meeting of the European Council resulted in an agreement to allow Denmark to opt out of the third stage of Economic and Monetary Union as well any Union measures that have defence implications.[53] This concession, together with the elaboration of the concept of subsidiarity, was intended to pave the way for Danish and British ratification of the TEU during 1993. Certainly, all the leaders at the Edinburgh meeting, including the Prime Minsters of Denmark and the United Kingdom, re-affirmed their commitment to the TEU.[54]

If Denmark or Britain still fail to ratify the TEU, it is unlikely that any further inducements will be offered by the other Member States to secure their adherence to the Treaty. Instead, the Treaty will be abandoned or, more likely, a two-tier Community will emerge that will permit the application of the TEU by those Member States who have ratified it.

In either case, the Treaty's institutional reforms will probably survive and be applied generally. If the TEU is abandoned, the Community will continue, under the original Treaties and the SEA, to enact legislation over a wide range of subjects. Thus, the loss of authority by the national parliaments and the democratic deficit within the Community will still be issues that must be confronted, and the solutions offered by the TEU through its reinforcement of Parliament's role, the principle of subsidiarity and the democratization of the Commission would remain relevant. Moreover, it is not these parts of the Treaty that are controversial. On the contrary, it would seem from the ratification debates that many critics of the TEU do not appreciate the extent to which it reforms the undemocratic system established by the original Treaties and perpetuated by the SEA. For this reason, it is likely that, in a two-tier Community, a non-ratifying Denmark or United Kingdom would apply at least the institutional provisions of the TEU.

However, if the TEU is not ratified, it will not be possible officially to apply its institutional provisions. Nor could the Member States single them out for application by an official and binding Community act to this effect, as the Court of Justice has

51 **Art. R(2) (TEU)**.

52 Arts. 236 (EEC); 204 (EAEC); 96 (ECSC); **R(2) (TEU)**.

53 Decision of the Heads of State and Government, meeting within the European Council, concerning certain problems raised by Denmark on the Treaty of European Union, *Edinburgh Summit Conclusions*, Part B, p. 4b.

54 *Edinburgh Summit Conclusions*, Part A, p. 2a.

ruled that "the essential elements of the Community structure as regards both the prerogatives of the institutions and the position of the Member States vis-à-vis one another" cannot be changed in this way.[55]

Pending negotiation of a new Treaty, a simple interim solution would be an informal agreement on the application of the TEU's institutional reforms.[56] This could take the form of a resolution or declaration by the Council, the Commission and the European Parliament under which they undertake to exercise their powers in accordance with the relevant provisions of the TEU. The conciliation procedure is applied by virtue of such an act,[57] and the European Council has called for a similar inter-institutional agreement on the effective application of **Article 3b (EC)**.[58] Moreover, the Court of Justice not only accepts the validity of such arrangements but has indicated that they may even create legal obligations as between the institutions involved.[59] Alternatively, the Representatives of the Governments of the Member States meeting within the Council could make a non-binding policy agreement to apply certain provisions of the TEU in the same way as they agreed under the 1966 Luxembourg Accords that the Council should act by unanimity whenever possible. Wherever the Member States are concerned directly, as with the appointment of the Commission, this latter procedure would have to be used. Otherwise, an inter-institutional agreement is probably the simplest and most effective solution. Under either procedure, the resulting arrangement would become part of the *acquis communautaire*, which new Member States would have to respect and apply.

All this means that, despite the uncertainty surrounding the entry into force of the TEU, we must take into account its provisions when discussing the legislative process in the European Community. At the same time, the form and way in which they may be applied is not yet completely clear. To deal with this ambivalent situation, we distinguish carefully in the text between the present procedures and those that are introduced by the TEU. Unless the contrary is stated, it is, however, to be assumed that there is no difference. Likewise, references to the EEC and the EEC Treaty include the EC and the EC Treaty unless there are discrepancies between the two. In the latter case, the terms EC and EC Treaty are used to refer to the amended Community set up by the TEU.[60] Treaty citations give both the original articles and the TEU's revisions and addenda. The latter are in bold type to alert readers to the fact that they may not yet be legally binding.

---

55 *Opinion 1/76 on the draft agreement establishing a European laying-up fund for inland waterway vessels*, [1977] E.C.R. 741 at 758.

56 These types of agreements are discussed in P.J.G. Kapteyn and P. Verloren van Themaat (ed. L.W. Gormley), *Introduction to the Law of the European Communities*, 2nd. ed., Deventer, 1989, at pp. 185-188 and pp. 205-206.

57 Joint Declaration of the European Parliament, the Council and the Commission on the conciliation procedure, OJ C 89/1975.

58 *Edinburgh Summit Conclusions*, Part A, p. 3a, Annex 1 to Part A, pp. 3-4.

59 *See Andersen et al* v. *European Parliament*, 260/80, [1984] E.C.R. 177 at 193 and 262/80, [1984] E.C.R. 195 at 207-208.

60 *See also* fn. 20.

1.7. What's in a Name?

Prior to the TEU, the official name for the association of the twelve Member States was the *European Communities*. If the three Communities are subsumed into a *European Union*, it would seem logical to assume that the latter term will become the official name. This may not, however, be the case. The official gazette of the association will retain the title of *Official Journal of the European Communities*, and the Council and Commission, despite their status as part of the single institutional framework of the Union, will still be called the Council and the Commission of the *European Communities*. It is also noteworthy that the TEU speaks only of the Union being "founded on the European Communities,"[61] while the Commission's draft spoke of it replacing them.[62] In the published record of its proceedings at Edinburgh, the European Council contributes to the uncertainty by using the term "Community" when it is clearly referring to the "Union".

This confusion over the name of the association is not new. In its early days, it was popularly known as the *Common Market*, which it was not yet, or as the *EEC*, which was only one of its three component parts, albeit by far the most important. As the success of the 1992 initiative began to weld the association into a genuine Community, the popular name became the *European Community* (used mainly by non-Europeans) or the *Community* (used mainly by Europeans). These names are still commonly used, but the advent of the European Union should encourage the tendency to refer to the association quite simply as *Europe*.

Given the uncertain fate of the European Union and the fact that almost all legislation is enacted under the auspices of the three Communities, we have chosen in this study to stick with the popular terms *Community* and *European Community*. The former is perhaps preferable as the latter may become the new name of the *European Economic Community* and its use could lead to confusion. The terms *European Union* or *Union* will only be used where it is necessary to single out the expanded association set up by the TEU.

2. LEGISLATIVE POWER AND THE COMMUNITY

2.1. Nature of Legislative Power

Legislative power is either primary or subordinate. Primary legislative power is a universal prescriptive authority that in most nation States is vested in the legislature. It entails the right to enact for all domains of human activity rules of any type or scope, subject in some States, however, to constitutional limitations designed to protect the rights of citizens or the division of power in a federal State. Primary legislation may address specific situations or persons, but more often it applies generally to everyone that comes within its scope.

Subordinate legislation implements or applies primary legislation. Subordinate implementing power is prescriptive in that it creates new rules, but, as these cannot

61. **Art. A (TEU).**
62. Art. B. The draft is published in *Europe*, Nr. 1715, May 31, 1991.

alter or exceed the primary rules which they implement, the subordinate prescriptive power is a limited one. Like primary legislation, subordinate implementing rules normally have general application.

The subordinate application of primary legislation does not involve making any new rules but rather applying those that already exist on a specific or general basis. This type of subordinate activity does not always take the form of legislation. The application of primary rules to specific situations or persons is frequently effected by executive decisions. Even the general application of legislation, which involves setting out the obligations and rights flowing from primary rules, may take the form of an administrative communication rather than a legislative act.

In nation States, subordinate legislative power is vested either in the Government to be exercised by Ministers or their officials or in special bodies set up for the purpose. Subordinate legislative power can only be granted by the primary legislative authority, which may, however, in some instances permit subdelegation. A body that acts pursuant to subdelegation can be said to be enacting "tertiary" legislation, as opposed to the "secondary" legislation of direct delegates of the primary authority. This tertiary legislation normally serves to implement or apply secondary rules.

2.2. Division of Legislative Power in the Community

The primary legislation of the Community consists of the various Treaties on which it is based. The most important of these are the Treaty of Paris (1951) setting up the ECSC, the two Treaties of Rome (1957) setting up the EEC and the EAEC, the various Accession Treaties, the Merger Treaty (MT) (1965) and the SEA (1986).[63] The TEU (1992) forms the additional part of the primary legislation of the European Union.

Any amendments to these Treaties, either to the original ones or the TEU, must be ratified by the Member States in accordance with their respective constitutional arrangements.[64] The Member States also have to ratify changes to the system for electing MEPs and the provisions on a system of own resources for the EEC as well as modifications to the TEU articles on Union citizenship and any proposal to bring justice and home affairs under the jurisdiction of the EC.[65] Although there are some minor changes that the Community is able to effect on its own,[66] it is essentially the Member States and not the Community institutions that possess the universal prescriptive authority within both the Community and the European Union.

63. Act concerning the Conditions of Accession and the Adjustments to the Treaties — Accession to the European Communities of the Kingdom of Denmark, Ireland and the United Kingdom, OJ L 73/1972; Act concerning the Conditions of Accession and the Adjustments to the Treaties — Accession to the European Communities of the Hellenic Republic, OJ L 291/1979; Act concerning the Conditions of Accession and the Adjustments to the Treaties — Accession to the European Communities of the Kingdom of Spain and the Portuguese Republic, OJ L 302/1985; Treaty establishing a Single Council and a Single Commission of the European Communities, (MT), OJ 152/1967. Citations for the other Treaties are given *supra* in the footnotes.

64. Arts. 236 (EEC); 204 (EAEC); 96 (ECSC); **N(1) (TEU)**.

65. *See* arts. 138(3), 201 (EEC); 108(3) (EAEC); 21(3) (ECSC); **8(e) (EC); K(9) (TEU)**.

66. *See* arts. 76, 90 (EAEC); **104c(14) (EC)**. Tables 1-3 indicate the subject matter of the legislation enacted pursuant to these Articles.

Subordinate legislative power is vested by the Community Treaties in the Council and the Commission, which since 1966 have operated as single institutions serving all three Communities.[67] Although the Council has the more important legislative role, at least in the EEC and EAEC, there is no inherent superiority in its legislative authority.[68] The Commission, like the Council, may in principle enact both general and prescriptive legislation.[69] Under the TEU, the European Parliament shares in the legislative power of the Council in the EC.[70]

Under the EEC Treaty, which is a framework treaty requiring extensive implementation, it is the Council, acting alone or, in the EC, jointly with Parliament, that is the predominant implementing body. It enjoys quite wide discretion in fulfilling this task.[71] The Council has a similar implementing role under the EAEC Treaty, but here its discretion is less because of the more detailed nature of the Treaty's provisions. Both the EEC and EAEC Treaties bestow on the Council the residual implementing power to enact whatever additional measures are necessary to attain the objectives of the two Communities.[72]

The Commission's implementing power under the EEC Treaty is restricted both in scope and the level of discretion it is accorded.[73] The only broad power it enjoys is under Article 48(3)(d), which permits the Commission to set down the conditions subject to which Community nationals can remain in another Member State after having been employed there. In practice, however, the Commission's regulations follow closely the Council's implementing legislation in this field.[74] Under the EAEC Treaty, the Commission's powers are restricted to setting up research and educational facilities.[75]

Both the EEC and EAEC Treaties do, however, grant the Commission a general power to enact tertiary legislation further implementing rules laid down in secondary implementing legislation enacted by the Council alone or jointly with Parliament. The grant of this power is implicit in Articles 155 (4th indent) and 124 (4th indent) of the two Treaties, respectively. The SEA amended Article 145 of the EEC Treaty to give the Council explicit authority to delegate tertiary implementing powers to the Commission,[76] but no equivalent amendment was made to the EAEC Treaty. This does not mean, however, that the Commission's powers are any less under the EAEC Treaty as the Court of Justice of the European Communities has consistently

67. Arts. 1, 9 (MT).
68. *See* arts. 189 (EEC); 161 (EAEC). The equivalent Article in the ECSC Treaty (art. 14) refers only to the Commission, thus underlining the Commission's legislative predominance in that Community — *see infra* at p. 12.
69. *See France, Italy and United Kingdom* v. *Commission*, 188—190/80, [1982] E.C.R. 2545 at 2572-2573.
70. **Art. 189b (EC).**
71. *See*, for example, its powers in the fields of agriculture and transport — arts. 43(2) and 75 (EEC), respectively.
72. Arts. 235 (EEC); 203(EAEC). But *see* fn. 6.
73. *See* arts. 33(7), 45(2) (EEC).
74. *Compare* Commission Regulation 1251/70 (OJ L 142/1970) with Council Directive 68/360 (OJ L 257/1968) and Council Regulation 1612/68 (OJ L 257/1968).
75. Arts. 8, 9 (EAEC).
76. Art. 10 (SEA).

affirmed the Council's implicit authority to sub-delegate.[77] In fact, the amendment serves to incorporate into the EEC Treaty the jurisprudence of the Court.

Under the ECSC Treaty, it is the Commission that is the main implementing body. Significantly, Article 8 of the Treaty sets out the Commission's role in the European Coal and Steel Community in the same words that Article 145 of the EEC Treaty employs for the Council. The Council has, however, the implementing power with respect to particularly sensitive matters,[78] and it must endorse implementing legislation of the Commission where the importance of the subject matter requires its involvement.[79] The Council also has the responsibility to act where the Commission fails to do so.[80] The residual implementing power that the other two Treaties bestow on the Council is also exercised by the Commission under the ECSC Treaty, albeit subject to the unanimous consent of the Council.[81] This predominance of the Commission is due partly to the nature of the ECSC Treaty, which is very detailed and leaves less discretion to the implementing authority, and partly to the more supranational character of the Coal and Steel Community.

Like other subordinate legislative bodies, the Community institutions must remain within the limits of their authority when enacting their implementing legislation.[82] This requirement has been particularly closely scrutinized in the case of the Commission when it enacts tertiary legislation implementing Council rules.[83] Nevertheless, the Council, acting alone or, in the EC, jointly with Parliament, may grant the Commission a considerable margin of discretion as long as this does not include the power to set rules that go beyond the "essential general aims" laid down by the Council.[84]

The application of primary Community law involves the enforcement of the rules of the Treaties, the granting of derogations and the administration of the various safeguard provisions.[85] As a general principle, this task is the responsibility of the Commission,[86] but the Council is also involved in many instances. It administers, for example, a number of derogations and safeguard provisions under both the EEC and EC Treaties,[87] and it will become responsible for the EC's economic guidelines

77. *See ACF Chemiefarma* v. *Commission* , 41/69, [1970] E.C.R. 661 at 688; *Rey Soda* v. *Cassa Conguaglio Zucchero* , 23/75, [1975] E.C.R. 1279 at 1300-1301.

78. *See* arts. 58(3), 59(2), 72 (ECSC). The Commission enjoys a tertiary implementing power with respect to these matters, which it derives either from its general power under Article 8 or from a specific provision, such as Article 59(2) (ECSC).

79. *See* arts. 53(b), 58(1), 59(5) (ECSC).

80. *See* arts. 58(1), 59(5), 59(6), 61(c), 95 (ECSC).

81. Art. 95 (ECSC).

82. **Art. 3b, first paragraph (EC)**. This is the principle of the attribution of powers that makes up part of the concept of subsidiarity. *See infra* at pp. 4-6.

83. *See Rey Soda* , 23/75, at 1302-1303.

84. *Association générale des producteurs de blé et autres céréales (AGPB)* v. *Office national interprofessionel des céréales (ONIC)*, 167/88, [1991] 2 C.M.L.R. 61 at 82. *See also Rey Soda*, 23/75, at 1301 and 1303. Where the Commission does exceed these "essential general aims", the act in question will be declared void — *see Handelsonderneming Vreugdenhil B.V.* v. *Minister van Landbouw en Visserij*, 22/88, [1991] 2 C.M.L.R. 461.

85. **Article 3b (EC)** does not apply to the application of Community law — *see infra* at pp. 5-6.

86. *See* arts. 155 (EEC); 124 (EAEC). The Commission's wide powers under Article 8 of the ECSC Treaty also include the authority to apply the Treaty rules.

and government deficit rules.[88] The Commission has general responsibility for the tertiary application of the Council's implementing rules[89] and specific authority to administer the latter's rules on transport, competition and derogations from the technical harmonization measures enacted under Article 100A of the EEC Treaty.[90]

In applying both primary and secondary Community law, the Community institutions often act by way of administrative decisions or by issuing a legislative act directed at a specific recipient. At the same time, however, both the Council and the Commission are empowered to apply Community law by enacting legislation of general application.[91] They also have specific authority to do this for certain matters, such as the enactment of block exemptions from the competition rules by the Commission[92] and the application of the Treaty rules on state aids by the Council.[93]

The Commission's general legislative power is strictly declaratory in this instance and cannot be used to create new rules. In *France* v. *Commission*, Advocate-General Tesauro questioned the Commission's right to enact Directive 88/301[94] on this ground, suggesting that the legislation did create new rules and thus went beyond the Commission's power under Article 90(3) to enact directives on the *application* of EEC Treaty rules to public and privileged undertakings.[95] The Court of Justice followed the Advocate-General's reasoning and ruled that paragraph 3 of Article 90 restricts the Commission to setting out in legislative form the obligations and rights flowing from paragraphs 1 and 2 of the Article.[96] Directive 88/301 is thus valid only to the extent that it does not exceed this declaratory authority.[97]

The application of Community law also involves the very important task of ensuring that Member States implement Community directives and enforce all directly applicable Community laws.[98] This is primarily the Commission's responsibility, and under the EEC and EAEC Treaties it is given the right to bring recalcitrant Member States before the Court of Justice.[99] Where the Commission fails to act, Member States can bring each other directly before the Court.[100] Over a thousand

87. *See* arts. 100a(5), 108(2) (EEC); **8b(1),(2), 73c(2), 73f, 100c(2), 103a(1) (2), 109h(2), 130s(5) (EC)**. In some instances, however, the Council's authority is limited to amending or revoking decisions of the Commission or the Member States — *see* arts. 108(3), 109(3) (EEC); **109h(3), 109i(3) (EC)**.
88. **Arts. 103(4), 104c (EC)**.
89. Arts. 155 (EEC); 124 (EAEC). A similar authority is implicit in Article 8 (ECSC).
90. *See* arts. 79(4), 87, 100A(5) (EEC), respectively.
91. For the Commission, this power is inherent in Articles 155 (EEC); 124 (EAEC). A similar authority is implicit in Article 8 (ECSC). The Council's authority is inherent in Article 145 (EEC), although the equivalent provisions of the ECSC and EAEC Treaties are less clear — *see* arts. 26 (ECSC); 115 (EAEC).
92. Art. 89(1) (EEC).
93. Art. 94 (EEC).
94. OJ L 131/1988. This Directive opens up the telecommunications terminal equipment market.
95. Case 202/88, pt. 54 (of the official court transcript).
96. Case 202/88, pt. 21.
97. The same is true of Commission Directive 90/388 (OJ L 192/1990) on competition in the telecommunications services market, which was also enacted by the Commission pursuant to Article 90(3) (EEC).
98. *See infra* at pp. 16-17 for a discussion of the Community's legal acts.
99. Arts. 169 (EEC); 141 (EAEC).

cases are examined each year by the Commission. The great majority of these are settled through informal discussions, but over a hundred usually lead to the opening by the Commission of formal infringement proceedings. Normally, the offending Member State rectifies the situation upon receiving the Commission's reasoned opinion as to what it should do. A few matters nevertheless come before the Court of Justice. Member States rarely refuse to comply with the ensuing judgment, although some take longer than others to implement the Court's ruling. One example of non-compliance, which caused particularly bad feelings between two Member States, was France's refusal to lift its ban on British lamb imports as required by the Court's ruling in Case 61/81, [1982] E.C.R. 2601. The TEU addresses this problem for the first time; it provides that, where a Member State does not comply with a finding by the Court that it has failed to apply Community law properly, the Commission may ask the Court to fine that State.[101]

2.3. Preeminence of Council Legislation

The Commission's legislative powers are more akin to the subordinate legislative authority that is often enjoyed by national Governments. That is to say, they are exercised within relatively strict parameters set by the enabling legislation, whether this be the Treaties or acts of the Council. The Commission's secondary implementing authority is limited both in scope and discretion. Even under the ECSC Treaty, where its powers are more extensive, the Commission acts pursuant to quite detailed Treaty provisions and in important matters it must seek the assent of the Council. The Commission's tertiary implementing authority may be wider in scope, but its decisions have to be referred to the Council where they differ from those of a management or regulatory committee.[102] It also has to remain within the basic principles set by the Council, whose secondary legislation it is implementing. Finally, when the Commission applies Community law by a general legislative act, it must be careful to state only the obligations and rights flowing from the law; it cannot create any new rules.

By contrast, the Council, acting alone or, in the EC, jointly with the European Parliament, wields what has become in effect a primary legislative power. Theoretically, this power still belongs to the Member States, who are solely responsible for enacting the Treaties pursuant to which the Council legislates. However, although the Council must remain within the parameters of these Treaties when enacting its secondary legislation, the scope of the Community's legislative competence has been so widened that it now resembles a federal area of jurisdiction akin to section 91 of the 1867 Canadian Constitution Act.[103] It should be noted that the TEU

100. Arts. 170 (EEC); 142 (EAEC). Such actions are rare, but one example is *France* v. *United Kingdom*, 141/78, [1979] E.C.R. 2923.

101. **Arts. 171 (EC); 143 (Revised EAEC)**. This particular revision does not extend to the ECSC Treaty.

102. *See infra* at pp. 112-114.

adds to this development but is not responsible for it.

The focus of this study is on the general legislation of the Community, most of which is enacted by the Council, acting alone or, in the EC, jointly with Parliament. The legislative procedures of the Council are thus given pride of place. The Commission nevertheless does issue legislation of general application, some of which is even prescriptive in nature, and for this reason a brief description of its legislative procedure is included at the end of this study.

The third stage of Economic and Monetary Union is not scheduled to start until at least 1997 and may well be delayed until 1999. For this reason, the study only considers the legislative process as it is now and will become during the second stage, which is due to start on January 1, 1994 if the TEU is ratified.[104]

3. THE LEGISLATIVE PROCESS OF THE COMMUNITY— AN OVERVIEW

3.1. The Institutions

Community legislation is enacted by the Council, the Commission or jointly by the Council and the European Parliament,[105] although the Parliament's legislative function will be restricted to the EC. Later, in the third stage of Economic and Monetary Union, the European Central Bank (ECB) will acquire a legislative role, but this development is beyond the scope of this study and in any case requires that the TEU be ratified.

There are differences in the manner in which these three Community institutions enact legislation and in the other roles they play in the legislative process. The Commission, for instance, is the sole initiator of most Community legislation, although the European Parliament, the Member States and the Council have, in varying degrees, some power of initiation. The European Parliament has a major and the Commission a minor consultative role. Other bodies that are involved in Community legislation in an advisory capacity are the Monetary Committee,[106] the Economic and Social Committee (ECOSOC), the Court of Auditors and, within the European Union, the Committee of Regions (COR) and the European Monetary Institute (EMI).[107] In addition, the Committee of Permanent Representatives (COREPER)

103. The British North America Act, 30 &31 Vict., c. 3, is now called the Constitution Act, 1867 by virtue of the Canada Act, (U.K.), 1982, c. 11. It sets out, *inter alia,* the division of powers between the federal and provincial legislatures. The point made here is highlighted by comparing Section 91 with Articles 2 and 3 (EEC) setting out the Community's areas of legislative competence. The statement by the European Council in the *Edinburgh Summit Conclusions* (Annex 1 to Part A, p.2) that "national powers are the rule and the Community's the exception" is thus somewhat misleading. In fact, despite subsidiarity, the Community's powers are no more an exception than federal powers are an exception under the Canadian and United States constitutions.

104. Presumably, the start of the second stage will now be delayed until a year after the TEU finally enters into force.

105. Arts. 189 (EEC); 161 (EAEC); 14 (ECSC); **189 (EC)**.

106. Pursuant to **Article 109c(2) (EC)**, the Monetary Committee will be replaced by an Economic and Financial Committee at the start of the third stage of Economic and Monetary Union.

prepares the work of the Council, in which task it will be assisted, in an as yet undetermined way, by the Monetary Committee and the Coordinating Committee for Justice and Home Affairs (CCJHA) once the TEU enters into force.

Standing aloft above this multi-faceted institutional structure but intimately connected with it is the European Council, which comprises the heads of government or state of the Member States and the President of the Commission.[108] The Ministers for Foreign Affairs of the Member States and an additional member from the Commission also attend its meetings. When it discusses Economic and Monetary Union, the European Council will be further expanded to include the Economic and Finance Ministers of the Member States.[109] The European Council has existed for over twenty years, but it was only given official status at the time of the SEA. Despite its august composition, it has no legislative function although, under the EC Treaty, it will be called upon to provide its views on the Council's draft guidelines for economic policy before they are enacted as a recommendation.[110] The real purpose of the European Council is to provide political leadership for the Community and to resolve conflicts between the Member States.[111] Although it has certainly contributed to the Community's development, the European Council has nevertheless been criticized for undermining the Council's authority and reducing the role of both the Commission and the European Parliament.[112]

Only four of the bodies mentioned above are Community institutions. These are the Court of Justice, the Council, the Commission and the European Parliament.[113] The others, with the exception of the European Council, do not possess either the same status or the same rights and immunities. They do, however, play important roles in the legislative process. The TEU elevates the Court of Auditors to the status of a Community institution.[114]

3.2. The Form of Legislation

Community legislation takes three forms.[115] Regulations are directly applicable in all Member States and have the force of law without the need for national implementing measures. Decisions have the same effect as regulations but are mainly used for legislative acts directed at specific persons, undertakings or Member States, except in the ECSC where decisions of general application take the place of

107. The EMI commences its functions at the start of the second stage of Economic and Monetary Union — *see* **art. 109f(1) (EC)**. Pursuant to Article **109l (2) (EC)**, the EMI will be replaced by the ECB at the start of the third stage of Economic and Monetary Union. During the first stage, its consultative role is filled by the Committee of Governors — *see* **art. 109f(8) (EC)**.
108. Art. 2 (SEA). This Article is replaced by the TEU with **Article D (TEU)**.
109. **4th Declaration (TEU)**.
110. **Art. 103(2) (EC)**.
111. On this point, *see* Emile Noël, *Working Together. The Institutions of the European Community*, Luxembourg, 1988, at p. 27.
112. *See* Kapteyn and Themaat, *Introduction to the Law of the European Communities* at pp. 107-108.
113. Arts. 4(1) (EEC); 3(1) (EAEC); 7(ECSC).
114. **Arts. 4(1) (EC); 3(1) (Revised EAEC); 7(Revised ECSC)**.
115. Arts. 189 (EEC); 161 (EAEC); 14 (ECSC).

regulations.

Directives, which are used extensively in the EEC and EAEC, are binding instructions to Member States to enact particular provisions. In principle, directives have no legal force in a Member State until they are implemented by national legislation. However, the Court of Justice has ruled that provisions of Community directives that are "unconditional and sufficiently precise" may be relied on directly before national courts in the absence of implementing legislation.[116] In a very important judgment rendered on November 19, 1991, the Court of Justice went further and recognized an individual citizen's right to damages against a national Government where he or she has suffered loss as a result of the failure of that Government to implement a Community directive.[117] The TEU, of course, will permit the Court of Justice to fine recalcitrant Member States on an application from the Commission.[118]

In the ECSC, the term "recommendation" is used instead of "directive". There is no provision in the TEU for taking court action against Member States that fail to implement ECSC recommendations.

Regulations and directives usually have general application, whereas decisions generally have specific addressees. The contrary may, however, apply, particularly in the ECSC where decisions with general application are common and are used instead of regulations. Specific legislation normally involves the application of the rules of the Treaties and the granting of derogations and safeguard measures. In this study, however, the emphasis is on general legislation and especially general prescriptive legislation.

The Communities also issue non-binding acts in the form of recommendations and opinions. The ECSC, of course, only issues opinions as its recommendations are the equivalent of directives under the other two Treaties. Although non-binding measures are sometimes very influential and is likely to become even more so if the EC gets to exercise its new powers of coordination in the area of economic policy,[119] this study is concerned with legislation. Non-binding acts are normally issued by the Council under the traditional procedure.

3.3. The Legislative Procedures

The legislative procedures of the Community are set out in the three Community Treaties, as revised by the MT and the SEA and to be revised by the TEU. The latter two introduce, respectively, the Cooperation and Co-decision Procedures, which enhance the role of the European Parliament and, in the case of Co-decision, give it a legislative function. The MT will be largely repealed by the TEU.[120]

The procedure that was established originally for all Council legislation calls for

116. *See Pubblico Ministero* v. *Tullio Ratti*, 148/78, [1980] 1 C.M.L.R. 96 at 110

117. *Francovich & Ors* v. *Italian Republic*, 6 and 9/90 (not yet reported). *See also* D. Curtin, "Directives: The Effectiveness of Judicial Protection of Individual Rights", 27 *C.M.L.Rev.* 709.

118. **Arts. 171 (EC Treaty); 143 (Revised EAEC Treaty)**.

119. **Art. 103 (EC)**.

120. **Art. P(1) (TEU).**

the Commission to submit a proposal to the Council, which then enacts the legislation in accordance with the proposal or in a modified form. In most instances, the Council must obtain the opinion of the European Parliament before legislating. Other bodies that may also have to be consulted by the Council are ECOSOC, the Court of Auditors and, on one occasion, the Commission. The TEU introduces the obligation of consulting COR and the EMI in a few instances. None of these consultations bind the Council, which is free to accept or reject the opinions that it is given, including those from Parliament. This traditional procedure is thus relatively simple and consists of three steps: proposal, consultation, enactment. The Council acts by a simple majority, a qualified majority or by unanimity. It must act by unanimity if it wishes to enact legislation that deviates from the Commission's proposal. The procedure is still used for numerous matters in the EEC and remains the only way for the Council to enact legislation in the ECSC and the EAEC. Table 1 sets out all the Treaty provisions that use the traditional procedure.

The Cooperation Procedure makes the consultation of Parliament an integral part of the legislative process and introduces a second round of activity. In the first round, the Commission submits its proposal to the Council as before and Parliament gives its non-binding opinion, or First Reading as it called here. Other bodies may also be consulted by the Council. When the Council finally acts, it adopts a Common Position, which is in essence a draft legislative act, and submits it to Parliament for a Second Reading. Parliament may approve the Common Position, amend it or reject it. The final enactment of the legislation is up to the Council. It acts by a qualified majority under this procedure unless it is modifying the Commission's proposal or overriding Parliament's rejection of the Common Position, in which two cases it must act by unanimity. The Cooperation Procedure is used only in the EEC. Table 2 sets out the Treaty provisions where it occurs.

The Co-decision Procedure will give Parliament a much greater input into legislation and the power of veto. The first round proceeds as under the Cooperation Procedure, but there are significant changes in the second round if Parliament does not approve the Common Position as is. If Parliament rejects the Common Position outright, that is the end of the matter unless the Council can persuade it to change its mind at a meeting of the Conciliation Committee, which consists of equal numbers of representatives from the two institutions. If Parliament amends the Common Position and the Council does not accept all its amendments, the Conciliation Committee meets to put together an alternative text, which, however, can only become law if it is approved by both Parliament and the Council. If the Conciliation Committee fails to reach agreement, the Council may confirm its Common Position, possibly with the inclusion of parliamentary amendments, which becomes law unless Parliament rejects it anew within six weeks. The Council acts normally by a qualified majority, unless it needs unanimity to deviate from the Commission's views, and Parliament by a majority of votes cast. The Co-decision Procedure will be used only in the EC. Table 3 sets out the Treaty provisions where it occurs.

When the Commission enacts legislation, its procedures resemble those it uses to draw up proposals and which are discussed in the next chapter.

Chapter II. Stage 1: The Commission Proposal

1. STRUCTURE OF THE COMMISSION

The Commission is a collegiate body made up at present of seventeen members.[121] Each Member State has a right to one Commissioner and, by convention, the five largest countries furnish two Commissioners each.[122] Commissioners are supposed to act independently of their Governments,[123] and as a general rule it is true that they are influenced more by their political views than their national loyalties. One exception was the controversial proposal in 1989 to introduce a uniform withholding tax on interest earned on bank accounts (OJ C 141/1989), which was vigorously opposed by the Luxembourg Commissioner because it threatened his country's importance as a banking center. A similar controversy surrounded the Commission's decision in October 1991 to block the acquisition of DeHavilland by a Franco-Italian consortium, although it is significant that in this latter case the French President of the Commission publicly supported the decision.

At present, both the Commissioners and the President of the Commission are appointed by the Member States, acting unanimously, for renewable terms of four and two years, respectively.[124] The European Parliament officially has no say in these appointments, but its Rules of Procedure require the Council to consult with it on the choice of the President of the Commission and the new Commission to submit itself to a vote of confidence by a majority of votes cast.[125] The other two institutions have followed these Rules, but they are not bound by them. However, under the terms of the TEU and starting with the Commission whose term of office commences on January 7, 1995, the procedure will change substantially and become more democratic. It will comprise three steps,[126] which largely follow the suggestions of the Commission and the European Parliament.[127]

121. Art. 10(1) (MT). This Article is replaced by the TEU with **Articles 157(1) (EC); 126(1) (Revised EAEC); 9(1) (Revised ECSC)**. *See also* art. 1 of the Rules of Procedure of the Commission (ROPComm), which are contained in Commission Regulation 63/41 (OJ 181/63), as amended. The Member States are to review the number of Commissioners according to the **15th Declaration (TEU)**. On the Commission's Rules of Procedure, *see also infra* at pp. 22-23.

122. *I.e.* France, Germany, Italy, Spain and the United Kingdom — *see* arts. 10(1) (MT); **157(1) (EC); 126(1) (Revised EAEC); 9(1) (Revised ECSC)**.

123. Arts. 10(2) (MT); **157(2) (EC); 126(2) (Revised EAEC); 9(2) (Revised ECSC)**.

124. Arts. 11, 14 (MT), respectively.

125. Rule 29(1),(2). The latest edition of the Rules of Procedure of the European Parliament (ROPParl) was published by the European Parliament in February 1991 but is subject to amendments adopted on March 13, 1991 and January 15, 1992.

126. These are set out in **Articles 158(2)(EC); 127(2) (Revised EAEC); 10(2) (Revised ECSC)**.

127. *See* Commission Opinion of 21 October 1990 on the proposal for amendment of the Treaty establishing the European Economic Community with a view to political union, COM (90) 600, at pt.

As a first step, the Member States, acting by unanimity, will nominate a candidate for President of the Commission in consultation with the European Parliament. As Parliament will ultimately be called upon to approve this nominee, the Member States will be constrained to use the consultation process to ascertain which person is likely to receive sufficient support from MEPs. In practical terms, therefore, the nomination may well become a joint decision of Parliament and the Member States.

Once a suitable candidate for President has been nominated, the second step is for the Governments of the Member States to nominate the other sixteen Commissioners in consultation with the nominee for President. Although the nominee will have no power of veto over the decisions of the Member States, this should not mean that the latter will continue to have a free hand in choosing the Commissioners. The Presidency of the Commission now requires a person of considerable stature, and such a person is likely to be able to exploit the right to be consulted in order to influence the make-up of the Commission. Moreover, Parliament must approve the choice of Commissioners, and it may not do so where there is disagreement between the presidential nominee and the Member States. It should be noted in this context that Parliament had advocated giving the presidential nominee the right to appoint the other Commissioners in agreement with the Council.[128]

The final step in the new procedure is the subjection of all the nominees as a body to a vote of approval by Parliament, after which the Member States, acting by unanimity, formally appoint the new Commission. At this stage, Parliament is supreme. If it does not approve the make-up of the Commission, the Member States cannot appoint it; if it does approve, the Member States are obliged to appoint. All members of the Commission, including the President, will now serve for renewable terms of five years.[129] The European Parliament cannot reject individual Commissioners under this new procedure, but nor can most national parliaments pick and choose when they are called upon to express their confidence in a new government.

The procedure for appointing Vice-Presidents of the Commission will be changed with immediate effect.[130] Their number will be reduced from six to one or two, and they will be appointed by the Commission for five years instead of by the Member States for two years.

These new procedures have no impact on the method of determining the areas

(note 127, continued)

III,1; Parliament's Resolution of 13 December 1990 on the powers of the Commission, on the executive powers of the Commission (comitology) and the role of the Commission in the Community's external affairs, in Part II of *1993. The New Treaties. European Parliament's Proposals*, Luxembourg, 1991, at pts. 23.and 24; Resolution of 11 July 1990 on the European Parliament's guidelines for a draft constitution for the European Union, OJ C 231/1990, at pt. 9. *See also* Article 158 of the Amendments to Articles of the EEC Treaty Proposed by the European Parliament (EP Draft Treaty). These amendments make up Part II of *1993. The New Treaties. European Parliament's Proposals*.

128. Art. 158 (EP Draft Treaty). *See also* Resolution of 13 December 1990 on the powers of the Commission at pt. 24. The Conference of Parliaments of the European Community supported this view — *see* pt. 18 of the proceedings of the Conference in Part III of *1993. The New Treaties. European Parliament's Proposals*.

129. **Arts. 158(1) (EC); 127(1) (Revised EAEC); 10(1) (Revised ECSC)**.

130. **Arts. 161 (EC); 130 (Revised EAEC); 11 (Revised ECSC)**

of responsibility, or portfolios, of the individual Commissioners.[131] In principle, it is the Commission, i.e. the Commissioners acting collectively, that allocates the portfolios,[132] but the President plays an increasingly dominant role in this process.[133] The Member States have no official role, but they often attempt to influence the allocation in favor of their nationals.

Although it is the Commissioners who make the decisions, the real work of the Commission is carried out by its permanent staff. The Commission services consist of twenty-three Directorates-General (DGs), which each deal with specific areas.[134] These DGs are further divided into Directorates and Divisions.[135] It is the Division that is the basic unit to which, as a general rule, all tasks are confided.[136] In addition to the DGs, there are the Secretariat-General of the Commission, the specialized services and the cabinets of the individual Commissioners.[137] The cabinets consist of about six officials who the Commissioner appoints personally[138] and who normally share his or her nationality. The Commission and its services are based in Brussels, except for the statistical office, the office for the Community's official publications, parts of DGs XIII, XVII and XIX and DG XVIII, all of which are based in Luxembourg.

Where a Commissioner is assigned a field of activity that coincides with that of a DG or a specialized service, he or she takes charge of that DG or service[139] This leads sometimes to an accumulation of DGs by one Commissioner. Two or more Commissioners may also share a DG or service.

The Commission is under the political control of the European Parliament.[140] Parliament may soon have a power of veto over the composition of the Commission, and it can already force its collective resignation at any time by passing a vote of

131. For a brief discussion of this process, *see* T.C. Hartley, *The Foundations of European Community Law*, Oxford, 1988, at p. 10.
132. Art. 13 (ROPComm) (suspended).
133. On this point, *see* the account of the allocation of portfolios for the 1993-1995 Commission in *The Financial Times*, December 23, 1992, pp. 1-2.
134. The DGs are: I — External Relations; II — Economic and Financial Affairs; III — Internal Market and Industrial Affairs; IV — Competition; V — Employment, Industrial Relations and Social Affairs; VI — Agriculture; VII — Transport; VIII — Development; IX — Personnel and Administration; X — Information; XI — Environment; XII — Science, Research and Development; XIII — Telecommunications, Information Industries and Innovation; XIV — Fisheries; XV — Financial Institutions and Company Law; XVI — Regional Policy; XVII — Energy; XVIII — Credit and Investments; XIX — Budgets; XX — Financial Control; XXI — Customs Union and Indirect Taxation; XXII — Coordination of Structural Policies; XXIII — Enterprise Policy, Distributive Trades, Tourism and Cooperatives. Consumer Affairs, which until February 1989 was a Directorate within DG XI, now functions as a separate service.
135. Art. 18 (ROPComm) (suspended).
136. Art. 20 (ROPComm) (suspended).
137. Arts. 15, 16, 18 (ROPComm) (suspended). The specialized services are the Legal Service, Spokesman's Service. Joint Interpreting and Conference Service, Translation Service and Consumer Policy Service.
138. Art. 15 (ROPComm) suspended).
139. Art. 13 (ROPComm) (suspended).
140. *See European Parliament* v. *The Commission* , 302/87, [1988] E.C.R. 5637 at 5640 — *see also* arts. 143, 144 (EEC); 113, 114 (EAEC); 24 (ECSC). *See also* Kapteyn and Themaat, *Introduction to the Law of the European Communities* at pp. 139-140.

censure. This requires, however, a two-thirds majority of votes cast representing a majority of MEPs,[141] which may account for the fact that, although four motions of censure have been tabled, none has ever passed.[142] The use of the vote of censure has also been discouraged by the fact that Parliament has no control over the Commission's replacement.[143] This should change, of course, after January 1995, and it will be interesting to see whether there is a greater use or threatened use of the vote of censure.

In fact, the vote of censure is too radical and disruptive a measure to permit an effective control of the Commission's day-to-day activities, and Parliament exercises more control over the Commission by virtue of the latter's obligations to submit to it the annual general report on the Communities,[144] to respond to questions from MEPs[145] and to take note of Parliament's amendments and resolutions.[146] Parliament can also bring the Commission before the Court of Justice for failure to act,[147] and, under the TEU, it acquires the right to request the submission of legislative proposals.[148] Despite all this, the Commission nevertheless retains a certain independence due to its exclusive initiatory power and its role as honest broker between Parliament and the Council, although this latter role will have decreased importance in the Co-decision Procedure.

2. OPERATION OF THE COMMISSION

The Commission has the authority to establish its own procedures.[149] A comprehensive set of rules was enacted in 1963,[150] but a significant portion of the rules dealing with the inner workings of the Commission was suspended in 1967[151] and has since been replaced by confidential, internal regulations. Although the general thrust of the suspended enactments is still followed, there would appear to a breach of the requirement in the Treaties that the Commission publish its Rules of Procedure.[152] Certainly, the transparency of the Commission's procedures has been impaired,

141. Arts. 144 (EEC); 114 (EAEC); 24 (ECSC) — *see also* Rule 30 (ROPParl.)
142. As from February 10, 1992, a motion of censure requires the support of one-tenth of current MEPs before it can be put to a vote — *see* Rule 30(1) (ROPParl).
143. D. Freestone and J.S. Davidson, *The Institutional Framework of the European Communities*, London and New York, 1988 at p. 79 discuss the vote of censure and rather aptly call it a "blunt weapon." *See also* Kapteyn and Themaat, *Law of the European Communities* at p. 139 and pp. 268-269 and Hartley, *Foundations of Community Law* at pp. 34-35.
144. Arts. 143 (EEC); 113 (EAEC); 24 (ECSC).
145. Arts. 140 (EEC); 110 (EAEC); 23 (ECSC) — *see also* Rules 58-61 (ROPParl).
146. *See European Parliament* v. *Commission*, 302/87, at 5640 — *see also* Rules 39-42, 52 (ROPParl). *See also infra* at pp. 62-63 and pp. 92-99 for a discussion of how the Commission reacts to Parliament's amendments.
147. Arts. 175 (EEC); 148 (EAEC). Parliament does not have this right under the ECSC Treaty.
148. **Arts. 138b (EC); 107a (Revised EAEC); 20a (Revised ECSC)**.
149. Art. 16 (MT). This Article is replaced by the TEU with **Articles 162(2) (EC); 131(2) (Revised EAEC); 16 (Revised ECSC)**.
150. Commission Regulation 63/41 (OJ 181/1963).
151. Commission Decision 67/426 (OJ 147/1967), as amended by Commission Decisions 73/1 (OJ L 7/1973), 75/461 (OJ L 199/1975), 81/2 (OJ L 8/1981) and 86/61 (OJ L 72/1986).
152. Arts. 16 (MT); **162(2) (EC); 131(2) (Revised EAEC); 16 (Revised ECSC)**.

which runs counter to the **17th Declaration (TEU)** that "transparency of the decision-making process strengthens the democratic nature of the institutions and the public's confidence in the administration." According to this Declaration, the Commission will have to submit a report on transparency to the Council by the end of 1993. It will be interesting to see how it evaluates its own practices.[153]

The Commission acts collectively,[154] and the ensemble of Commissioners is referred to in Brussels jargon as the "College". There is a limited authority to delegate power to individual Commissioners to take, in the name of and subject to the control of the Commission, "clearly defined measures of management or administration".[155] In practice, this means measures that do not require the exercise of any discretion, such as the variable agricultural levies, which are fixed according to certain established criteria.

The Commission is supposed, as a general rule, to make its decisions in full session at the weekly meetings of the Commissioners.[156] Occasionally, the Commissioners may meet more frequently. The quorum for these meetings is nine, and matters are decided by a simple majority vote.[157] In fact, the Commissioners strive to reach their collective decisions by consensus and only take a formal vote when the issue is a controversial one, such as in the case of the proposal on a uniform withholding tax for investment income.[158] Meetings of the Commissioners in full session are not open to the public, but Commission officials from the "services" (i.e. the DGs and the specialized services) may be invited to attend and, exceptionally, even outsiders.[159]

The 1992 process has increased substantially the workload of the Commission, and this has led to a greater use of the written procedure for making collective decisions.[160] This procedure, which was originally intended for dealing with more routine matters, involves the circulation of a text by the responsible DG to all the Commissioners, who then have a prescribed time in which to make known their objections or amendments. If, within the time limit, no comments are forthcoming and no Commissioner objects to the use of the procedure, the text is deemed adopted and noted as such in the minutes of the next full session of the Commission. The time limit depends on the type of written procedure that is used. The normal procedure sets a period of five working days, but there is an accelerated procedure for

153. In response to the urging of the European Council at its 1992 Birmingham meeting, the Commission has already taken some steps towards greater openness and transparency. These include producing an annual work program in October, allowing for wider debate and input from national parliaments, seeking closer consultation with the Council on the annual legislative program, wider consultation before making proposals, greater use of green papers and making Commission documents public in all Community languages. Greater openness in its decision-making processes is not, however, among these initiatives.
154. Art. 1 (ROPComm).
155. Art. 51 (ROPComm), as amended by Commission Decision 75/461 (OJ L 199/1975), art. 1.
156. Arts. 2, 3 (ROPComm).
157. Art. 17 (MT). This Article is replaced by the TEU with **Articles 163 (EC); 132 (Revised EAEC); 13 (Revised ECSC)**. *See too* arts. 6, 7 (ROPComm), as last amended by Commission Decision 86/61 (OJ L 72/1986), art. 1.
158. *See supra* at p. 19.
159. Arts. 8, 9 (ROPComm).
160. This procedure is authorized by Article 11 (ROPComm).

urgent matters where the period is reduced to three days. If all Commissioners have previously studied the dossier, the period can be further shortened to one or two days.

An important operating feature of the Commission is the committees involving members of the Commissioners' cabinets that help expedite the business of the Commission. Special inter-cabinet committees deal on an on-going basis with the various dossiers under active consideration. They consist of the member from each cabinet who is responsible for a particular dossier and the Commission official who is handling it for the services. These committees assure an exchange of views and information between the services and the various Commissioners and their DGs, which helps prevent disagreements or misunderstandings that might otherwise retard the Commission's decisions. There is also a weekly meeting of the chefs de cabinet[161] that prepares the weekly meeting of the Commission and permits technical and non-controversial matters to be settled at cabinet level.[162] As long as the chefs de cabinet reach a unanimous decision, the Commission will normally adopt the measure without further ado. Somewhat confusingly, both types of cabinet committees are referred to as meetings of the "chefs".

3. INITIATION OF COUNCIL LEGISLATION

3.1. Importance of the Initiatory Power

The Commission plays the role of both initiator and legislator in the legislative process of the Community, Its legislative role is limited in scope, but it has an almost exclusive right of initiation, which enables it to control the legislative agenda of the Council and Parliament. Practically all general legislative acts of the Council, including those that it will enact under the TEU, must be based on an initiating proposal from the Commission.[163] There are only two exceptions. The European Parliament is responsible for making the proposal for Council action on a uniform voting procedure for Parliament,[164] while, in the European Union, the Member States must initiate legislation on judicial cooperation in criminal matters, customs cooperation and police cooperation.[165] The Member States, however, share with the Commission the right to initiate Council action ending production quotas under the ECSC Treaty[166] as well as legislation in the European Union on asylum policy, border controls, immigration, drug addiction, international fraud and judicial coopera-

161. This is one of the many French expressions used in current Eurojargon. The tendency now is not to italicize them.

162. The Spierenburg Report (D. Spierenburg, *Proposals for Reform of the Commission of the European Communities and its Services*, Brussels, 1979) criticized the role of the chefs de cabinet, alleging that they obstruct communication between the Commissioners and their staff in the services.

163. *See* Tables 1-3. In the case of Article 126 (EEC), the Commission delivers an opinion rather than submitting a proposal and, under **Article 100c(2) (EC)**, it makes a recommendation. The procedure for adopting a recommendation or delivering an opinion is less complex and resembles the enactment of secondary legislation by the Commission — *see infra* at pp. 111-112.

164. Arts. 138(3) (EEC); 108(3) (EAEC); 21(3) (ECSC).

165. **Art. K.3(2) (TEU)**.

166. Art. 58(3) (ECSC).

tion in civil matters.[167]

The European Council has confirmed that the Commission's right of initiative is not called into question by **Article 3b (EC)**,[168] but the Commission will nonetheless be bound by these provisions. Thus, although the Commission will continue to decide alone on the content of its legislative proposals, these must remain within the parameters of the Treaties and respect the principles of proportionality and subsidiarity.[169] Furthermore, the TEU imposes upon the Commission the additional obligation of ensuring that a proposal can be financed within the limit of the Community's own resources.[170]

The Commission is free to amend or withdraw its proposals. The power of amendment is contained in Article 149(3) (EEC)[171] and the second paragraph of Article 119 (EAEC). There is no equivalent provision in the ECSC Treaty, but it is accepted that the power of amendment is implicit in the Commission's general authority under Article 8. The power of withdrawal is contained within the amending power; if the Commission has the right to alter a proposal completely, it surely follows that it can set it aside instead. It should, however, be noted here that the Commission has no such control over legislative proposals made by Parliament or the Member States.

There is disagreement over the scope of the Commission's right to amend and withdraw its proposals. Council jurists contend that the Commission cannot amend or withdraw a proposal once the Council has adopted a Common Position, whereas the Commission maintains that it is free to act at any stage in the legislative process.[172] It has been supported in this contention by Parliament, whose Rules of Procedure presently require the President of Parliament to request the Commission to withdraw its proposal when Parliament has rejected the Common Position.[173] The problem is that the Treaty Articles are ambiguous and admit of either interpretation, although it is fair to say that Article 119 (EAEC) tends more to support the Council and Articles 149(3) (EEC) and **189a(2) (EC)** the Commission. However, in the following discussion of the Commission's role, it will become clear that it has to be able to withdraw or amend legislation at any stage under all the legislative procedures in order properly to look after the Community interest. This is reason enough

167. **Art K.3(2) (TEU)**.

168. *Edinburgh Summit Conclusions*, Annex 1 to Part A, p. 10.

169. The Commission is already obliged to respect the principles of attribution of powers and proportionality as they are part of the jurisprudence of the Court of Justice (*see supra* at pp. 4-5). However, under **Article 3b (EC)**, this obligation is a made a formal prerequisite for Community action.

170. **Arts. 201a (EC); 173a (Revised EAEC)**.

171. This Article is replaced by the TEU with **Article 189a(2) (EC)**.

172. There is no dispute, of course, over the Commission's right to issue a Re-examined Proposal under Article 149(2)(d) (EEC). On the difference between a Re-examined Proposal and an amended proposal, *see infra* at p. 96. Article 149(2) (EEC) is replaced by the TEU with **Article 189c (EC)**.

173. Rule 50(3) (ROPParl). In Article 188a(1) (EP Draft Treaty), Parliament advocated limiting the Commission's right to amend and withdraw to the period prior to the completion of Parliament's First Reading. This change of attitude is explained by the nature of the Co-decision Procedure suggested by Parliament. Significantly, this amendment is not taken up by the TEU.

to interpret the ambiguities of the Treaties in favor of the Commission, as many other academic writers have done.[174]

The Council can only amend a Commission proposal unilaterally if it is able to act by unanimity,[175] although the new Co-decision Procedure permits such amendments to be made by a qualified majority in order to reach an accommodation with Parliament within the Conciliation Committee.[176] Where the Council wishes to amend one of its previous legislative acts, it must also act by unanimity unless the Commission agrees to produce a proposal for amendment. These unilateral amendments cannot alter the substance of the proposal to which they relate, which means that they cannot depart from the subject matter or alter the objectives set by the Commission.[177] Unanimity is not easy for the Council to achieve, and so normally it has to rely on the Commission agreeing to produce an amended proposal. Even where the Council does achieve the required unanimity or if it is able to act by a qualified majority under the Co-decision Procedure, the Commission can still thwart it by withdrawing the proposal from the legislative agenda.[178]

The Council has a general power under the Community Treaties to request the Commission to submit proposals for legislation,[179] and it will acquire a specific power to do so in connection with economic and monetary matters that it will share with Member States.[180] Member States can also elicit proposals on tariffs for coal and steel products,[181] changes to the EAEC Treaty rules on the supply of materials and the Community's right of ownership[182] and safeguard application procedures for the nuclear sector.[183] They are given by the TEU the same right with respect to visas,[184] and Parliament, acting by an absolute majority of MEPs, is given the right to request the Commission to submit proposals where it considers this necessary in order to implement the Treaties.[185] Although the wording of the Treaty provisions

174. *See e.g.* R. Bieber, "Legislative Procedure for the Establishment of the Single Market", (1989), 26 *C.M.L.Rev.* 711 at pp. 718 and 722; Van Hamme, "The European Parliament and the Cooperation Procedure Impact on Lobbying", in *Gestion 2000*, 4, (1988), at p. 135. *Contra* Glaesner, "La procédure de coopération", in Louis/Waelbroek (eds.), *Le Parlement Européen*, at p. 77.

175. Arts. 149(1) (EEC); 119 (EAEC). The same principle applies under the ECSC Treaty — *see e.g.* art. 58(3). On the Council's right to change the legal base of proposed legislation, *see infra* at p. 73. Article 149(1) (EEC) is replaced by the TEU with **Article 189a(1) (EC)**.

176. **Art. 189a(1) (EC)**. This conciliation procedure is discussed *infra* at pp. 102-103 and pp. 106-107.

177. This, at least, is what the Commission has always maintained — *see Commission* v. *Council*, 355/87, [1991] 1 C.M.L.R. 586 at 608. In this case, neither the Court of Justice nor the Advocate-General were prepared to support the Commission's view expressly but nonetheless upheld the Council's amendments to a Commission proposal on the ground that they did not affect its substance. Bieber in "Legislative Procedure" argues in favor of the Commission's viewpoint by pointing out at p. 718 that "the very notion of "amendment" presupposes the continued existence of the identity of a proposal".

178. It did this, for example, in 1988 with its proposal on a general right of residence for Community nationals (OJ C 171/85).

179. Arts. 152 (EEC); 122 (EAEC); 26 (ECSC).

180. **Art. 109d (EC)**.

181. Art. 72 (ECSC).

182. Arts. 76, 90 (EAEC).

183. Art. 85 (EAEC).

184. **Art. 100c(4) (EC)**.

185. **Arts. 138b (EC); 107a (Revised EAEC); 20a (Revised ECSC)**. This right of request does not extend to home and justice affairs — *see* **art. K.8(1) (TEU)**.

does not suggest that the Commission is obliged to accede to these requests for legislative proposals,[186] the Council, the European Parliament and the Member States can bring it before the Court of Justice if it fails to make a proposal where required by the Community interest.[187] No-one, however, including the Court of Justice, can dictate the content of Commission proposals[188] or prevent the Commission from subsequently withdrawing them.

The Commission's initiatory power is one of the most effective means it has for fulfilling its task of ensuring the proper functioning and development of the Community.[189] It enables the Commission to bring before the Council and Parliament whatever legislative proposals it considers necessary to advance the process of economic integration, thereby, to some extent, forcing the Council's hand. At the same time, the Commission's amending and withdrawal powers permit it to protect the integrity of the Community and the vital interests of individual Member States and to ensure that the other institutions act consistently. The advent of a single Commission has also facilitated consistency between the legislation of the three Communities.[190]

3.2. Emergence of the Idea

The majority of ideas for new legislative proposals emerge within the Commission itself from the highest level down to individual Division officials, although many of these ideas may have their genesis in informal contacts with national and European interest groups, officials from Member States, other Community bodies and even individuals. Some ideas are prompted by specific instructions for action in the Treaties or secondary legislation;[191] others, like the three hundred or so proposals in the 1985 White Paper, arise from the Commission's general responsibility for the proper functioning and development of the Community. As part of its commitment to openness and transparency, the Commission will now publish every October an annual work program setting out its intended initiatives.

Other Community bodies do have a means of input into the Commission's legislative program, which they exploit to varying degrees. The Council is given explicit authority under the Community Treaties to request the Commission to sub-

186. On this point, *see* Kapteyn and Themaat, *Introduction to the Law of the European Communities* at pp. 252-253.

187. Arts. 175 (EEC); 148 (EAEC); 35 (ECSC). The European Parliament, however, has no right of action with respect to matters falling within the ECSC Treaty.

188. This point has never been settled by the Court of Justice, but it can be implied from the Court's decision in *Commission* v. *Council*, 355/87. If the Council cannot change the substance of a proposal, it would not seem open to it to dictate the whole content of Commission proposals. *See also* Bieber, "Legislative Procedure" at p. 718.

189. It is given this task by Articles 155 (EEC); 124 (EAEC). *See also* art. 8 (ECSC).

190. The importance of consistency in all the activities of the Union is emphasized by **Article C (TEU)**.

191. *See* art. 87(1) (EEC), which requires proposals on the implementation of the Treaty's competition rules. The Commission's proposal for a uniform withholding tax on interest payments (OJ C 141/1989) was made pursuant to Article 6(5) of Council Directive 88/361 (OJ L 178/1988).

mit legislative proposals on a particular subject matter,[192] while the Monetary Committee and the Court of Auditors are empowered to submit observations or opinions on their own initiative, which may on occasion contain ideas for legislation.[193] Both the European Parliament and ECOSOC have given themselves the same right to own-initiative opinions in their Rules of Procedure,[194] and this is officially sanctioned by the TEU, which extends the right to COR and the EMI.[195] ECOSOC, however, only operates for the EC, EEC and EAEC, the Monetary Committee only for the EC and EEC, and the EMI only for the EC, should it come into being. The various advisory and consultative committees set up by the Council or Commission are also often empowered to make suggestions for legislative proposals.[196]

The Member States may stimulate ideas for legislation by collective action through the European Council, which often gives the impulse for new legislative proposals and sometimes even requires specific measures to be introduced. Individual Member States on occasion use the European Council as a means for advancing their own agendas. France, for example, used the European Council to have the provision calling for a proposal on a uniform withholding tax inserted into Council Directive 88/361 on the free movement of capital.[197] Despite its exalted status, the European Council cannot require secondary legislation that exceeds the parameters of the Treaties or, upon its entry into force, otherwise violates the principles set out in **Article 3b (EC)**.[198] Under the TEU, the Member States can also influence the Commission's legislative program by means of their right to request proposals for legislation on visas and economic and monetary policy.[199]

Frequently, the Commission is able to reverse these various processes by using them to elicit proposals. The many action programs that the Council has adopted on the basis of Commission proposals, for example, empower the latter to make a wide array of further proposals.[200] The Community Social Charter, which was adopted at

192. Arts. 152 (EEC); 122 (EAEC); 26 (ECSC). However, the Commission has now indicated that it will henceforth decline to accept informal requests from the Council for legislative proposals—*see Edinburgh Summit Conclusions*, Annex 2 to Part A, p. 5. It is difficult to appreciate the reason for this move, which the Commission justifies somewhat inexplicably on the basis of the subsidiarity provisions in **Article 3b (EC)**.

193. Arts. 105(2), 206a(4) (EEC); 180a(4) (EAEC); 78f(4) (ECSC). These Articles are replaced by the TEU with, respectively, **Articles 109c(1), 188c(4) (EC); 160c(4) (Revised EAEC); 45c(4) (Revised ECSC)**.

194. Rules 63 (individual MEPs and parliamentary groups), 121 (committees) (ROPParl); Article 20 of the Rules of Procedure of the Economic and Social Committee and Rule 1.2. of the Standing Orders of its Bureau. The Rules of Procedure of the Economic and Social Committee (ROPEcosoc) are found in OJ L 228/1974, as amended by OJ L 366/1980, OJ L 127/1981, OJ L 19/1982 and OJ L 354/1986.

195. **Arts. 138b, 198, 198c, 109f(4) (EC); 107a, 170 (Revised EAEC); 20a (Revised ECSC)**.

196. *See* Council Regulation 1408/71 (OJ L 149/1971), art. 81(g) (Administrative Commission on Social Security for Migrant Workers); Commission Decision 87/305 (OJ L 152/1987), art. 2 (Advisory Committee on Public Procurement).

197. *See* fn. 191.

198. But *note* that the comment in fn. 169 also applies to the European Council.

199. **Arts. 100c(4), 109d (EC)**.

200. *See, e.g.*, Council Decision 88/524 (OJ L 288/1988) on an action program for the information services market .

the instigation of the Commission in December 1989 by eleven of the Governments making up the European Council, also calls for legislative proposals.[201]

As a general rule, neither individuals nor national and European organizations have a formal avenue of approach to the Commission and are limited to acting through ECOSOC or informal contacts. An example of the latter approach was the 1989 proposal to permit public offer prospectuses to be used as stock exchange listing particulars in other Member States,[202] which was drawn up largely as a result of informal representations from the European securities industry. Under the Social Policy Agreement, however, the Commission will actually be obliged to consult with management and labor "on the possible direction of Community action" before submitting proposals in the social policy field,[203] which will obviously allow a privileged input into the Commission's future legislative ideas.

3.3. Preliminary Study

Sometimes the Commission will carry out a study of a particular issue or area before making any specific legislative proposals. These studies may involve more than one DG. They are conducted either internally by the Commission services or externally by a single academic, a group of academics, firms of consultants or other experts working in the field. Particularly elaborate studies, which may cover all the legal, technical, social and economic ramifications involved, are called "Green Papers."[204] Most studies are published by the Commission as COM documents, which means that they have to be formally adopted by the Commission. The written procedure is normally used for this purpose.

Where the Commission services undertake a study internally, they may consult with the appropriate advisory or consultative committee where one exists. There is, however, no obligation to do so at this stage, even where consultation is required by the Treaties or the Council before the proposal is adopted by the Commission in its final form. The services may also consult on a voluntary basis with other Community bodies, notably the European Parliament or ECOSOC.[205] In the case of Green Papers, these latter two bodies often issue formal opinions on them even if they have not been formally consulted. Other DGs, European trade, professional and other organizations as well as Member States may also be solicited for their views. Three European organizations that are frequently consulted are UNICE (the European employers' group), ETUC (the European trades unions) and BEUC (the

201. Title II, at pt. 28. *See, e.g.*, the proposal on working time (OJ C 254/1990) and that on the protection of pregnant women at work (OJ C 281/1990). The United Kingdom was the lone dissenter from the Charter and has opposed much of the social legislation proposed by the Commission pursuant to it.

202. OJ C 101/1989, as amended by OJ C 70/1990. The proposal was ultimately enacted as Council Directive 90/211 (OJ L 112/1990).

203. **Art. 3.2 of the 14th Protocol (TEU)**.

204. *See, e.g.*, the Green Papers on telecommunications (COM (87) 90) and copyright (COM (88) 172). As part of its commitment to openness and transparency, the Commission has decided to make more use of Green Papers—*see Edinburgh Summit Conclusions*, Part A, p. 4a.

205. Arts. 198 (EEC); 170 (EAEC). *See also* Rule 36 (ROPParl). Under Article 19 (ECSC), the Commission has the option of consulting the Consultative Committee.

European consumers' group). In the area of social policy, the Commission will again be obliged to consult with management and labor if action is being taken under the Social Policy Agreement.[206]

The Commission is now committed to consulting more widely before deciding to make a proposal, particularly with respect to Member States and perhaps even national parliaments.[207] Moreover, in its consultations at this preliminary stage, the Commission is likely to seek out views on the subsidiarity aspect of its initiative once **Article 3b (EC)** is in force.

3.4. Preliminary Draft Proposal

The preliminary draft proposal is drawn up by a Commission Working Party in a process that can take from a few weeks to several years. The Working Party will generally include outside experts as well as members of the Commission services; it is always chaired by the Commission official responsible for the dossier.[208] The outside experts may, at the Commission's option, be independent or nominees of the Governments of the Member States. The presence of Government nominees, who are often civil servants, has the advantage of making known to the Commission the various national views and priorities. This affords a useful preview of what is likely to transpire in the Council, and it enables the Commission to devise a proposal that will enjoy the widest possible support among the Member States while still serving the Community interest. There are some undertones of negotiation at this stage, but the national nominees have no official status and cannot bind their respective Governments.

It is important to stress that at this stage the Commission is still in sole control of the process and under no obligation to involve any of the advisory or consultative committees that may have competence for the dossier in question. Most of these committees are in any case quite inappropriate for the task at hand. Those established by the Treaties do not even provide for Commission representation,[209] with the exception of the Monetary Committee, whose primary purpose, however, is to make known the views of the Member States to the Commission.[210] The committees set up by the Council, despite frequent provision for a Commission Chairman,[211] for representation of the Commission services[212] and for the creation of Working

206. **Art. 3.2 of the 14th Protocol (TEU)**.

207. *Edinburgh Summit Conclusions*, Annex 1 to Part A, p. 10.

208. Art. 14 (ROPComm) (suspended).

209. For example, ECOSOC (arts. 193 (EEC); 165 (EAEC)); the Transport Advisory Committee (art. 83 (EEC)); the Scientific and Technical Committee (art. 134 (EAEC)); and the Consultative Committee (art. 18 (ECSC)); and also COR (**art. 198a (EC)**).

210. This committee consists of two representatives from each Member State and the Commission — *see* arts. 105(2) (EEC); **109c(1) (EC)**.

211. *See* Council Decision 74/235 (OJ L 185/1974), art. 6(1) (Advisory Committee on Safety, Hygiene and Health Protection at Work); Council Decision 75/320 (OJ L 147/1975), art. 3(3) (Pharmaceutical Committee).

212. *See* Council Decision 74/235, art. 6(5) (Advisory Committee on Safety); Rules of Procedure of the Administrative Commission on Social Security for Migrant Workers (OJ C 61/1982), art. 3(1).

Parties,[213] are equally inappropriate. They rarely have the composition that the Commission desires and, above all, are beyond its control. The members are appointed by the Council or the Member States[214] and, where there is a Commission Chairman, he or she may not have a vote.[215] Council committees also normally record their opinions on a matter formally by vote,[216] which is a procedure more adapted to considering a final text than drawing one up.

Advisory committees which the Commission itself has established may be used to draft proposals where they have the appropriate structure.[217] The disadvantage of these committees is that the nature of their composition is fixed by the enabling legislation and may not correspond to what the Commission desires in a particular instance.[218]

Before the Working Party starts its series of meetings, the DG responsible for the dossier will establish a Working Document setting out the issues that have to be settled by the legislation. This document is amended and re-submitted after each meeting of the Working Party. The Commission services like to set down draft articles as soon as possible in order to focus the discussions of the Working Party and expedite the process. These draft articles are very sketchy at first and are filled in gradually as the Working Party progresses in its deliberations. The preamble to the legislation, which will eventually include a justification of the measure's relevance in terms of the subsidiarity provisions of **Article 3b (EC)**, must also be elaborated at this stage. Finally, unless the dossier proves intractable or is shelved for political reasons, a preliminary draft proposal will emerge that is circulated to other interested Commission services, Member States and the relevant European and national organizations. It is rarely published by the Commission, but usually a copy can be obtained from national Government departments or trade and professional organizations.[219]

This is the most fluid stage in the whole legislative process. The Commission's ideas are not yet set in any particular direction, and it is nearly always receptive to outside input, particularly from European trade, professional and other organizations. It has indicated that it will now also be more receptive to the views expressed in national parliaments.[220] The Commission itself, however, has rarely consulted beyond the Working Party at this stage, but this should change under its new commitment to wider consultation. In politically sensitive cases, the Commissioner in charge of the responsible DG will also become closely involved in the drafting

213. *See* Council Decision 74/235, art. 6(4) (Advisory Committee on Safety); Rules of Administrative Commission on Social Security, art. 4.

214. *See* Council Decision 74/235, art. 4(3) (Advisory Committee on Safety); Council Decision 75/320, art. 3(1) (Pharmaceutical Committee); Council Regulation 1408/71, art. 80(1) (Administrative Commission on Social Security).

215. *See* Council Decision 74/235, art. 6(1) (Advisory Committee on Safety).

216. *See* Council Decision 74/235, art. 7(2) (Advisory Committee on Safety); Rules of Administrative Commission on Social Security, art. 8(1).

217. *See* Commission Decision 87/305, setting up the Advisory Committee on Public Procurement, which provides for a Commission chairman (art. 7), representation of Commission officials (art. 10(2)) and Working Parties (art. 9)

218. *See, e.g.*, Commission Decision 87/305, arts. 3, 4 (Advisory Committee on Public Procurement).

219. It is not clear whether the Commission's new commitment to making its documents public (*see* fn. 153) applies to preliminary draft proposals.

220. *Edinburgh Summit Conclusions*, Part A, p. 4a.

process. Once the preliminary draft has been finalized, it becomes more difficult to change the basic thrust of the proposal.

A slight digression is necessary before proceeding further in order to deal with the different procedures laid down in the Social Policy Agreement. Under the Agreement, the Commission will be obliged to elaborate its proposal in consultation with management and labor, and the latter will have to forward to the Commission their opinion or recommendation on its content.[221] Management and labor are even permitted to take the matter out of the Commission's hands and to attempt to regulate the issue between themselves.[222] The time limit set for these private discussions is nine months, after which time the matter reverts to the Commission unless all three parties agree to extend the time limit. Any agreement between management and labor will be concluded at Community level and implemented either privately or, at the joint request of the signatory parties, by a Council Decision taken on a proposal from the Commission.[223]

Even if the TEU is ratified, the Social Policy Agreement will not apply to the United Kingdom. It is not at all clear how this country will fit into the new arrangements, particularly as regards occupational health, which is the one area of social policy that can be enacted by a qualified majority under the EEC Treaty[224] and to which the United Kingdom does not object as a matter of principle. If the Social Policy Agreement is used, the measures will not apply to the United Kingdom, but if the EC Treaty is used, the new procedures cannot be exploited. Presumably, recourse will be had in such cases to both the Agreement and the parallel provisions of the Treaty, but this is, to say the least, an untidy solution.

3.5. Final Draft Proposal

Returning to the normal procedures, the Working Party continues in session to prepare the final draft of the Commission's proposal. This is the stage that involves extensive consultation and compromise on the basis of the preliminary draft. It is a difficult period for the Commission, as the Working Party under the Division official responsible for the dossier must absorb all the various inputs and come up with a generally acceptable final version.

Mandatory consultation takes place within and outside the Commission. Pursuant to Article 21 of the Commission's Rules of Procedure, the views of other interested services must be considered and an attempt made to accommodate them. Failing this, divergent views must be mentioned in the final draft. The Commissioner in charge of the responsible DG must also be consulted.[225] Although not a legal requirement, the preliminary draft proposal will normally be circulated to the other Commissioners so that it can be discussed in the special cabinet committees.

In some instances, consultation of outside committees is required at this stage

221. **Art. 3(3) of the 14th Protocol (TEU).**
222. **Art. 3(4) of the 14th Protocol (TEU).**
223. **Art. 4 of the 14th Protocol (TEU).**
224. Art. 118a(2) (EEC).
225. Art. 22 (ROPComm) (suspended).

under the Treaties, namely the Monetary Committee,[226] ECOSOC,[227] the Scientific and Technical Committee[228] and the Consultative Committee[229] (*See* Table 4). Some of the committees set up by the Council may also have to consulted before a proposal is finalized.[230] The Commission will have to consult yet again with management and labor for proposals to be submitted under the Social Policy Agreement. Even where consultation is not mandatory, the Council may refuse to act on a proposal that has not been referred to the appropriate committee where one exists. Whenever consultation has taken place, this fact is indicated in the preamble to the legislation.[231]

These consultative committees normally comprise either Government representatives,[232] Government-appointed experts[233] or a wide spectrum of interest groups.[234] Independent experts are more often found in advisory committees set up by the Commission.[235] Most consultative committees act by delivering official opinions on the basis of a majority vote.[236]

In addition to its obligations to consult, the Commission is given the option of consulting the Court of Auditors[237] and the various committees set up by the Treaties[238] or the Council.[239] It may also choose to consider the opinion of one of its own advisory committees or, more rarely, the appropriate committee of the European Parliament.[240] Sometimes, it may canvass the views of Member States and seek input from European organizations. The Commission continues at this stage to be receptive to representations from national bodies, companies and even individuals. Indeed, it is committed to being even more receptive, particularly as regards the

226. Art. 69 (EEC). Under the TEU, this Article is to be repealed as from January 1, 1994 — *see* **art. 73a (EC)**
227. *See* arts. 43(2) (EEC); 31, 41, 96 (EAEC).
228. *See* art. 31 (EAEC). More precisely, the Commission has to consult a group of experts appointed by the Scientific and Technical Committee.
229. *See* art. 58(3) (ECSC).
230. *See* Council Decision 75/320, art 2 (Pharmaceutical Committee).
231. *See* Council Directive 80/836 (OJ L 246/1980), which was the subject of mandatory consultation of the Scientific and Technical Committee, and Council Directive 89/391 (OJ L 183/1989), where there was optional consultation of the Advisory Committee on Safety.
232. *See* arts. 105(2) (EEC), **109c(1) (EC)** (Monetary Committee); Council Regulation 1408/71, art. 80(1) (Administrative Commission for Social Security)
233. *See* art. 83 (EEC) (Transport Advisory Committee); Council Decision 75/320, art. 3(1) (Pharmaceutical Committee).
234. *See* arts. 193 (EEC), 165 (EAEC) (ECOSOC); 18 (ECSC) (Consultative Committee); Council Decision 74/235, art. 4(3) (Advisory Committee on Safety)
235. *See* Commission Decision 87/305, art. 4 (Advisory Committee on Public Procurement)
236. *See* art. 45 (ROPEcosoc); Council Decision 74/235. art. 7(2) (Advisory Committee on Safety). The Rules of the Administrative Commission for Social Security, on the other hand, require decisions to be taken unanimously — *see* art. 8(2),(3).
237. Arts. 206a(4) (EEC); 180a(4) (EAEC); 78f(4) (ECSC); **188c(4) (EC); 160c(4) (Revised EAEC); 45c(4) (Revised ECSC).**
238. *See* arts. 105 (2) (EEC), **109c(1) (EC)** (Monetary Committee); 198 (EEC), 170 (EAEC) (ECOSOC); 83 (EEC) (Transport Advisory Committee); 134(1) (EAEC) (Scientific and Technical Committee); 19 (ECSC) (Consultative Committee); and **198c (EC)** (COR).
239. *See* Council Regulation 1408/71, art 80 (Administrative Commission on Social Security).
240. Under Rule 36(1) (ROPParl), it is up to the President of the European Parliament to refer requests for consultation from the Commission to the appropriate parliamentary committee.

views expressed in national parliaments. As at earlier stages in the process, all these consultations, whether mandatory or not, will likely bear as well on the subsidiarity aspect of the proposal.

The Working Party will consider all these opinions, views and representations and attempt to find the common ground on which to base its final draft. This can often take some time and involve several prior drafts. The Commission is not, however, obliged to incorporate any of the suggestions that it has received, even when they emanate from a process of compulsory consultation. This would impinge on its exclusive initiatory power. Eventually, unless the dossier is abandoned or put aside, a final draft will be agreed upon. However, before this document can be submitted for the collective approval of the Commissioners, it needs a fiche d'impact.

The fiche is an economic impact audit, which requires the Working Party to consider the effect that the proposal will have on business generally and on small to medium-sized businesses in particular. It must weigh such matters as what businesses are likely to be affected, how they will be affected and the qualitative and quantitative nature of these effects. It must pay special attention to the administrative burdens that the proposal creates for small and medium-sized enterprises. Even where the Working Party considers that a proposal has no impact on business, it must still append a fiche to this effect.

The fiche d'impact is sent for evaluation to DG XXIII. This is an important step in the Community legislative procedure, as DG XXIII has the right to hold up a proposal until it receives a fiche with which it concurs. Its authority is, however, limited to insisting on a proper evaluation of the business impact; it cannot require changes to the proposal. In October 1991, DG XXIII indicated that it had modified the fiche d'impact system and would concentrate on those legislative proposals that have a significant impact on business.

Once the Division official responsible for the dossier receives the approval of DG XXIII, the proposal is sent to the Commissioner in charge of the DG accompanied by its fiche. It will normally pass by way of the Heads of Division and Directorate, who have the right to amend the proposal but rarely do so.[241]

3.6. Commission Proposal

The adoption of proposals for Council legislation involves the exercise of discretionary power and has to be carried out by the Commission as a body. It is not a function that can be delegated under Article 27 of the Commission's Rules of Procedure to an individual Commissioner. The responsibility for securing a draft proposal's adoption lies with the Commissioner in charge of the particular area to which it relates.

All draft proposals pass through the relevant special cabinet committee, and the results of these meetings give the responsible Commissioner a good idea of the likely reaction of the other Commissioners to the proposal. Where there appears to be a consensus of opinion, the written procedure is likely to be used. Otherwise, the draft proposal is set down for a full meeting of the Commission.

241. Art. 22 (ROPComm) (suspended).

All draft proposals that are to be considered in full session come first before the weekly meeting of the chefs de cabinet. The chefs attempt to reach agreement on outstanding technical and non-controversial issues so that the Commissioners can concentrate on the major points of contention. Unless the draft proposal is referred back to the Commission services for further work or set aside for later consideration, it will be formally adopted by the Commissioners by consensus or, more rarely, by majority vote.[242]

The adopted proposal is now sent to the Legal and Translation Services to receive its final form. This process is normally a mere formality, but sometimes legal problems as to the basis of the proposed legislation or the sufficiency of its provisions can cause a delay and even necessitate a further meeting of the Commission. Finally, the proposal is published as a COM document, together with an Explanatory Memorandum that analyzes and justifies the proposal both from the point of view of its substance and, eventually, its compliance with the subsidiarity provisions of **Article 3b (EC)**. It is then submitted to the Council. Later it will appear in the 'C' series of the Official Journal, without the Memorandum but with the date on which it was transmitted to the Council.

242. The Luxembourg Accords, which are found in the *9th General Report on the Activities of the European Communities (1966)* at pp. 31-33, call in point a(1) for the Commission to inform the Permanent Representatives of the Member States before any "important" proposal is adopted. This idea has been largely ignored.

Chapter III. Stage 2: The First Consultations

1. THE EUROPEAN PARLIAMENT

1.1. The Development of Parliament's Role

The Assembly, as it was initially called, was given little influence over the legislative process by the original Community Treaties. In the first place, they provided only for the traditional legislative procedure under which Parliament is assigned a very subordinate role. The Council is not obliged to follow Parliament's opinion under this procedure and sometimes does not even have to consult at all.[243] Also, under the traditional procedure, Parliament cannot reject a Commission proposal, as any rejection is considered by the Council to constitute an Opinion and to satisfy the procedural requirement for consultation. Thus, the Council felt able to enact Council Regulation 3945/87 on the radioactive contamination of foodstuffs on December 22, 1987 despite Parliament's rejection of the Commission's proposal on December 16, 1987.[244] The other notable features of Parliament's original role are that there is no provision for optional consultation by the Council and no say in the initiation of legislation.

The effect of the original Treaties is to make Parliament entirely dependent on the Commission if it wishes to influence the type and final form of Community legislation. The Commission has to agree to initiate legislation desired by Parliament and to cooperate with Parliament in the legislative procedure. Unless it espouses Parliament's amendments, the Council can only incorporate them by unanimity and

243. There is no obligation to consult under Articles 28, 51, 55, 59, 69, 70(1), 79(3), 94, 100, 101, 103(2), 103(3), 112(1), 113(2),(4), 128, 138(3) (EEC); 24(1), 41, 42, 54, 69, 92, 108(3) (EAEC); 21(3), 58(3), 59(2), 72, (ECSC); **8a(2), 73c(2), 73f, 100c(2), 103a(1), 106(5) (EC)**. Note, however, that under Articles 138(3) (EEC), 108(3) (EAEC) and 21(3) (ECSC), it is Parliament that submits the proposal and that, under the TEU, it must also give its assent to the final act — *see* **arts. 138(3) (EC)**; **108(3) (Revised EAEC)**; **21(3) (Revised ECSC)**. The assent of Parliament is also needed under **Articles 8a(2), 106(5) (EC)**. The TEU introduces the obligation to consult Parliament for Articles 94 and 100 (EEC) — *see* **arts. 94**, **100 (EC)**. *See* Table 4 for a complete list of the consultation provisions of the Treaties.

244. *See* OJ L 371/1988 and OJ C 13/1988. Parliament challenged the validity of this regulation before the Court of Justice, but, interestingly enough, its objection was to the legal base rather than the disregard of its rejection of the proposal — *Re Radioactive Food: European Parliament* v. *The Council*, 70/88, [1992] 1 C.M.L.R. 91. Parliament did, however, propose that, under the Co-decision Procedure, the Council would have to act unanimously if it wanted to adopt a Common Position on the basis of a proposal rejected by Parliament — *see* art. 188b(b) (EP Draft Treaty); Resolution of 11 July 1990 on the Intergovernmental Conference in the context of Parliament's strategy for European Union, OJ C 231/1990, at pt. 33. This proposal was not accepted. *See also* Bieber, "Legislative Procedure" at p. 716.

is more likely to ignore them completely. Even if the Commission accepts the amendments, they will not necessarily find favor with the Council, which may either persuade the Commission to drop them or overrule them by unanimity. In either case, Parliament relies on the Commission to be its advocate as there is no provision for a direct dialogue between it and the Council.

The change of name to the *European Parliament* in 1962 was the first step in Parliament's campaign to become more influential. The advent of direct elections in 1979, which made Parliament the only directly-elected Community institution, gave real substance to its claims.[245] Two years previously, Article 203 of the EEC Treaty had been amended to give Parliament the right to adopt the Community budget.[246] This specialized procedure is beyond the scope of this study, but its introduction highlights Parliament's increasing influence. On the practical side, Parliament introduced various procedural devices aimed at strengthening its meagre role in the legislative process.

One of the changes brought about by Parliament's Rules of Procedure was a provision for optional consultation by the Council.[247] The Council agreed to this addendum to the Treaties and nowadays refers all legislative proposals to Parliament as a matter of course.[248] What is perhaps more important, Parliament also designed its Rules to exploit the fact that, where its Opinion or First Reading is mandated by the Treaties, this is an essential procedural requirement that must be fulfilled before the Council can act on a proposal. Otherwise the legislative act is liable to an action for annulment.[249] This allows Parliament to pressure the Commission into accepting parliamentary amendments or withdrawing its proposal at Parliament's request by threatening to delay completion of its consultation.[250] However, although the Treaties set no time limit for Parliament's first consultation, the Court of Justice has indicat-

245. *See* the Preambles to the European Parliament's Resolution of 17 April 1980 on the relations between the European Parliament and the Commission of the Community with a view to the forthcoming appointment of a new Commission, OJ C 117/1980, at p. 53; Resolution of 9 July 1981 on relations between the European Parliament and the Council, OJ C 234/1981, at p. 52; Resolution of 9 July 1981 on the right of legislative initiative and on the role of the European Parliament in the legislative process of the Community, OJ C 234/1981, at p. 64; and Resolution of 14 December 1983 on the draft second joint declaration of the European Parliament, the Council and the Commission on the conciliation procedure, OJ C 10/1984, at p. 34. *See also* Resolution of 11 July 1990 on the European Parliament's guidelines for a draft constitution for the European Union at pt. 5. Parliament's Declaration of Fundamental Rights and Freedoms, OJ C 120/1989, at pt. 17(2) states: "Every public authority must be directly elected or answerable to a directly elected parliament".

246. This was done by Article 12 of the Treaty Amending Certain Financial Provisions (OJ L 359/1977).

247. Rule 36(1) (ROPParl) is in fact couched in neutral language, which allows for both mandatory and optional consultations.

248. Parliament has called — so far, unsuccessfully — for this practice to be enshrined in the Treaties — *see* Resolution of 9 July 1981 on relations between the European Parliament and the Council at pt. 8.

249. *See* arts. 173 (EEC); 146 (EAEC); 33 (ECSC). *See also Roquette Frères* v. *Council*, 138/79, [1980] E.C.R. 3333 at 3360-3361; *Maizena GmbH* v. *Council*, 139/79, [1980] E.C.R. 3393 at 3424-3425.

250. *See* Rules 39, 40 (ROPParl).

ed that Parliament cannot delay the legislative process indefinitely.[251] Nevertheless, the threat of obstruction has considerably strengthened Parliament's position vis-à-vis the Commission.

Other procedural devices aimed at augmenting Parliament's influence over the legislative process are the rules on re-consultation and conciliation. Parliament's Rules provide for re-consultation wherever, after the first consultation, a proposal is replaced or substantially amended or Parliament's original opinion has become outdated.[252] The Conciliation Procedure establishes a direct dialogue between the Council and Parliament in order to overcome differences of opinion between them.[253] The procedure is not without its deficiencies and, under the TEU, it may become restricted to the Co-decision Procedure where its use is institutionalized.[254] It is discussed in detail later in this chapter.

The SEA further increased Parliament's role in the legislative process by introducing the Cooperation Procedure for certain matters in the EEC Treaty.[255] Under this procedure, Parliament is guaranteed a first consultation and in addition has the right to a Second Reading, which enables it to re-introduce amendments from its First Reading that were disregarded as well as adopt new amendments.[256] These amendments may continue to be disregarded by the Council, but in practice a substantial minority are incorporated into the final legislation. Furthermore, the Council is supposed under this procedure to explain its attitude to the parliamentary amendments that it has not incorporated into its Common Position, and the Commission must express its opinion on those amendments from Parliament's Second Reading that it has not accepted.[257] These particular provisions go a long way towards ensuring that the Council properly considers Parliament's views.

Parliament can also reject proposed legislation at its Second Reading.[258] This time, the Council can only override Parliament's rejection by a unanimous vote, which is difficult to achieve, and so the Second Reading gives Parliament what almost amounts to a power of veto. On the one occasion that Parliament has used its

---

251. *See Roquette Frères* v. *Council* , 138/79, at 3360-3361; *Maizena GmbH* v. *Council* , 139/79, at 3424-3425. In these two cases, the Council had enacted a regulation without waiting for Parliament to deliver its Opinion. The Court of Justice held this to be a breach of an essential procedural requirement as the Council had not availed itself of all the means available to force Parliament to act, notably by invoking the urgency procedure (Rule 75 (ROPParl)) or by requesting an extraordinary plenary session pursuant to Article 139 (EEC). The clear implication of the judgment is that the Council is able to act unilaterally where Parliament refuses to cooperate in the legislative process. This is also the view taken by Freestone and Davidson, *Institutional Framework of the European Communites* at p.77 and pp. 98-99. Article 188b(a) (EP Draft Treaty) suggests a six-month limit for Parliament to act in the first round.
252. Rule 42 (ROPParl). *See also* OJ C 167/1988 at p. 63 and *infra* at pp. 53-54.
253. *See* Rule 43 (ROPParl) and the Joint Declaration on the conciliation procedure.
254. **Art. 189b (EC)**.
255. *See* arts. 7, 49, 54(2), 56(2), 57, 100a(1), 100b(1), 118a(2), 130e, 130q(2) (EEC); 6(1) (SEA). Under the TEU, Articles 49, 54(2), 56(2), 57(1), 57(2), 100a(1) and 100b(1) adopt the Co-decision Procedure. **Article 130i(4) (EC)**, by contrast, will use the traditional procedure whereas the SEA provides for the Cooperation Procedure — *see* arts. 130k, 130q(2) (EEC). *See also* Table 2.
256. Arts. 149(2)(c) (EEC); **189c(c) (EC)**; Rule 51 (ROPParl.). Parliament has, however, placed limits on its right to adopt new amendments — *see infra* at pp. 85-86 and p. 87.
257. Arts. 149(2)(b),(d) (EEC); **189c(b),(d) (EC)**.
258. Arts. 149(2)(c) (EEC); **189c(c) (EC)**; Rule 50 (ROPParl)

power of rejection under the Cooperation Procedure, the Council was indeed unable to achieve the unanimity needed to override Parliament, and the proposal was abandoned.[259]

The changes wrought by the SEA certainly enhance Parliament's stature and make its amending power more meaningful, but they do not alter its essential dependence on the Commission.[260] If the Commission does not accept Parliament's amendments under the Cooperation Procedure, the Council is still unlikely to do so by unanimity. Moreover, the Commission remains Parliament's advocate before the Council. It must also be remembered that the Cooperation Procedure only displaces the traditional procedure for certain EEC matters.[261] The SEA does not give Parliament any role in the initiation of legislation.

The TEU continues where the SEA left off. It introduces the Co-decision Procedure, which follows the same steps in the first round as the Cooperation Procedure but strengthens Parliament's position in the second round. Now, if Parliament rejects the Common Position, the legislative process is ended unless the Council can persuade Parliament to change its mind in the Conciliation Committee.[262] The rejection can no longer be overridden by the Council acting unanimously. Likewise, if the Council does not accept Parliament's amendments at its Second Reading, it cannot press on regardless but must meet representatives of Parliament in the Conciliation Committee in order to work out a joint, compromise text. This text must be formally accepted by both institutions, otherwise the act is not adopted as legislation.[263] Where conciliation fails to produce an agreed text, the Council can re-confirm its original Common Position, but it will not become law if Parliament rejects it anew by an absolute majority of MEPs.[264]

This new procedure will give Parliament a right of veto and substantially reduce its dependence on the Commission, as it will now deal directly with the Council during the second round on the basis of equality. Above all, the Co-decision Procedure will finally give the European Parliament a legislative function, at least in the EC, and this is reflected in the new terminology of the Treaty provisions. **Article 137** of the EC Treaty refers now to Parliament's "powers" without the limiting words "advisory and supervisory."[265] Wherever there is reference to the legislative organs of the Community, there is also mention of acts adopted jointly by the European Parliament and the Council.[266] Community legislation enacted under the Co-decision Procedure will have to be signed by both the President of the Council and the

259. In October 1988, Parliament rejected at its Second Reading the proposed Directive on the protection of workers exposed to benzene at work.

260. The European Parliament has criticized the SEA as not being a valid response to the problem of the democratic deficit — *see* Resolution of 8 October 1986 on relations between the European Parliament and the Council, OJ C 283/1986, at pt. 1. T.C. Hartley, *Foundations of Community Law*, echoes this criticism at pp. 33-34.

261. *See* Table 2 and fn. 255.

262. **Art. 189b(2)(c) (EC)**.

263. **Art. 189b(2)(d),(3),(4),(5),(6) (EC)**.

264. **Art. 189b (6) (EC)**.

265. The EAEC and ECSC Treaties, however, retain the old language — *see* arts. 107 (EAEC); 20 (ECSC).

266. **Arts. 172, 173, 184, 189, 190 (EC)**.

President of Parliament, and the European Parliament is now included as one of the Community institutions that can be brought before the Court of Justice for failure to act.[267]

The TEU makes other significant changes. It extends the use of the Cooperation Procedure[268] and requires Parliament's assent for Council legislation on the exercise of the general right of movement and residence, changes to the Statute of the European System of Central Banks (ESCB), the organization of the structural Funds and the uniform voting procedure for the European Parliament.[269] It also gives Parliament the right to request the Commission to submit legislative proposals that Parliament considers necessary for the implementation of the Treaties.[270]

Despite all these changes, the TEU falls short of giving Parliament the full part in the legislative process that it had wanted.[271] In the first place, the new Co-decision Procedure does not replace but complements the existing Cooperation Procedure[272] and is limited to certain EC matters.[273] More important, neither Co-decision nor the requirement for Parliament's assent give it an independent legislative power but only a right to share in or control the Council's power. Parliament will still require the Commission's cooperation during the first round, where the procedure remains unchanged. Moreover, Parliament's new right to request the Commission to make a legislative proposal will not permit it to dictate the content of the ensuing proposal or to make the proposal itself if the Commission does not act within a set time limit, which powers Parliament had specifically requested. [274]

The Co-decision Procedure itself, as established by the TEU, also differs from Parliament's model in a way that effectively reduces Parliament's role and keeps it inferior to the Council.[275] These are the salient differences:

---

267. **Arts. 191(1), 175 (EC).**
268. *See* **arts. 75(1), 84(2), 104a(2), 104b(2), 125, 127(4), 130e, 130s(1) (EC).**
269. **Arts. 8a(2), 106(5), 130d, 138(3) (EC); 108(3) (Revised EAEC); 21(3) (Revised ECSC).**
270. **Arts. 138b (EC); 107a (Revised EAEC);20a (Revised ECSC).**
271. *See* Resolution of 16 January 1986 on the position of the European Parliament on the Single Act approved by the Intergovernmental Conference on 16 and 17 December 1985, OJ C 36/1986, at pt. C; Resolution of 17 June 1988 on the democratic deficit in the European Community, OJ C 187/1988, at pt. 21; Resolution of 14 March 1990 on the Intergovernmental Conference in the context of Parliament's strategy for European Union, OJ C 96/1990, at pt. 3(h); Resolution of 11 July 1990 on the Intergovernmental Conference in the context of Parliament's strategy for European Union at pt. 3.
272. Parliament had intended the Co-decision Procedure to replace the Cooperation Procedure — *see* art. 188c (EP Draft Treaty).
273. *See* Table 3 and fn. 255.
274. *See* art. 188a (2) (EP Draft Treaty); Resolution of 9 July 1981 on the right of legislative initiative at pt. 3; Resolution of 11 July 1990 on the Intergovernmental Conference in the context of Parliament's strategy for European Union at pt. 34.
275. Parliament's suggestions are set out in Article 188b (EP Draft Treaty) and its Resolution of 22 November 1990 embodying Parliament's opinion on the convening of the Intergovernmental Conferences on Economic and Monetary Union and Political Union, in Part I of *1993. The New Treaties. European Parliament's Proposals* at pt. 33.

— the Council is not required to act by unanimity when it adopts a Common Position after Parliament has rejected the Commission's proposal at its First Reading;[276]
— there is no provision for the Council to proceed directly to enact the legislation in the first round instead of adopting a Common Position where Parliament and the Council are in agreement on the text;
— Parliament needs to muster an absolute majority of MEPs against the Common Position in order to bring the Conciliation Committee into operation instead of a simple majority of votes cast;
— Parliament's failure to act during its Second Reading still amounts to an approval by default of the Common Position, whereas under the EP Draft Treaty the Conciliation Committee would meet in this situation;
— the EP Draft Treaty does not give the Council the right to re-confirm its Common Position where conciliation fails, which procedure forces upon Parliament a third reading and the need to muster an absolute majority of MEPs to prevent the text from becoming law.[277]

The TEU also creates one new problem. Under the Social Policy Agreement, it is possible for management and labor to negotiate directly and to have their agreement implemented by a Council Decision.[278] In this case, Parliament would be side-stepped as there is no provision for consultation by the Council.

1.2. Structure and Operation of Parliament

The European Parliament represents the peoples of the Member States in the legislative process, just as the Commission represents the Community as a whole and the Council the Governments of the Member States.[279] The 518 MEPs are elected directly by universal suffrage[280] with the number of seats per Member State being roughly based on population. There are 81 seats for France, Germany, Italy and the United Kingdom, 60 for Spain, 25 for the Netherlands, 24 for Belgium, Portugal and Greece, 16 for Denmark, 15 for Ireland and 6 for Luxembourg.[281] The calculation is, however, far from equitable. In Germany, for example, almost one million votes are needed to elect a single MEP, whereas in Luxembourg it takes less than seventy thousand votes. The TEU includes a Declaration committing the Member States to

276. It should be noted, however, that, under Article 188b(a) (EP Draft Treaty), Parliament would need an absolute majority of MEPs to reject the Commission's proposal at its First Reading instead the simple majority of votes required at present.
277. Parliament, in fact, severely criticized this provision in its Resolution of 11 July 1990 on the Intergovernmental Conference in the context of Parliament's strategy for European Union at pt. 32. *See also infra* at p. 99.
278. **Art. 4(2) of the 14th Protocol (TEU).**
279. *See* arts. 137 (EEC); 107 (EAEC); 20 (ECSC). *See also* the Act Concerning the Election of the Representatives of the European Parliament by Direct Universal Suffrage, (OJ L 278/1976), art. 1
280. Act Concerning the Election, art. 1. There have been three direct elections; in 1979, 1984 and 1989.
281. Act Concerning the Election, art. 2.

review the present number of MEPs with a view to making changes in time for the 1994 elections.[282] This review has now taken place, and at Edinburgh the European Council agreed to increase the number of MEPs to 567 and to re-allocate the number of seats held by Member States. The new arrangement will give 99 seats to Germany (a gain of 18 seats), 87 to France, Italy and the United Kingdom (a gain of 6 seats), 64 to Spain (a gain of 4 seats), 31 to the Netherlands (a gain of 6 seats), 25 to Belgium, Greece and Portugal (a gain of 1 seat), 16 to Denmark (no change), 15 to Ireland (no change) and 6 to Luxembourg (no change).

The MEPs are divided into transnational political groups, a development that is encouraged by the parliamentary rules, which specify that a political group must comprise either twenty-three MEPs from one, eighteen from two or twelve from three or more Member States.[283] The EC Treaty gives official recognition to these European political parties, which it sees as contributing to forming "a European awareness."[284] There are limits to this transnationalism, however, and some issues still provoke a regrouping along national lines. An example is agricultural policy reform, which all British MEPs support regardless of party affiliation and which most French MEPs oppose.

On the Left are the Socialists, the Left Unity Group (orthodox Communists and allies), the European Unitarian Left (progressive Communists and allies) and the Rainbow Group, which gathers together an assortment of ecological and left-wing movements although some ecologists now sit in a separate Green Group. The Right is also fragmented and comprises the European People's Party (Christian Democrats together with the British and Danish Conservatives[285]), the Liberal Democratic and Reformist Group (Liberals[286] and Centrists), the European Democratic Alliance (French and Irish Conservatives) and the European Right, which consists mainly of the French and Italian far-right parties. There is also a Non-Attached Group, which includes such diverse movements as the Italian Radicals and the Dutch Calvinists. In fact, the European Parliament is dominated by the Socialists and the Christian Democrats, which accounts for its strong bias in favor of a social market economy. One week per month is set aside for meetings of the political groups, except during the summer break.

The representation of the various political groups in the present European Parliament is as follows:

282. **15th Declaration (TEU).**

283. Rule 26(5) (ROPParl). It is possible that these figures will be changed as a result of the increase in the number of MEPs.

284. **Art. 138a (EC).**

285. Under Mrs. Thatcher's leadership, the British Conservatives were refused membership of the EPP and constituted, together with the Danish Conservatives, the European Democrats. Significantly, they and their Danish colleagues were admitted into the EPP on April 9th, 1992, the day that Mrs Thatcher's successor, John Major, was confirmed in office. They have sat under the EPP banner since May 1992.

286. The Liberals in the European Parliament are to the political right of the British and Canadian Liberal Parties.

Socialists	180
European People's Party	162
Liberal Democratic and Reformist Group	45
European Unitarian Left	29
Greens	27
European Democratic Alliance	21
Rainbow Group	15
European Right Group	14
Left Unity	13
Independents	12

In addition to the political groups, there are also parliamentary inter-groups for certain issues that cut across both national and political lines. Examples are the groups for institutional reform, research and development and the internal market. These pressure groups exert considerable influence in Parliament. Like the political groups, they meet once a month, normally in Brussels.

Parliament's Opinions and First Readings are decided in its plenary sessions, but it is the parliamentary committees that carry out the detailed examination of the Commission's proposals and prepare the reports that form the basis for the plenary session's debate and vote. There are nineteen of these committees, each of which comprises between twenty and sixty MEPs and deals with a particular subject area.[287] Commission officials from the Secretariat-General and the responsible DGs regularly attend committee meetings to explain the Commission's position, and other experts and representatives of specialist organizations may also be invited to attend.[288] The committees are also assisted by administrators from DG II of Parliament's General Secretariat, who are responsible for seeing proposals through the committee stage. Parliamentary committees are not obliged to hold their meetings in public but many do so.[289] When a committee is given the power of decision over a matter, its meetings must be open to the public [290]

The European Parliament usually takes about six months to deliver its Opinion or First Reading, but the Council or the Commission can request a proposal to be dealt with on an urgent basis.[291] Efficiency remains, however, a major problem. The twelve periods of monthly plenary sessions, including the budget session, take place

287. The parliamentary committees are: I — Foreign Affairs and Security (formerly Political Affairs); II — Agriculture, Fisheries and Rural Development; III — Budgets; IV — Economic and Monetary Affairs and Industrial Policy; V — Energy, Research and Technology; VI — External Economic Relations; VII — Legal Affairs and Citizens' Rights; VIII — Social Affairs, Employment and the Working Environment; IX — Regional Policy, Regional Planning and Relations with Regional and Local Authorities; X — Transport and Tourism; XI — Environment, Public Health and Consumer Protection; XII — Youth, Culture, Education, the Media and Sport; XIII — Development and Cooperation; XIV — Civil Liberties and Internal Affairs; XV — Budgetary Control; XVI — Institutional Affairs; XVII — Rules of Procedure, the Verification of Credentials and Immunities; XVIII — Women's Rights; XIX — Petitions. The terms of reference of these committees are found in Annex VI (ROPParl).

288. Rule 124 (3) (ROPParl).

289. Rule 124 (2) (ROPParl).

290. Rule 37(4) (ROPParl).

291. Art. 139 (EEC); Rule 75 (ROPParl).

in Strasbourg, while the committees meet in Brussels and the General Secretariat is based in Luxembourg. Although the European Parliament attempts now to coordinate its activities with the legislative programs of the Commission and the Council, it is still hamstrung by these institutional arrangements.[292] Unfortunately, it is up to the Member States, acting by common accord, to determine the seat of the European Parliament,[293] and they confirmed these illogical arrangements at the Edinburgh summit.[294] The only concession was to allow Parliament to continue holding additional plenary sessions in Brussels.[295] It seems likely, therefore, that the long-overdue reorganization of Parliament has been delayed indefinitely.

It is the President of the European Parliament who directs its activities[296] and who represents the Parliament in its relations with the other Community institutions.[297] He or she is elected by an absolute majority of votes cast by MEPs.[298] If a fourth ballot is required, it is confined to the two leading candidates. The President also decides on the admissibility of proposed amendments at both the First and Second Readings.[299] The Bureau of the Parliament, which includes the President and the fourteen Vice-Presidents, is responsible for the delicate task of ensuring a fair representation of the Member States and the political groups on the parliamentary committees.[300]

1.3. Parliament's Opinion/First Reading

The parliamentary procedures are largely the same whether Parliament is delivering an Opinion under the traditional procedure or undertaking its First Reading in the

292. *The Economist* (October 14th, 1989, p. 58) describes the problems thus:

> Deputies and Eurocrats waste days each month just travelling. Many services have to be performed three times over. The work of the committees is delayed because they cannot meet in the week of the plenary sessions. Lorries cart trunks of documents from one city to another, yet still deputies often find they lack the document they need (the library and research departments are in Luxembourg). The direct cost of all this was estimated in 1987 at 40 m. ecus ($46 m.).

293. Arts. 216 (EEC); 189 (EAEC); 77 (ECSC). The Court of Justice has confirmed that Parliament cannot unilaterally change its instititutional arrangements — *see Luxembourg* v. *European Parliament*, 230/81, [1983] E.C.R. 255 at 262. In its Resolution of 11 July 1990 on the Intergovernmental Conference in the context of Parliament's strategy for European Union at pt. 41, Parliament called for these Treaty Articles to be amended in order to give it the right to fix its own seat. This idea was not taken up in the TEU.
294. Decision Taken by Common Agreement between the Representatives of the Governments of the Member States on the Location of the Seats of the Institutions and of Certain Bodies and Departments of the European Communities, art.1(a) (*Edinburgh Summit Conclusions*, Annex 6).
295. The Court of Justice had already endorsed this practice in *France* v. *European Parliament*, 358/85 and 51/85, [1990] 1 C.M.L.R. 309 at 336.
296. Rule 18 (ROPParl).
297. Rules 39, 42, 43 (ROPParl).
298. Rule 13(1) (ROPParl).
299. Rules 51(2), 70(3) (ROPParl.).
300. Rules 21(1), 110(1) (ROPParl).

Cooperation and Co-decision Procedures.[301] Both consultations are designated subsequently in this text as Parliament's opinion except where it is necessary to make a distinction. Unless the contrary is stated, all votes taken in committee or in plenary session with respect to Parliament's opinion are decided by a simple majority of votes cast.[302] In the event of a tie, a motion stands rejected. Although it is the Council that has the obligation to consult Parliament, it is in fact the Commission that both sends the proposal to Parliament and reacts to its opinion.[303]

Once the proposal has been received by Parliament, it is referred to the appropriate committee for consideration.[304] Up to two other committees may be asked to furnish the responsible committee with their opinions on the proposal.[305] The designation of these committees is the responsibility of the President, but a committee may refer any dispute over its role to the full Parliament.[306] In practice, the areas of competence for each committee are set out in sufficient detail in Annex VI to the Parliament's Rules of Procedure that disputes are rare. For example, services and corporate law always involve the Legal Affairs Committee as the responsible committee and the Economic and Monetary Affairs Committee as the committee giving an opinion.

When a proposal is referred to committee, Parliament may, upon a proposal from the President, twenty-three MEPs or a committee, delegate to the responsible committee the power to take a decision unless one tenth of MEPs object.[307] Under this delegation procedure, the committee's report containing its resolution and amendments, if any, to the Commission's proposal is put before Parliament and deemed adopted unless one tenth of MEPs, belonging to at least three political groups, express their disapproval.[308] In this latter event, the report is considered by Parliament in accordance with its normal procedure.

The responsible committee must first decide on its procedure. Upon the recommendation of the President or the committee Chairman, it may decide to approve the proposal without a report or to empower its Chairman to draw up a draft report.[309] These quicker procedures are used mostly in the case of routine legislation, but neither can be used where the committee wishes to propose amendments to the Commission's proposal or if at least four members of the committee object to their use.[310] The no-report procedure is recommended by the Rules for urgent matters.[311] The Chairman's draft report consists of a procedural section, a draft legislative reso-

301. Rule 44 (1) (ROPParl). Articles 149(2)(a) (EEC) and **189b(2)** and **189c(a) (EC)** in fact continue to use the term "Opinion" when referring to the First Reading of Parliament.
302. Rule 90(4) (ROPParl).
303. *See* Rules 39 and 40 (ROPParl). **Article 189b(2) (EC)** now recognizes this practice for the first time.
304. Rule 36(1) (ROPParl). This committee is officially called the "committee responsible," but the inversion is reversed in the text for stylistic reasons.
305. Rules 112(3), 120 (ROPParl).
306. Rules 36(1), 112(2), 120(1) (ROPParl).
307. Rule 37(1),(2) (ROPParl). The figure of twenty-three MEPs may change with the increase in the overall number of MEPs.
308. Rule 37(5) (ROPParl).
309. Rule 116(1), (2) (ROPParl).
310. Rule 116(3) (ROPParl).
311. Rule 75(5) (ROPParl).

lution and a brief explanatory statement.[312] It cannot suggest amendments, but the draft legislative resolution can recommend that Parliament reject the proposal. It is sent to all the members of the committee and is considered adopted unless four or more members object to it within a set time limit, which must not be less than fourteen days. In the latter event, the full report procedure with a Rapporteur must be used.[313]

The committee may, of course, decide at the outset to appoint a Rapporteur to assist it in preparing a full report.[314] This is the procedure that is normally followed for any significant legislative proposal. It must be followed if four or more committee members object to either of the other two procedures or if the committee wishes to propose amendments. The Rapporteur draws up a draft report containing any suggested amendments to the Commission's proposal, including the legal base, and a draft legislative resolution, which is made up of a statement as to whether Parliament approves, rejects or proposes amendments to the proposal plus any procedural requests.[315] In the meantime, the other committee (or committees) prepares its opinion, which it (they) must submit within the time limit set by the responsible committee if it is to be taken into account by the latter.[316] The responsible committee cannot, however, reach its final conclusion before this time limit has expired.

Both the Rapporteur's draft report and the opinion of the other committee(s) are considered by the responsible committee meeting in plenary session. Any MEP, whether or not a member of the committee, may table additional amendments to the Commission's proposal or to the draft legislative resolution for consideration by the responsible committee, but only current members of the committee may vote on them.[317] Amendments may not seek to delete or replace the whole of a text,[318] which precludes changes to the tenor of the Rapporteur's draft legislative resolution. As there is no provision in the Rules for MEPs to table a motion for the committee to reject the proposal, this means that only the Rapporteur may propose rejecting the Commission's proposal. However, the responsible committee can always reject the proposal on its own initiative by simply failing to approve the Rapporteur's recommendation that it be accepted. In this case, the Rapporteur must alter the draft legislative resolution in order to record the committee's rejection of the Commission's proposal.

The responsible committee first examines the legal base chosen by the Commission for the proposed measure.[319] If it approves an amendment calling for a change to the legal base, it refers the matter to the Legal Affairs Committee for its

312. Rule 116(2) (ROPParl.).
313. Rule 116(3) (ROPParl).
314. Rule 117 (ROPParl).
315. Rule 117(3) — *see too* Rule 36(5) (ROPParl).
316. Rule 120(4) (ROPParl).
317. Rule 69(1) and note to Rule 37 (ROPParl).
318. *See* Rules 70(1)(b) and 123(4) (ROPParl).
319. Rule 36(3) (ROPParl). It is a moot point whether the European Parliament will expand its examination to include all the aspects of subsidiarity as laid down in **Article 3b (EC)**. It must be borne in mind that Parliament has never shown any particular sensitivity towards encroachments on the legislative competence of the Member States, and it is significant that the European Council foresees no particular role for Parliament in the application of **Article 3b** beyond its participation in an interinstitutional agreement.

opinion.[320] Thus, the responsible committee referred the Commission's proposal on the radioactive contamination of foodstuffs,[321] as it wished to replace Article 31 (EAEC) with Article 100A (EEC) as the legal base. As is frequently the case, this also involved exchanging the traditional procedure for the Cooperation Procedure. If the opinion of the Legal Affairs Committee is supportive, the matter is then brought before the full Parliament, which will vote on whether to call upon the Commission to change the legal base accordingly.[322] The support of the Legal Affairs Committee is not essential, but there is little chance that Parliament will approve a challenge to the legal base without its support. In the case of the proposal on the radioactive contamination of foodstuffs, the Legal Affairs Committee voted unanimously in favor of a change to the legal base. Where the Commission decides not to make the change in conformity with Parliament's resolution, the change is still usually submitted by the responsible committee to Parliament as one of its proposed amendments. This happened with the above proposal on foodstuffs. The Commission insisted on keeping Article 31 as the legal base of the proposal, but the responsible committee nevertheless submitted Article 100A as an amendment, which was adopted by Parliament.

Once this particular legal issue has been dealt with, the responsible committee proceeds to examine the substance of the Commission's proposal. It considers both the suggestions contained in the Rapporteur's draft report as well as the amendments tabled by MEPs. Where there are many amendments tabled, the committee may suspend its considerations and instruct the Rapporteur to submit a new draft report taking these amendments into account.[323]

Even where the Rapporteur has recommended rejecting the proposal, the Rules provide that the committee votes first on amendments to the proposal, then on the proposal as amended, then on amendments to the paragraphs of the draft legislative resolution and the individual paragraphs as amended and only at the very end on the draft resolution as a whole.[324] This sequence of voting means that committee members give their final opinion on the Commission's proposal only after they have been given ample opportunity to amend it to their satisfaction. This practice reflects the reluctance of Parliament to reject proposals on a first consultation. Not only is rejection often counter-productive in that it may eliminate legislation necessary to advance the Community, but there is a good chance that it will provoke a confrontation with the Commission and may in any case be ignored by the Council. Except in the case of disputes over the legal base, it is rare for a responsible committee to recommend that a proposal be rejected. Under the Cooperation and Co-decision Procedures, there is even less reason to do so as a rejection by Parliament of the Common Position at its Second Reading has much more effect.

After the responsible committee has completed its voting, the Rapporteur prepares a final report incorporating the committee's decisions, to which he or she will

320. Rule 36(3) (ROPParl).

321. OJ C 174/1987.

322. The resolution calling for the Commission to change the legal base of its proposal on the radioactive contamination of foodstuffs is found in OJ C 305/1987 at p. 33.

323. Rule 123(5) (ROPParl).

324. Rules 90(1), 123(4) (ROPParl). At the Second Reading, by contrast, both the responsible committee and the full Parliament vote first on any resolution to reject the Common Position — *see* Rules 90(2), 123(4) (ROPParl).

append an explanatory statement setting out the reasons for them and indicating clearly any minority opinion.[325] The report must also set out the views of committees asked for an opinion insofar as these differ from that of the responsible committee.[326] In practice, the report will often include the whole opinion(s). In the event that a committee asked for an opinion is dissatisfied with the report as it is submitted to Parliament, it is no longer able to table its own set of amendments[327] but presumably can always propose additional amendments at the plenary session under Rule 69(1).

Once a proposal has been considered by the appropriate committee, it is up to the plenary session of Parliament to deal with it on the basis of the committee report,[328] unless it has delegated this decision-making power to the committee. Where the responsible committee so requests or where it has used the simpler procedures (no report/Chairman's report), Parliament dispenses with a debate and votes immediately unless at least twenty-three MEPs lodge a protest in advance.[329] Since February 10, 1992, however, a responsible committee cannot ask for an immediate vote where it is proposing amendments that have been opposed in committee by more than three dissenting votes.[330]

Where the responsible committee has approved a proposal without a report and Parliament decides on a debate, the proposal is referred back to the committee for reconsideration and the preparation of a report.[331] The responsible committee is not expressly required now to appoint a Rapporteur, but this would seem to be implied as the Chairman's report is not intended for use in connection with a parliamentary debate.[332] For this reason, it would seem that a Chairman's report should also be referred back when a debate is called for, although Rule 38(2) does not require this.

When a debate in Parliament takes place on a committee report, additional amendments either to the Commission's proposal or to the draft legislative resolution are only admitted if they are supported by a political group, a committee or at least twenty-three MEPs.[333] All other amendments proposed by MEPs must be made through the responsible committee and can no longer be brought directly before Parliament.[334] There is no provision for MEPs to table a motion for Parliament to

325. Rule 119(1) (ROPParl).
326. Rule 120(3) (ROPParl).
327. Rule 120(6a) (ROPParl).
328. Rules 36(4), 116(2) (ROPParl).
329. Rule 38(1),(2) (ROPParl). The figure of twenty-three MEPs may change with the increase in the overall number of MEPs. Debate is perhaps too strong a word for what actually takes place. Due to the extreme time restraints under which the European Parliament operates, political groups may be allotted as little as three minutes and individual MEPs even less time in which to express their points of view. For an example of the allocation of speaking times, *see* OJ C 39/1992 at p.8.
330. Rule 38(2), 2nd. subparagraph. Where the simpler procedures are being used, this Rule will not apply as they cannot be used to propose amendments to the Commission's proposal — *see supra* at pp. 46-47.
331. Rule 38(2) (ROPParl.)
332. *See* Rule 116(2) (ROPParl.).
333. Rule 69(1) (ROPParl). The figure of twenty-three MEPs may change with the increase in the overall number of MEPs.
334. Rule 69(1) (ROPParl). Until February 10, 1992, such amendments could, if rejected by the responsible committee, nevertheless be brought before the full Parliament if there were at least four votes cast in their favor by committee members

reject the Commission's proposal.[335] Thus, a vote to reject the proposal is only possible if this is the tenor of the responsible committee's draft legislative resolution, although a proposal also stands rejected if it fails to secure the support of a majority of votes cast by MEPs.[336] It is rare for a Commission proposal to fail to make it through Parliament's first consultation for the same reasons that it is exceptional for the responsible committee to recommend rejection.[337]

Where there are overall more than twenty additional amendments for Parliament to consider in plenary session, the President must refer them back to the responsible committee unless Parliament decides otherwise on a proposal from the President or the Chairman or the Rapporteur of the committee.[338] The responsible committee then examines the additional amendments and puts both them and any compromise amendments it itself proposes to a vote. A written supplementary report is submitted to Parliament containing the full text of all amendments considered by the committee and the result of the vote on them. Amendments that are rejected by the committee at this stage are only put before the full Parliament if this is requested in writing by a committee or at least twenty-three MEPs.[339] Additional amendments that aim to change the legal base of a Commission proposal must first be referred to the Legal Affairs Committee for its opinion before they can be considered by Parliament.[340]

After the debate has taken place, Parliament votes on the Commission's proposal and the draft legislative resolution in exactly the same sequence as the responsible committee.[341] Once again, and for the same reasons, a draft resolution to reject the proposal is not voted on until the end.[342] Parliament does not vote on the explanatory statement or the opinions of other committees contained in the report. Once the vote on the draft legislative resolution has been taken, the consultation procedure is concluded and the text of the proposal as approved (or rejected) by the European Parliament together with its legislative resolution are forwarded by the President to both the Council and the Commission.[343] The proposal is rejected if a legislative resolution to this effect is passed by a simple majority of votes cast by MEPs or if the draft resolution approving the proposal does not secure a simple majority of votes.[344] In the latter case, a new resolution indicating Parliament's rejection of the proposal will have to be adopted in order to complete Parliament's consultation.

Parliament's vote on the draft legislative resolution may, however, be postponed in certain circumstances. Firstly, any MEP, and *a fortiori* any political group or committee, can request that a proposal be referred back to committee.[345] If this request is

335. At the Second Reading, by contrast, MEPs are expressly given the right to propose that the Common Position of the Council be rejected — *see* Rule 50(1) (ROPParl).
336. Rules 39(1), 90(4). (ROPParl).
337. *See supra* at p. 48.
338. Rule 71(2) (ROPParl).
339. Rule 71(4) (ROPParl). The figure of twenty-three MEPs may change with the increase in the overall number of MEPs.
340. Note to Rule 36(3) (ROPParl).
341. Rules 36(5), 90(1) (ROPParl).
342. *See supra* at p. 48.
343. Rule 36(5), (7) (ROPParl).
344. Rules 39(1), 90(1)(d), 90(4) (ROPParl).
345. Rule 103 (ROPParl).

accepted, it entails suspension of the debate and the vote until the committee reports back. Parliament can set a time limit for reporting back but is not obliged to do so. Only one request for referral back to committee may be made during a debate.

Secondly, where Parliament rejects the Commission's proposal, the President of Parliament must request the Commission to withdraw its proposal and the formal vote on the draft legislative resolution is postponed until the Commission has indicated whether or not it intends to comply with this request.[346] It is important for Parliament to secure this withdrawal, as this is the only way of bringing the legislative process to a definitive end. As we have seen, the Council is not bound by Parliament's rejection of the Commission's proposal on its first consultation and may go on to enact the legislation or adopt a Common Position, depending on which procedure is being used. As yet, Parliament has rarely rejected Commission proposals when delivering its Opinion and, for the reasons given earlier,[347] never at a First Reading.

If the proposal is withdrawn, no vote on the draft legislative resolution takes place and the President informs the Council that the consultation procedure has become superfluous. Otherwise, the rejected proposal is referred back to committee for a maximum period of two months while a compromise is sought with the Commission, which would take the form of a new or substantially amended proposal. Failing agreement at this stage, Parliament may vote to keep the proposal in committee in order to put pressure on the Commission. Parliament cannot, however, delay legislation indefinitely; sooner or later it must either vote on the legislative resolution or risk being sidetracked.[348]

Where Parliament approves a Commission proposal in amended form, the vote on the draft legislative resolution is likewise postponed until the Commission has indicated its intentions with respect to modifying its proposal.[349] If the Commission does not adopt all of Parliament's amendments, which is the usual case, the proposal may be referred back to committee at the request of the Rapporteur for a maximum period of two months. At this stage, only amendments tabled by the responsible committee with the aim of reaching a compromise with the Commission are admissible. Further referrals back to committee are possible where no compromise is forthcoming, but, here again, Parliament has to weigh its desire to have its own way against the risk of being sidetracked. Where there is no likelihood of the Commission bowing to its wishes, Parliament may, exceptionally, reject the proposal. It did this with the proposal on the radioactive contamination of foodstuffs in the face of the Commission's refusal to incorporate its amendment changing the legal base.[350]

The Council sometimes interferes with these interchanges between the Commission and Parliament. It may, for example, act immediately Parliament has passed its legislative resolution without waiting for the Commission to submit the amendments that have been agreed upon. Depending upon the procedure used, this means either reaching a Common Position or enacting the legislation on the basis of

---

346. Rule 39 (ROPParl).
347. *See supra* at p. 48.
348. *See supra* at pp. 38-39
349. Rule 40 (ROPParl).
350. *See supra* at pp. 47-48.

the unamended proposal from the Commission. Parliament has formally requested that the Council refrain from such precipitation,[351] but, in fact, the close and relatively collegial relations between the Council and the Commission virtually rule it out. What does happen, however, is that the Council starts its deliberations before Parliament has delivered its opinion. The result is that the amendments passed subsequently by Parliament may be politically unfeasible in view of developments that have already taken place in the Council. Thus, in the case of the Second Banking Directive, Parliament's desire, expressed at its First Reading, for a management committee instead of a regulatory committee could not be accommodated by the Commission as the Council had already decided to follow the original proposal.[352] It would seem that such premature decisions by the Council constitute at least a technical violation of the Treaties, which require Parliament to be consulted before any part of a Common Position or piece of legislation is adopted, but the practice has not yet been challenged before the Court of Justice.

1.4. Follow-Up Procedures

Parliament's Rules of Procedure charge the Chairman and the Rapporteur of the responsible committee with ensuring that the Commission respects any agreement to amend its original proposal.[353] In practice, the follow-up procedure is much broader in scope and involves monitoring the progress of the proposal right up to the moment of its enactment or the adoption of a Common Position by the Council. Both the Council and the Commission are expected to cooperate with the committee by furnishing all necessary information.[354] In the event that Parliament's opinion is disregarded, the committee can request Parliament to call for withdrawal of the proposal by the Commission, re-consultation of Parliament by the Council or the initiation of the Conciliation Procedure.[355] Alternatively, the committee can request the President to call for re-consultation directly without any prior vote in Parliament.[356] A proposal for re-consultation can also be put before Parliament by a political group or at least twenty-three MEPs.[357]

Parliament will normally call for withdrawal of a proposal subsequent to giving its opinion when the traditional procedure is being used and it is clear that the Council is going to adopt legislation that is seriously at odds with Parliament's view. Under the Cooperation (and Co-decision) Procedures, the issue is not so urgent as Parliament can always reject the Common Position at its Second Reading. It is up to the Commission alone to make the final decision. It is more apt to cooperate with

351. Resolution of 9 July 1981 on relations between the European Parliament and the Council at pt. 12; Resolution of 9 July 1981 on the right of legislative initiative at pt. 6.
352. *See* OJ C 84/1988, art. 20(2) (original proposal); OJ C 96/1989, art. 20(2) (First Reading); OJ C 167/1989, art 20 (2) (amended proposal); Co. Doc. 7835/89, art. 22(2) (Common Position).
353. Rule 41(1), (3) (ROPParl).
354. Rule 41(2) (ROPParl).
355. Rule 41(4) (ROPParl).
356. Rule 42 (ROPParl).
357. Rule 42, 2nd para. (ROPParl). The figure of twenty-three MEPs may change with the increase in the overall number of MEPs.

Parliament where there is a measure of agreement between them on the substance of the proposal; it is less likely to withdraw a proposal where Parliament is insisting on amendments that the Commission accepted reluctantly or not at all.

Re-consultation of Parliament entails repeating the whole consultation procedure, including, if necessary, further amendments by the Commission to the proposal or even its withdrawal. It is the President who must request re-consultation by the Council, acting either at the behest of the responsible committee or on a request from the full Parliament.[358] Re-consultation is requested of the Council as it is the Council that has the legal obligation to consult Parliament. Parliament's Rules call for re-consultation where a) the Commission withdraws its proposal after Parliament has expressed its opinion on it and replaces it with a new proposal; b) the proposal as approved by Parliament is substantially amended by the Commission or the Council; or c) Parliament's opinion has become out-dated through either the passage of time or changes in circumstances.[359] As far as Parliament is concerned, the right to re-consultation applies to both its Opinion and its First Reading, but this view has not yet been officially endorsed by the other two institutions.[360]

There is no dispute over Parliament's right to deliver a new opinion on a replacement proposal, but in the other two instances the Commission and the Council take a much more restrictive attitude than Parliament and require a fundamental change before agreeing to the need for re-consultation. Parliament has repeatedly argued in favor of its own position,[361] but, despite support from the Court of Justice,[362] to no avail. There is nothing, of course, to prevent Parliament from undertaking a second opinion on its own initiative, as it did in the case of the proposal for a Second Non-Life Insurance Directive,[363] but it needs the cooperation of the other two institutions if it wishes a proposal to be amended or withdrawn.

The problem with requiring re-consultation whenever a proposal is modified is that such modifications are an intrinsic part of the horse-trading that characterizes the Council's decision-making process. Throughout the Council's deliberations, the Commission is constantly refining its proposal in order to secure sufficient support for its enactment or the adoption of a Common Position. The Community legislative process would be considerably lengthened and perhaps fatally weakened if all the various compromise formulae first had to be approved by Parliament. Despite its earlier call for re-consultation in the case of all subsequent changes made to a proposal,[364] Parliament now seems to accept that this is unrealistic except where the

358. Rule 42 (ROPParl).

359. Rule 42 (ROPParl).

360. *See* Rule 44 and the note to Rule 45(1) (ROPParl). *See also* Bieber, "Legislative Procedure" at pp. 717-718.

361. *See* its Resolution of 9 July 1981 on relations between the European Parliament and the Council at pt. 11 and its Resolution of 9 July 1981 on the right of legislative initiative at pt. 5.

362. In *ACF Chemiefarma N.V.* v. *Commission*, 41/69, [1070] E.C.R. 661 at p. 662 (pt. 31) and p. 691 (pts. 68, 69), the Court stated that there was no need for re-consultation of Parliament as long as the final text adopted by the Council was substantially the same as that on which Parliament gave its opinion.

363. *See* OJ C 167/1988 at p. 63. In this case, Parliament gave its approval without requiring further amendments.

364. Resolution of 9 July 1981 on relations between the European Parliament and the Council at pt. 11(b).

changes alter the fundamental nature of the proposed measure. In the case of the Public Offers Directive, Parliament did not request re-consultation even though the Common Position differed considerably from the text that it had approved at its First Reading.[365] It has, however, asked the Commission to consult with the responsible committee when it proposes changes to a text already approved by Parliament.[366]

Under the Cooperation (and Co-decision) Procedures, Parliament has the right to a Second Reading, and its Rules of Procedure now permit new amendments to those parts of the Common Position that differ from or were not included in the Commission's proposal as submitted to Parliament for its First Reading.[367] Previously, Parliament had unilaterally limited its power of amendment on a Second Reading to the reintroduction of amendments from its First Reading and the facilitation of a compromise with the Council.[368] This change enables Parliament to react with greater flexibility to the necessary machinations of the Council and the Commission. Nevertheless, Parliament still insists on its right to re-consultation after its First Reading whenever a proposal has undergone a fundamental change.[369]

The Conciliation Procedure was inaugurated in 1975 by a Joint Declaration of the European Parliament, the Council and the Commission.[370] It is also part of Parliament's Rules of Procedure.[371] It is supposed to be used whenever the Council intends to depart from Parliament's opinion and is initiated by Parliament on its own or at the Council's request.[372] It involves setting up a conciliation committee made up of an equal number of representatives from the Council and Parliament.[373] The committee's task is to work out a compromise between Parliament and the Council. The Commission participates in the work of the committee and plays the role of honest broker.[374] The advantages of the Conciliation Procedure are that it establishes a dialogue before any changes are made to a proposal and permits direct negotiations between the two antagonists. In the case of re-consultation, Parliament normally finds itself before a *fait accompli* and also has to rely on the Commission to place its views before the Council. Although the Conciliation Procedure was introduced before the advent of the Cooperation (and Co-decision) Procedures, Parliament's Rules also provide for its use in the context of the First Reading.[375] This extended use of the Conciliation Procedure seems to have been tacitly accepted by the other two institutions and is perhaps more effective where Parliament's position is strengthened by its power to reject the Council's Common Position at its Second Reading. It

365. *Compare* OJ C 125/1982, p. 177 (First Reading) and Co. Doc. 4017/1989 (Common Position)
366. Draft Joint Declaration by the European Parliament and the Commission on relations between the two institutions, OJ C 283/1986, at pt. 7.
367. Rule 51(2)(c) (ROPParl).
368. Rules 51(2)(a),(b) (ROPParl).
369. *See* note to Rule 45(1) (ROPParl)
370. OJ C 89/1975.
371. Rule 43 (ROPParl).
372. Joint Declaration at pts. 3,4; Rule 43(1),(2) (ROPParl). This departure from Parliament's opinion is normally signalled by the recommendation of COREPER to the Council — *see infra* at p. 79.
373. Joint Declaration at pt. 5; Rule 43(3) (ROPParl).
374. Joint Declaration at pt. 5; Rule 43(1) (ROPParl).
375. This is the effect of Rules 43 and 44(1) (ROPParl).

may also serve to reduce the possibility of Parliament rejecting the Common Position.[376]

Unfortunately, despite some successes such as the restructuring of the European Social Fund in 1983, the Conciliation Procedure has not been very effective.[377] In the first place, there is disagreement over its scope. Parliament's Rules provide for it to be used in the case of all important Community acts,[378] whereas the Joint Declaration restricts its use to legislative proposals that have appreciable financial implications.[379] The European Parliament has frequently urged the Council to agree to extend the scope of the procedure,[380] but so far to no avail despite the promise of action by the European Council at its Stuttgart meeting in 1983.[381]

The procedure itself is also flawed. The conciliation committee is empowered to function for up to three months, but there are no provisions for dealing with a failure to reach a compromise.[382] Worse still, Parliament does not even have a right to re-consultation unless the positions of the two institutions are "sufficiently close."[383] This effectively means that once it has initiated conciliation, Parliament is powerless if the procedure does not yield a satisfactory result. It is not surprising, therefore, that Parliament wishes to have a guaranteed right to re-consultation whenever disagreement persists after conciliation.[384] It has also called for the Council's representatives to have proper negotiating authority and for the Council to make its final decision within a fixed time after the end of conciliation.[385] Parliament would like to reactivate the procedure established on October 4, 1971 for exchanging views between the Council and Parliament as a way of making the Conciliation Procedure more effective or even in order to replace it.[386]

The TEU institutionalizes a form of conciliation procedure in the context of the second round of the Co-decision Procedure.[387] There is no limitation on its scope here, and the flaws in the original process have been removed. No action can be

376. *See* Bieber, "Legislative Procedure" at pp. 720-721. This point is also mentioned by Parliament in the Preamble to its Resolution of 16 February 1989 on the conciliation procedure, OJ C 69/1989, at p. 152.
377. This is also the view of Freestone and Davidson, *Institutional Framework of the European Communities* at pp. 99-100 and Hartley, *Foundations of European Community Law* at pp. 31-32. For a brief review of the use of the Conciliation Procedure, *see also* Kapteyn and Themaat, *Introduction to the Law of the European Communities* at pp. 263-265.
378. This is the effect of Rules 43 and 44(1) (ROPParl).
379. Joint Declaration at pt. 2.
380. *See* Resolution on of 9 July 1981 relations between the European Parliament and the Council at pt. 16(a); Resolution of 9 July 1981 on the right of legislative initiative at pt. 10(a); Resolution of 14 December 1983 on the draft second joint declaration on the conciliation procedure at pt.2; Resolution of 16 February 1989 on the conciliation procedure at pt. 2.
381. 2.3.6. EC Bull. 6 (1983), at pp. 24-29.
382. Joint Declaration at pt. 6.
383. Joint Declaration at pt. 7.
384. Resolution of 16 February 1989 on the conciliation procedure at pt. 8.
385. Resolution of 9 July 1981 on relations between the European Parliament and the Council at pt. 17(d),(g).
386. *See* Resolution of 8 October 1986 on relations between the European Parliament and the Council at pt. 13; Resolution of 16 February 1989 on the conciliation procedure at pts. 4, 5. This procedure is discussed briefly *infra* at pp. 79-80.
387. **Art. 189b(2)(c), (3)-(6) (EC)**.

taken without the approval of Parliament if conciliation fails. It is not clear whether this institutionalized procedure, which we shall refer to as the "Conciliation Committee Procedure," is intended to operate alongside the Conciliation Procedure or replace it. The latter result would be unfortunate as it would limit conciliation to the second round of the Co-decision Procedure. If the Conciliation Procedure survives, it would, on the other hand, be available during the first round under all three legislative procedures. This is surely useful, as conciliation at any state helps expedite the passage of legislation and encourages a harmonious and constructive relationship between the Council and Parliament.

1.5. Consultation of Parliament under Article K.6 of the TEU

Article K 3(2) (TEU) provides for the Council to legislate on home and justice affairs. In doing so, the Council will act under an informal procedure whereby the Presidency consults with Parliament and is obliged to ensure that its views are taken into consideration.[388] There will be no consultation by the Council as such, and there is no provision for a formal Opinion from Parliament. It is not clear as yet how much influence this new procedure will permit Parliament to exercise, particularly in view of the fact that the TEU only requires consultation on the principal aspects of the Council's activities.

1.6. The Assent of Parliament

The TEU introduces the requirement for Parliament's assent in the case of four matters that otherwise come under the traditional procedure. These are legislation on the general right of movement and residence, changes to the Statute of the ESCB, the organization of the Structural Funds and a uniform voting procedure for the European Parliament.[389] In the case of the Structural Funds, Parliament will also have to be consulted. The uniform voting procedure will require, as previously under the original Treaties, the ratification of the Member States in addition to Parliament's assent.[390] The parliamentary procedures for giving an assent will probably follow those for adopting an opinion.

2. THE ECONOMIC AND SOCIAL COMMITTEE (ECOSOC)

2.1. Structure and Operation of ECOSOC

ECOSOC comprises 189 members drawn from a broad spectrum of economic and social groups.[391] They are appointed by the Council on the basis of lists drawn up by

388. **Art. K.6 (TEU)**.

389. **Arts. 8a(2), 106(5), 130d, 138(3) (EC); 108(3) (Revised EAEC); 21(3) (Revised ECSC)**.

390. *Compare, e.g.,* arts. 138(3) (EEC) and **138(3) (EC)**.

391. Arts. 193 (EEC); 165 (EAEC). Apparently, the numerical structure of ECOSOC will not be changed despite the revision of the number and allocation of MEPs.

the Member States for renewable terms of four years.[392] The number of members from each Member State is weighted according to population.[393] Members of ECOSOC are bound to act independently of their national Governments.[394]

ECOSOC was put into the EEC and the EAEC Treaties somewhat as an afterthought, and it is not officially a Community institution.[395] Originally, it was not even allowed to deliver own-initiative Opinions or publish its Opinions in the Official Journal, but these limitations were tacitly lifted.[396] The TEU officially recognizes the right of ECOSOC to meet on its own initiative and also provides that its Rules of Procedure no longer have to be approved by the Council.[397] The equivalent body under the ECSC Treaty is the Consultative Committee, but it is not involved in the legislative function of the Council.[398]

Consultation of ECOSOC by the Council is mandatory under the EEC for numerous matters, to which the TEU adds others.[399] In all but two instances, however, consultation of ECOSOC complements an opinion from the European Parliament.[400] There is no mandatory consultation of ECOSOC by the Council under the EAEC Treaty. All three Treaties provide for optional consultation of ECOSOC.[401]

ECOSOC, like the European Parliament, is an advisory body whose Opinions are not binding.[402] Even where its involvement constitutes an essential procedural requirement, ECOSOC cannot emulate Parliament's delaying tactics as the Council can set a time limit for the Committee's deliberations. Absence of an Opinion from ECOSOC after the expiration of the allotted time, which must not be less than ten days, does not stall the legislative process.[403] The TEU extends this time limit to one month.[404]

The Commission rarely amends its proposals purely on the basis of ECOSOC's Opinions, although it does often include its suggestions where a proposal is amended for other reasons. In the case of the Commission's amended proposal for a Second Non-Life Insurance Directive, for example, several of ECOSOC's sugges-

392. Arts. 194, 195 (EEC); 166, 167 (EAEC).

393. Arts. 194 (EEC); 166 (EAEC). The numbers are 24 for France, Germany, Italy and the United Kingdom; 21 for Spain; 12 for Belgium, Greece, Netherlands and Portugal; 9 for Denmark and Ireland; and 6 for Luxembourg. Apparently, the numerical structure of ECOSOC will not be changed despite the revision of the number and allocation of MEPs.

394. Arts. 194 (EEC); 166 (EAEC).

395. Arts. 4 (EEC); 3 (EAEC). *See also Adam* v. *Commission*, 828/79, [1982] E.C.R. 269 at 290.

396. *See* arts. 20, 51 (ROPEcosoc).

397. **Arts. 196, 198 (EC); 168, 170 (Revised EAEC)**.

398. Art. 18 (ECSC).

399. ECOSOC must be consulted under arts. 49, 54(2), 63(2), 75(1), 75(3), 79(3), 84(2), 100, 100a(1), 100b(1), 118A(2), 126, 127, 128, 130q(1),(2), 130s (EEC); **99, 100, 125, 126(4), 127(4), 128(5), 129(4), 129a(2), 129d, 130(3), 130b, 130d, 130e, 130i(1), 130i(4), 130o, 130s(1), 130s(2), 130s(3) (EC)**. *See also* Table 4.

400. The exceptions are Articles 79(3) and 128 (EEC), which deal with employment in the transport sector and vocational training, respectively. Note, however, that the TEU places vocational training under the Cooperation Procedure — *see* **art. 127(4) (EC).**

401. Arts. 198 (EEC); 170 (EAEC); **198 (EC)**; **170 (EAEC)**.

402. Arts. 193 (EEC); 165 (EAEC).

403. Arts. 198 (EEC); 170 (EAEC).

404. **Arts. 198 (EC)**; **170 (Revised EAEC)**.

tions were incorporated into the text.[405] Despite its low profile, ECOSOC should not be dismissed as irrelevant,[406] as its views are a valuable indicator of the potential reactions of the various social groups throughout the Community to a particular piece of legislation. Thus, for the Commission, consultation of ECOSOC can complement and sometimes even replace separate consultations with a multitude of pan-European trade associations, professional bodies and trade union organizations.

In an attempt to insert itself more forcefully into the legislative process, an ad hoc committee of ECOSOC recommended in 1987 that ECOSOC make an effort to deliver its Opinion before Parliament considers a proposal.[407] This way, ECOSOC's suggestions could be taken into consideration by Parliament when delivering its opinion and thereby make more impression on the Commission.

ECOSOC decides upon its Opinions in plenary sessions, but the preparatory work is carried out by the nine Sections.[408] In addition, the members are divided into three groups, which meet separately to prepare their common approach to the work of the Sections and to decide on amendments that they wish to place before the plenary sessions. These groups are the Employers' Group, the Workers' Group (consisting mainly of trade union representatives) and the Miscellaneous Activities Group. The last-named group includes representatives from agriculture, small industries, science, the professions, consumers and environmental and family organizations. The groups are equally represented in all the Sections, whose members are chosen by the Chairman of ECOSOC.[409] There is also a General Secretariat that provides administrative support services for ECOSOC.

The Chairman of ECOSOC is elected in turn from among the three Groups.[410] To be elected, a candidate must obtain at least three quarters of the votes cast by members of the Committee in the first ballot but needs only a simple majority in subsequent ballots.[411]

2.2. Delivery of an Opinion by ECOSOC

Although it is the Council that is obliged to consult ECOSOC, it is the Commission that sends the legislative proposal to the Chairman of the Committee. The Chairman

405. *Compare* OJ C 204/1976 (Opinion of ECOSOC) and COM (78) 63 (Commission's amended proposal).
406. Freestone and Davidson, *Institutional Framework of the European Communities* at p.86 tend, like many writers, to be overly dismissive of ECOSOC.
407. *Report on the Status of the Economic and Social Committee in the Institutional Machinery Provided for in the Single Act*, Brussels, June 22, 1987.
408. The nine sections are: I — Agriculture; II — Industry, Commerce, Crafts and Services; III — Economic, Financial and Monetary Questions; IV — Social, Family, Educational and Cultural Affairs; V — Transport and Communications; VI — External Relations; VII — Energy, Nuclear Questions and Research; VIII — Regional Development and Town and Country Planning; IX — Protection of the Environment, Public Health and Consumer Affairs. The exact terms of reference of the various Sections are set out in Title I, Chapter III, Rule 3.2 of the Standing Orders of the Committee's Bureau.
409. Art. 12 (ROPEcosoc).
410. Art. 5 (ROPEcosoc).
411. Art. 6 (ROPEcosoc).

refers the proposal to the appropriate Section for an Opinion.[412] In some cases, the proposal may be referred to another Section for a supplementary Opinion, but ECOSOC now limits the use of supplementary referrals.[413] It is the Section responsible for drawing up the main Opinion that reports to the plenary session.[414]

The Sections operate in one of three ways.[415] The normal procedure is for a Section to appoint a Study Group of up to fifteen members together with a Rapporteur. Study groups arrive at their conclusions without voting. Their meetings are often attended by Commission officials. Less complex matters may be dealt with by a Drafting Group, which consists of the Rapporteur and some Co-rapporteurs. Simple or urgent matters are confided to a Rapporteur acting alone. Whichever procedure is chosen, the result will be a draft Opinion that the Rapporteur places before the whole Section.[416] Exceptionally, where clear divergences of opinion are immediately apparent, a Report setting out the various views may also be placed before the Section.[417]

The Section now debates the draft Opinion and the Report if there is one. Amendments to the draft Opinion may be proposed and put to the vote before the Section votes on the Opinion as a whole. No action is taken on the Report. The text of amendments that are not accepted but which received a quarter of the votes cast or which constitute a Counter-Opinion, is appended to the Opinion as adopted by the Section.[418] A Counter-Opinion exists where a Group or one of the categories of economic and social activity within the Groups adopt a uniform standpoint that differs from the majority view.[419] Except where the Section unanimously adopts an Opinion, the Rapporteur draws up another Report setting out the various views expressed at the Section meeting and appends it to the Opinion.[420]

Sections responsible for preparing supplementary Opinions follow the same procedure, but they are expected to complete their work in time for the main Section to consider the supplementary documentation before taking its decision.[421] Supplementary Opinions are appended at the Main Opinion.[422]

Once the main Section has completed its work, the Chairman of the Section forwards its Opinion together with the various appendices to the plenary session of ECOSOC.[423] The plenary session debates on the basis of the documents received from the Section. It does so in public unless the matter is considered confidential.[424] If the Section Opinion is rejected, the matter is referred back to the Section or a Rapporteur-General is appointed to draw up a new draft Opinion.[425] Otherwise,

412. Art. 22 (ROPEcosoc).
413. Art. 23 (ROPEcosoc); Title II, Chapter I, Rule 1.4.1 of the Bureau's Standing Orders.
414. Art. 23 (ROPEcosoc).
415. Art. 14 (ROPEcosoc).
416. Art. 34 (ROPEcosoc).
417. Art. 34 (ROPEcosoc); Title II, Chapter I, Rule 1.2.2.10 of the Bureau's Standing Orders.
418. Art. 30 (ROPEcosoc).
419. Art. 43 (ROPEcosoc).
420. Art. 30 (ROPEcosoc).
421. Art. 29 (ROPEcosoc); Title II, Chapter 1, Rule 1.4.5 of the Bureau's Standing Orders.
422. Art. 30 (ROPEcosoc).
423. Art. 31 (ROPEcosoc).
424. Art. 52 (ROPEcosoc).
425. Art. 39 (ROPEcosoc).

amendments to the Section Opinion are put to the vote and then the plenary session votes on the definitive text of the ECOSOC's Opinion. The text of any amendments that are not accepted but which received a quarter of the votes cast or which constitute a Counter-Opinion is appended to the Opinion.[426] The plenary session neither votes on the Section Report if there is one, nor draws up its own Report. Finally, the Chairman of ECOSOC sends to the Council and the Commission the Opinion as adopted by the plenary session, the documentation that was received from the main Section and the minutes of the plenary session meeting.[427] This concludes the consultation of ECOSOC.

3. OTHER CONSULTATIONS

3.1. The Committee of the Regions (COR)

COR is introduced into the EC by the TEU. Its 189 members will represent regional and local bodies in the Member States and be appointed in the same way as the members of ECOSOC.[428] Indeed, apart from the fact that COR's Rules of Procedure will have to be submitted to the Council for its unanimous approval, its structure, operation and the way it delivers its Opinions are intended to be exactly the same as for ECOSOC, with which it will share a common organizational structure.[429] Like ECOSOC, it will not be a Community institution.[430]

Consultation of COR will be mandatory in such areas as education, culture, public health, trans-European networks and regional aid.[431] Moreover, whenever ECOSOC is consulted, the Council will have to inform COR, which may thereupon issue its own opinion on the matter where it considers that regional interests are involved.[432] The EC Treaty also provides for optional consultation and own-initiative Opinions.[433]

3.2. The Court of Auditors

Despite its low profile, the Court of Auditors is important and, under the TEU, it becomes an official Community institution.[434] It has twelve members, one from each Member State, who are appointed by the Council acting unanimously and in consultation with Parliament.[435] The members of the Court are appointed for renewable

426. Art. 43 (ROPEcosoc).
427. Art. 44 (ROPEcosoc).
428. **Art. 198a (EC)**. *See supra* at pp. 56-57. Apparently, the numerical structure of COR will also not be changed despite the revision of the number and allocation of MEPs.
429. **Arts. 198a, 198b, 198c (EC)**. *See also* **16th Protocol (TEU)**.
430. **Art. 4(2) (EC)**.
431. **Arts. 126(4), 128(5), 129(4), 129d, 130b, 130d, 130e (EC)**. *See also* Table 4.
432. **Art. 198c (EC)**.
433. **Art. 198c (EC)**.
434. **Arts. 4(1) (EC); 3(1) (Revised EAEC); 7 (Revised ECSC)**.
435. Arts. 206 (EEC); 180 (EAEC); 78e (ECSC). These Articles are replaced by the TEU with **Articles 188b (EC); 160b (Revised EAEC); 45b (ECSC)**.

terms of six years and are obliged to act independently.

The Opinion of the Court of Auditors must be obtained by the Council before it proceeds to enact a financial regulation.[436] The Treaties do not provide for a time limit, but it is unlikely that the Court would be allowed to delay the Community legislative process any longer than Parliament. The Treaties also provide for optional consultation and own-initiative Opinions.[437]

The importance of the Court of Auditors has increased in recent years, and the TEU exhorts the other Community institutions to consider all appropriate ways of enhancing its effectiveness.[438] This presumably includes increased optional consultation and taking note of the Court's own-initiative Opinions on legislative proposals.

3.3. The European Monetary Institute (EMI)

The EMI is to be set up at the start of the second stage of Economic and Monetary Union on January 1, 1994 and will replace the Committee of Governors of the national central banks. It will comprise the central banks of the Member States and be directed and managed by a Council consisting of a President and the Governors of the national central banks.[439] The Governors will continue to be named solely by the individual Member States, but the President will be appointed by common accord of the Member States on a recommendation of the Council of the EMI (or, for the initial appointment, the Committee of Governors) and after consulting Parliament and the Council.

The EMI will have to be consulted by the Council on four specific occasions, and there will also be a general obligation to consult whenever monetary legislation is being considered.[440] The EMI will also have the right to give own-initiative Opinions.[441]

Until the EMI is established, its consultative role will be filled by the Committee of Governors.[442] At the start of the third stage of Economic and Monetary Union, the EMI will be dissolved and its role taken over by the ECB.[443]

3.4. The Commission

The Council is obliged to consult the Commission before setting consumption priorities and allocating resources under the ECSC Treaty.[444]

436. Arts. 209(a) (EC); 183(a) (EAEC); 78h(a) (ECSC).

437. Arts 206a(4) (EEC); 180a(4) (EAEC); 78f(4) (ECSC); **188c(4) (EC); 160c(4) (Revised EAEC); 45c(4) (Revised ECSC)**.

438. **21st. Declaration (TEU)**.

439. **Arts. 109f(1) (EC); 1.2 of the Statute of the EMI (4th Protocol (TEU))**.

440. **Arts. 73f, 104c(14), 106(5),(6) (EC)**. The general obligation is contained in **Article 109f(6) (EC)**. *See too* Table 4.

441. **Art. 109f(4) (EC)**.

442. **Art. 109f(8) (EC)**.

443. **Art. 109l(2) (EC)**.

444. Art. 59(2) (ECSC).

3.5. The Monetary Committee

The Monetary Committee is an advisory committee set up by the EEC Treaty and comprising two representatives from each Member State and the Commission.[445] The Council is not obliged to consult this committee but has the option of doing so.[446] The Committee also has the right to issue own-initiative Opinions.[447]

At the start of the third stage of Economic and Monetary Union, the Monetary Committee will be dissolved and its functions taken over by the Economic and Financial Committee (EFC).[448]

3.6. Coordinating Committee for Justice and Home Affairs (CCJHA)

The CCJHA is to be made up of senior officials from the Member States. Its main task will be to help prepare the work of the Council in the field of visas, justice and home affairs, but there is also provision for optional consultation by the Council and own-initiative Opinions.[449] There will be no mandatory consultation of the CCJHA.

4. REACTION OF THE COMMISSION

As we have seen, the Commission may be called upon to react to Parliament's Opinion or First Reading by amending or withdrawing its proposal. Otherwise, Parliament may hold up the legislative process or even, in very exceptional circumstances, censure the Commission. Certainly, a refusal by the Commission to cooperate to some extent with Parliament will in any case undermine their relationship.

In making its decision how to react to Parliament's first consultation, the Commission must consider the interests of the Community as a whole and, in the case of amendments to the proposal, balance as well the likely reaction of the Council to Parliament's amendments and its own view of them against the need to keep the good will of Parliament. Once the TEU enters into force, the Commission will also have to measure Parliament's amendments against the subsidiarity provisions of **Article 3b (EC)**.[450] In practice, Parliament and the Commission normally find an acceptable compromise that will permit the first round to be completed. The two institutions share broadly-speaking the same outlook on the Community and need each other's support. The Commission relies on Parliament to give its propos-

445. Arts. 105(2) (EEC); **109c(1) (EC)**.
446. Arts. 105(2) (EEC); **109c(1) (EC)**.
447. Arts. 105(2) (EEC); **109c(1) (EC)**.
448. **Art. 109c(2) (EC)**.
449. **Art. K.4(1) (TEU)**.
450. The Commission has confirmed that it will be tougher about rejecting parliamentary amendments that run counter to the proportionality principle (*Edinburgh Summit Conclusions*, Annex 2 to Part A, p. 5), but, oddly, it does not mention the principles of attribution of powers (**Article 3b, 1st paragraph**) or subsidiarity in the strict sense (**Article 3b, 2nd paragraph**). Presumably, though, the Commission will also reject parliamentary amendments that violate these two latter principles. *See also* the comments in fn. 169.

als a democratic legitimacy, while Parliament's amendments still require the Commission's support in most cases if they are to find their way into the final legislation. The Commission has in fact committed itself to acting as Parliament's ally in the legislative process and accommodating its wishes, whenever possible.[451] This does not mean, however, that it will take on all of Parliament's amendments or always withdraw a proposal that Parliament has rejected.

Previously the Commissioner in charge of a dossier defined the Commission's position with respect to Parliament's opinion, but now this is a decision that is taken collectively. Whenever possible, the matter is handled by the inter-cabinet committee responsible for parliamentary affairs. If no agreement is forthcoming at this level, the matter is referred to the weekly meeting of the chefs de cabinet. If disagreement persists, the Commissioners will have to take the necessary decision at their weekly meeting.

451. *See* Van Hamme in "The Cooperation Procedure" at p. 136. The Commission now openly acknowledges the fact when it amends a proposal in order to take Parliament's views into consideration — *see* OJ C 318/1990 at p. 13.

Chapter IV. Stage 3: The Council's First Round – *Common Position or Legislative Act*

1. STRUCTURE OF THE COUNCIL

Most important general legislation of the European Community is enacted by the Council, particularly in the EEC and the EAEC. The Council is made up of representatives of the Member States, each of which normally sends one or more of its Ministers to take part in the meetings.[452] Under the TEU, the members of the Council must be Government Ministers authorized to commit their Governments.[453] Although, strictly speaking, the Council is a single body, the practice is for different sets of Ministers to meet together to decide on matters within their competence. As a result, there are a number of separate Councils. The most important of these are the General (or Foreign) Affairs Council, the Agriculture Council, the Economic and Financial Council (Ecofin) and the Internal Market Council. The others are the Fisheries, Budget, Development, Environment, Energy, Research, Transport, Labor and Social Affairs, Education, Industry, Consumers, Health, Culture, Civil Protection, Telecommunications and Tourism Councils. On occasion, joint meetings are held of two or more Councils. Members of the Commission usually participate in meetings of the Council but can be excluded.[454] They have no vote but, as we shall see, they play a crucial role in the Council's deliberations.

Council meetings are held in private unless there is unanimous agreement to the contrary.[455] Although many acts are adopted without much discussion or even a formal vote,[456] there is often an element of horse-trading, and intense bargaining may attend the more controversial matters. As a result, public meetings of Council are rare. A written procedure exists for urgent matters but is used only with the agreement of all Member States and the Commission.[457] The Council meets in Brussels except in the months of April, June and October, when its meetings take place in Luxembourg.[458]

452. Art. 2 (MT). This Article is replaced by the TEU with **Articles 146 (EC); 116 (Revised EAEC); 27 (Revised ECSC)**.

453. **Arts. 146 (EC); 116 (Revised EAEC); 27 (Revised ECSC)**.

454. Art. 3(2) of the Rules of Procedure of the Council (ROPCo), which are contained in Council Decision 79/868 (OJ L 268/1979), as amended by Council Decision 87/508 (OJ L 291/1987). *See also* **art. K.4(2) (TEU)**.

455. Art. 3(1) (ROPCo).

456. Under Article 5(1) of the Council's Rules, a vote is not obligatory. Article 28 (ECSC) actually recommends that Council decisions be reached by consensus.

457. Art. 6 (ROPCo).

458. Decision on the Location of the Seats of the Institutions, Art. 1(b).

As part of the desire for greater openness and transparency in the Community's legislative process, the European Council decided at Edinburgh that henceforth major legislative proposals should, where appropriate, be the subject of a preliminary open debate.[459] Given that such a move still requires unanimous agreement in the Council and that the subsequent negotiations are to remain confidential, it does not appear to constitute a major step. Likewise, the decision of the European Council that the records of formal votes in the Council should be published[460] is no dramatic innovation. The record of such votes has usually been ascertained in the past by the press, and, in any case, many decisions are made by the Council without a formal vote.

Although it is the Council that ultimately has the power of decision,[461] much of the work is carried out by the Committee of Permanent Representatives (COREPER) and its dependent groups.[462] The aim is to secure the widest possible agreement at COREPER level before a matter comes before the Council. This procedure is essential if the Council is to meet its commitments, for its members are Government Ministers who do not have the time to devote to detailed preliminaries. For the same reason, where the Council reaches a political agreement on the basic outlines of a measure, it normally refers the dossier back for COREPER to settle the details. Likewise, if the Council discussion reveals serious differences of opinion, COREPER will be asked to take back the dossier in order to build some form of consensus.

COREPER meets in two different groups, one consisting of the Ambassadors of the Member States (COREPER II) and the other of the Deputy Permanent Representatives (COREPER I). There is no hierarchical relationship between the two groups; each is autonomous and acts as COREPER in the areas that fall within its competence. Although COREPER II deals with matters that are perhaps more politically sensitive, such as external affairs and financial services, COREPER I nevertheless has responsibility for high-profile areas like the internal market, environment, transport and social matters. Commission officials participate in meetings of COREPER unless the Council decides otherwise.[463]

COREPER is assisted in its task by Working Parties which it creates, instructs and supervises.[464] At any given time there are over one hundred of these Working Parties in existence, both standing and ad hoc. They are composed of desk officers from the Permanent Representations and national officials. The Member States appoint their own members, who act under instructions from their Government. Commission officials invariably participate as well.[465] For some areas there may be a standing committee that operates instead of a Working Party but along the same

459. *Edinburgh Summit Conclusions*, Annex 3 to Part A, p.1. It is not incumbent upon the European Council, however, to dictate to the Council, and so it will be up to this latter body to take up the suggestion or not.

460. *Edinburgh Summit Conclusions*, Annex 3 to Part A, p.1.

461. Arts. 145 (EEC); 115 (EAEC); 26 (ECSC).

462. Art. 4 (MT). This Article is replaced by the TEU with **Articles 151 (EC); 121 (Revised EAEC); 30 (Revised ECSC)**. *See also* art. 16(1),(2) (ROPCo).

463. Art. 16(3) (ROPCo).

464. Art. 16(2) (ROPCo).

465. Art. 16(3) (ROPCo). There are no representatives from the European Parliament, but Parliament has requested that the Commission representatives keep it informed — *see* Resolution of 8 October 1986 on relations between the European Parliament and the Council at pt. 12.

lines. For example, there is the Special Agricultural Committee for the Common Agricultural Policy, the Article 113 Committee for the Common Commercial Policy and the Education Committee.

The task of these Working Parties (or committees) is to undertake the preliminary examination of a dossier with a view to settling the technical details. COREPER then deliberates on the basis of the Working Party's conclusions. In essence, COREPER has to solve the political problems that have arisen out of the preparatory work and prepare the dossier for presentation to the Council. Both the Working Parties and COREPER will also have to consider the subsidiarity aspect of a proposal once the TEU enters into force.[466]

The TEU provides for two other bodies to be associated with the work of the Council. These are the Monetary Committee, which is charged with contributing to the preparatory work on some economic and monetary legislation, and the CCJHA, which has the same task with respect to immigration, home and justice affairs.[467] It is not clear what will be the modalities of the interaction between these two bodies and COREPER, but, according to the Treaty provisions, neither are supposed to interfere with the relationship between COREPER and the Council. Unlike the CCJHA and COREPER, the Monetary Committee includes representatives from the Commission, which will increase the latter's potential influence over the formation of monetary and economic policy.

The complex, multi-tiered organization that makes up what is collectively called "the Council" is under the control of the Council Presidency, which is held for six months by each Member State in turn.[468] The Presidency has become a crucial and influential office from which the collective work of the various Councils, COREPER, the Working Parties, the standing committees and all other ad hoc groups set up by the Council or COREPER is organized and coordinated. The Member State holding the Presidency of the Council furnishes the chairs of the various separate Councils and of the other bodies within the Council organization.[469] It is also up to the Presidency to set the number and dates of the meetings that are to take place at all levels of the Council during its six months.[470] In doing so, it has to ensure that preliminary work will be completed in time for COREPER, which is in permanent session, to prepare a particular dossier for the appropriate Council meeting. The dates for the meetings within the Council are supposed to be set seven months in advance, but in practice they are rarely finalized until just before a Member State commences its six-month Presidency.

Apart from the general control it exercises over the work of the Council, the Presidency exerts its influence in three other ways. In the first place, it sets the agenda of Council meetings[471] in close cooperation with COREPER, which it also chairs. Although all the Member States as well as the Commission can request the inclusion

466. *Edinburgh Summit Conclusions*, Annex 1 to Part A, p 12. *Note*, however, that the comments in fn. 169 also apply to the Council and its bodies.
467. **Arts. 100d, 109c(1) (EC); K.4(1) (TEU)**.
468. Arts. 2 (MT); **146 (EC); 116 (Revised EAEC); 27 (Revised ECSC)**.
469. Art. 16(4) (ROPCo).
470. Art. 1(2) (ROPCo).
471. Art. 2(1) (ROPCo).

of items on the agenda,[472] the Presidency is given a relatively free hand and can thus determine to a large extent which dossiers will progress during its term. The Presidency also decides when a matter will be put to the vote in Council meetings.[473] Since 1987, any Member State or the Commission can force a vote with the support of a majority on the Council,[474] but this is rarely done. This ability to stall or force issues reinforces the Presidency's influence over the progress of the Community's affairs and has enabled it in the past to control the use of the Luxembourg Accords.[475] Finally, it is the Presidency, working together with the Commission, that puts together the compromise formulae that create the necessary consensus within the Council for decisions to be made.

The Presidency of the Council thus plays a pivotal role. An efficient Presidency, like the German Presidency in the first half of 1988 and the Spanish Presidency in the first half of 1989, can do much to ensure the proper progress of the Community's affairs. Unfortunately, the converse is also true. The present arrangement is also coming under criticism for encouraging short-term strategies and parochialism.

A number of reforms have been suggested.[476] One is that the Presidency should be held for one year by the five larger Member States only. This idea is unlikely to be acceptable to Belgium, Denmark, Greece, Ireland, Luxembourg, the Netherlands or Portugal. Another possibility is a permanent executive body. This could either be the Commission, which is unlikely under the present political circumstances, or a Council modelled on the Security Council of the United Nations, which would comprise the larger Member States and representatives from the smaller States on a rotating basis. Another idea being floated in Brussels is that of regional presidencies. Britain, France, Germany and Italy would still be entitled to their own presidencies, but the others would share on a regional basis. There would be an Iberian and a Benelux Presidency, for example, and later a Scandinavian Presidency. However, the idea of a joint Greek-Turkish Presidency by early next century still boggles the imagination! Nevertheless, it is clear that some institutional change is necessary, particularly in view of the Community's plans for expansion.

The Council bodies are served by a General Secretariat under the direction of a Secretary General, who is appointed by the Council acting unanimously.[477] The General Secretariat comprises the Secretary-General's private office, a Legal Service and seven Directorates-General.[478] The various areas in which the Council

472. Art. 2(2),(5) (ROPCo). The Member States will also be able to exercise this right with respect to an examination of the conformity of a measure with **Article 3b(EC)** — *see Edinburgh Summit Conclusions*, Annex 1 to Part A, fn. 1 on p. 11.

473. Art. 5(1) (ROPCo). The agenda of Council meetings must indicate those items on which a vote may be requested — *see* art. 2(2) (ROPCo).

474. Art. 5(1) (ROPCo). Where a Member State or the Commission call for a vote, there is a two-step procedure. Firstly, a vote is taken on whether to put the substantive issue to a vote and then, if necessary, a vote is taken on the substantive issue itself. *See also* Hartley, *Foundations of European Community Law* at p. 20.

475. The Luxembourg Accords are discussed *infra* at pp. 74-76.

476. *See The Economist*, January 11, 1992 at p. 48.

477. Art. 17 (ROPCo). This arrangement is formalized by **Articles 151(2) (EC): 121(2) (Revised EAEC); 30(2) (Revised ECSC)**.

478. These DGs are: A — Administration; B — Agriculture, Fisheries; C — Internal Market, Customs Union, Industrial Policy, Approximation of Laws, Right of Establishment, Freedom to Provide Ser-

legislates are divided up among the seven DGs, and one or more Council officials are responsible for a particular measure as it moves through the Council's legislative machinery. The jurists-linguists, who vet Community legislation before it is officially adopted, are attached to Directorate III of DG A.

2. OPERATION OF THE COUNCIL

2.1. The Council's Dual Role

The Council operates in one of two ways during the first round. Under the traditional procedure, it proceeds directly to enact the legislation by a simple majority, qualified majority or unanimous vote. This signifies the end of the legislative process except on the few occasions where the act has to be ratified by the Member States before it can go into effect.[479] Under the Cooperation (and Co-decision) Procedures, on the other hand, the Council reaches a Common Position on the basis of a qualified majority or, exceptionally under the TEU, by unanimity.[480] This is not a legislative enactment but a statement of the Council's legislative *intention*. It is put before Parliament and may or may not be finally enacted into legislation depending on what happens during the second round.[481] Despite some discrepancy in the wording of the various language versions of the Treaty, unanimity is required for the Council to modify the Commission's proposal both when adopting a Common Position and enacting a piece of legislation.[482]

The Council is under no time restraints during the first round and may take as long as it likes to adopt the legislation or reach a Common Position.[483] The record is held by two tax proposals, which were put forward in 1969 and finally enacted into legislation in 1990.[484] The Council is also free to take no action at all if the requisite majority cannot be attained.

(note 478, continued)

vices, Competition Law, Intellectual Property; D — Research, Energy, Transport, Environment, Consumer Protection; E — External Relations, Development Cooperation; F — Relations with Parliament and the Economic and Social Committee, Institutional Affairs, Budget and Staff Regulations; G — Economic, Financial and Social Affairs.

479. *See* arts. 138(3), 201 (EEC); 108(3) (EAEC); 21(3) (ECSC); **8e (EC)**; **K(9) (TEU)**. *See also* Tables 1-3.

480. Arts. 149(2)(a) (EEC); **189c(a)**, **189b(2) (EC)**. Unanimity is required under the Co-decision Procedure for cultural matters and R&D framework programs — *see* **arts. 128(5) and 130i(1) (EC)**.

481. The European Parliament and the Commission had suggested eliminating this two-step procedure where there is agreement between the Council and Parliament — *see* art. 188b(d) (EP Draft Treaty); Resolution of 11 July 1990 on the Intergovernmental Conference in the context of Parliament's strategy for European Union at p. 33(d); Commission Proposals (Submitted to the Intergovernmental Conference) on the Parliament's powers and a new legislative procedure (Co-decision) at pt. 3.3.3. in *Europe*, Nr. 1694/95, March 5, 1991.

482. On this point, *see* Bieber, "Legislative Procedure" at pp. 718-719. Unanimity is not, however, required when the Council adopts a Common Position with the support of the Commission but in the face of Parliament's rejection of the proposal at its First Reading.

483. Parliament's had proposed in Article 188b(d) (EP Draft Treaty) that the Council be subject to a six-month time limit, after which time the Conciliation Committee would automatically meet.

484. *See* OJ C 39/1969 and OJ L 225/1990.

2.2. Consultations by the Council

Under the traditional procedure, the Council may have to consult Parliament, ECOSOC, the Court of Auditors or the Commission before it enacts legislation, where this is required by the Treaties (*see* Table 1). In the future, it may have to consult COR and the EMI as well, and on a few occasions it may even require Parliament's assent before proceeding to adopt the legislation.[485] Under the Cooperation (and Co-decision) Procedures, the Council must always obtain Parliament's opinion before reaching a Common Position, often that of ECOSOC and, upon the entry into force of the TEU, sometimes that of COR (*see* Tables 2-3). Even where a consultation is not mandatory, the Council may choose under any of the procedures to consult on a voluntary basis with the above-mentioned bodies as well as with the Monetary Committee and, within the European Union, the CCJHA. In the case of Parliament, the Council now always asks for its opinion before enacting legislation even where this is not a legal necessity. The Council may also be presented with own-initiative opinions. All these various consultation provisions are set out in Table 4.

The Council is not obliged to take account of any of the suggestions it receives as a result of these consultations, although it will need unanimity to reject them where they are supported by the Commission.[486] Moreover, the Court of Justice has ruled that failure to carry out a mandatory consultation of Parliament can always be cured retroactively by obtaining an opinion after the Council has acted.[487] Parliament cannot, however, be forced to cure in this way the breach of an essential procedural requirement. The same principles must apply to consultation of the other bodies.

2.3. Voting in the Council

The Council takes its decisions by a simple majority, qualified majority or unanimous votes. A Member State that is prevented from sending a Minister to represent it at a Council meeting may always vote by proxy.[488] Although the Treaties lay down simple majority voting as the normal procedure,[489] it is used rarely for general legislation and only for implementing a common vocational training policy in the EEC.[490] The end of the transitional period on January 1, 1970 and the coming into force of the SEA on July 1, 1987, however, significantly increased the use of *qualified* majority voting, which is now the most widely-used procedure. The TEU will further add to this development when it comes into effect. A breakdown of the vot-

485. *See* **arts. 8a(2), 106(5), 130d, 138(3) (EC); 108(3) (Revised EAEC); 21(3) (Revised ECSC)**. *See also* Table 1.

486. *See supra* at p. 26.

487. *Tunnel Refineries* v. *Council*, 114/81, [1982] E.C.R. 3189 at 3210.

488. Arts. 150 (EEC); 120 (EAEC); 28 (ECSC); 4, 5(3) (ROPCo).

489. Arts. 148(1) (EEC); 118(1) (EAEC); 28 (ECSC).

490. It is used for general legislation only in Articles 128 (EEC); 24(1), 42, 92 (EAEC); 58(3) (ECSC). The TEU, somewhat oddly, abolishes simple majority voting for general legislation in the EEC by putting vocational training measures under the Cooperation Procedure — *see* **art. 127(4) (EC)**.

ing procedures for the Council is given in Tables 1-3.

Simple majority voting in the EEC and the EAEC requires only that a majority of Member States vote in favor of the measure.[491] In the ECSC, on the other hand, there has to be an absolute majority of at least two Member States in favor, and this majority must include two Member States that each produce at least one-ninth of the total value of the Community's coal and steel output.[492] Abstentions in simple majority voting situations are equivalent to a negative vote.

Under the qualified majority voting procedure, each Member State casts a number of votes that are loosely based on its relative size. The votes are weighted as follows:[493]

Germany, France, Italy, United Kingdom	10 votes each
Spain	8 votes
Belgium, Greece, Netherlands, Portugal	5 votes
Denmark, Ireland	3 votes
Luxembourg	2 votes
TOTAL VOTES	76

A qualified majority normally requires fifty-four votes in favor of a measure out of the total of seventy-six,[494] except under the Social Agreement where the non-involvement of the United Kingdom will reduce the majority to forty-four out of sixty-six votes.[495] The ECSC Treaty requires that the fifty-four votes in favor be cast by not less than eight Member States,[496] as does the TEU with respect to justice and home affairs.[497] This is also the rule where the Council acts by a qualified majority without a proposal from the Commission, which never happens, however, in the case of general legislation (*see* Tables 1-3). Abstentions in a qualified majority voting situation are equivalent to a vote against the measure; whether a Member State votes against or abstains, its votes do not contribute to the fifty-four needed to enact the legislation. Such a Member State also cannot figure among the eight States needed to cast their vote in favor, where this is a requirement.

Qualified majority voting serves the general purpose of ensuring that the more important decisions are taken by a majority that reflects the relative importance of the Member States.[498] Also, by allocating forty votes to the larger Member States and thirty-six votes to the smaller States, the system has the more specific aim of maintaining a balance between the interests of these two groups. On the one hand, it prevents the larger States from pushing a measure through. Where three larger States are in favor, they can only muster thirty votes and must find twenty-four votes from

491. Arts. 148(1) (EEC); 118(1) (EAEC).

492. Art. 28 (ECSC).

493. *Note* that the voting strengths of the Member States in the Council have not been changed to reflect the re-allocation of seats in the European Parliament.

494. Arts. 148(2) (EEC); 118(2) (EAEC); 28 (ECSC).

495. **Point 2 of the 14th Protocol (TEU).**

496. Art. 28 (ECSC).

497. **Art. K.4 (3) (TEU).**

498. The distribution of votes does, however, favor the smaller Member States, which receive 13.1% of the votes for their 4.3% of the Community population and 1.8% of its GDP.

among the smaller States. Even if all four larger Member States are in favor, passage of the legislation still requires fourteen additional votes. Conversely, the smaller States with their combined thirty-six votes can never secure the passage of legislation without the support of at least two larger States. Nor it is that easy for a few smaller states to muster the necessary votes to hold up Community legislation.

Nowadays, it is usually the general purpose that is served by qualified majority voting. The Member States rarely divide up into larger States versus smaller ones, so qualified majority voting functions more as a way of ensuring that important measures are not enacted without substantial support. In practice, Member States tend to avoid being outvoted in the Council. Where they realize that they are unlikely to assemble the twenty-three votes necessary to block a measure, they often prefer to acquiesce. It is in their interest to abandon an isolated position in return for present concessions or future considerations.[499] The same reasoning applies to simple majority voting situations.

The role of the Commission is crucial in both simple and qualified voting situations in order to prevent any abuse and to encourage compromise.[500] As the Council cannot amend a Commission proposal where it lacks unanimity,[501] the latter is able to support individual Member States whose legitimate national interests are at stake by refusing to cooperate with the other States. This often secures an acceptable compromise. Two points should be noted, however. Firstly, under the Co-decision Procedure, the Council will be able to amend a Commission proposal by a qualified majority in order to reach agreement with Parliament in the Conciliation Committee.[502] The Commission is still able to withdraw its proposal, but it will need a very good reason to defy Parliament and the Council in this way. Secondly, the increasing impetus of the integration process within the Community in recent years has created a more dynamic political atmosphere. The need for consensus is no longer perceived as absolute and, ultimately, action by qualified or simple majorities is now thwarted by the Commission in most cases only where it considers that this is in the Community interest as a whole.

Little needs to be said about unanimous voting, which is still frequently used in all three Communities (*see* Table 1) and is also required where the Council wishes to modify a Commission proposal unilaterally or override a rejection of its Common Position under the Cooperation Procedure.[503] Abstentions under the EEC and EAEC Treaties do not prevent the adoption of legislation by unanimity as long as the abstaining Member State is present or represented,[504] whereas in the ECSC unanimity requires all Member States to vote in favor, except in the case of financial regulations enacted under Article 78h(a).[505] Abstentions never prevent the Council overriding the Commission or Parliament.

---

499. *See also* Freestone and Davidson, *Institutional Framework of the European Communities* at p. 68 and Noël, *Working Together* at p. 24.
500. *See* Noël, *Working Together* at p. 29.
501. Arts. 149(1) (EEC); 119 (EAEC); **189a(1) (EC)**. *See also* art. 58(3) (ECSC) and *supra* at p. 26.
502. **Art. 189a(1) (EC)**.
503. Unanimity is not required to adopt a Common Position in the face of Parliament's rejection of the Commission's proposal at First Reading, as Parliament had suggested — *see* fnn. 275, 276.
504. Arts. 148(3) (EEC); 118(3) (EAEC).
505. Art. 28 (ECSC).

2.4. The Council and the Legal Base of Legislation

There is some controversy over the voting requirements where the Council changes the legal base of proposed legislation. Although such unilateral changes by the Council do not involve the substance of the proposal and are thus permissible,[506] some legal writers have suggested that, as unilateral amendments, they nevertheless require a unanimous vote in the Council.[507] This is not so. The Court of Justice has made it quite clear that the legal base is a separate matter from the content of the proposal and is not something over which the Commission has any special rights. It must be based on objective factors, and, in the case of a dispute, it is ultimately for the Court of Justice to determine the correct legal base of a particular legislative act.[508] Legislation that has been enacted pursuant to an incorrect legal base will normally be declared void by the Court[509] unless the wrong legal base did not alter the way in which the Council made its decision.[510]

It is thus clearly open to the Council, acting by a simple majority, to replace the legal base chosen by the Commission if it considers that it is incorrect. If the Commission wishes to insist on its position, it can always take the matter to the Court of Justice, which may declare the legislation void, as in the case of Council Directive 87/64.[511] Member States may similarly challenge the validity of legislation on this ground before the Court.[512] In practice, the objections from members of the Council to the legal base of acts tend to be directed at resisting the Commission's efforts to enact legislation by a qualified majority rather than by unanimity. Thus, in the case of the proposal on the contained use of genetically modified micro-organisms, the Council exchanged Article 100A of the EEC Treaty for Article 130S, which entailed replacing the Cooperation Procedure with the traditional procedure.[513] Sometimes, members of the Council will trade acceptance of a contested legal base for concessions on the substance of the proposal, which were the tactics adopted by the United Kingdom with respect to the Commission's proposal on the organization of working time.[514]

---

506. *See* Bieber, "Legislative Procedure" at p. 714.
507. Glaesner, "La procédure de coopération" at p. 71 suggests that a change to the legal base cannot be disassociated from an amendment to the proposal. *Contra* Bieber, "Legislative Procedure" at p. 714.
508. In *Commission* v. *Council*, 45/86, [1988] 2 C.M.L.R. 131 at 153, the Court of Justice declared that "the legal base for a measure may not depend simply on an institution's conviction as to the objective pursued but must be based on objective factors which are amenable to judicial review."
509. *See Commission* v. *Council*, 131/87, [1991] 1 C.M.L.R. 780, where Council Directive 87/64 was declared void because the Council had enacted it pursuant to Articles 43 *and* 100 (EEC) instead of just Article 43.
510. In *Commission* v. *Council*, 165/87, [1990] 1 C.M.L.R. 457, the Council had incorrectly included Article 235 (EEC) in addition to Articles 28 and 113 (EEC) as the legal base. As Article 28 already required unanimity in the Council, the use of Article 235 with its requirement of unanimity did not change the Council's decision-making procedure and the validity of Council Decision 87/369 was upheld. The legal base, however, was changed by the Court.
511. *See* fn. 509.
512. *See Greece* v. *Council*, 62/88, [1991] 2 C.M.L.R. 649.
513. *Compare* OJ C 198/1988 and Council Directive 90/219 (OJ L 117/1990).
514. *See* OJ C 254/1990 and OJ C 124/1991.

2.5 The Council and the Application of Article 3b (EC)

Once the TEU enters into effect, the Council will be responsible for ensuring that all Community legislation that it is being asked to enact complies with the concept of subsidiarity as set out in **Article 3b**.[515] At its Edinburgh meeting, the European Council stated that any Council decision on subsidiarity should be taken "at the same time as the decision on substance and according to the voting requirements set out in the Treaty".[516]

This statement by the European Council has two implications. Firstly, it suggests that the Council can unilaterally amend a Commission proposal in order to render it compatible with **Article 3b**. This is acceptable as long as the Council modifies rather than changes the substance of the proposal.[517] The second implication is that the Council needs to act by unanimity in order to effect this modification. In other words, the Council does not have the same freedom regarding the compatibility of a proposal with **Article 3b** as it does with respect to the legal base. This also seems correct. Whereas the legal base is a separate matter from the content of a proposal, subsidiarity has to do with the proposal's substantive provisions. However, it should be borne in mind that it is not the European Council but the Court of Justice that has the last word on these issues.

2.6. The Luxembourg Accords

The increase in qualified majority voting after the end of the second stage of the transitional period on January 1, 1966[518] was opposed by France, which provoked a severe crisis within the Community. The French boycott of Council meetings was eventually ended by the so-called Luxembourg Compromise or Accords.[519] All six signatories agreed that, where very important interests of a Member State are at stake, every effort should be made to secure unanimous agreement for Council action.[520] The signatories did not, however, agree on what should happen if it is impossible to achieve such agreement within a reasonable time. The French view that discussions should continue until agreement is reached[521] was not supported by the other Member States but, due to France's preponderance at the time, it was accepted as the guiding principle of the Accords. As a result, majority voting is effectively suspended under the Accords whenever important national interests are at stake. Moreover, it is left up to each Member State to define its own important interests.[522]

515. *Edinburgh Summit Conclusions*, Annex 1 to Part A, pp.11-12. But *note* the comments in fnn. 169 and 466.
516. *Edinburgh Summit Conclusions*, Annex 1 to Part A, p.11.
517. On the Council's inability to change the substance of a Commission proposal, *see supra* at p. 26.
518. The following Articles in the EEC Treaty were made subject to qualified majority voting: 43(2), 54(2), 57(1), 63(2), 75(1), 87(1), 101.
519. *9th General Report on the Activities of the EC (1966)* at pp. 31-33.
520. Luxembourg Accords at pt. a(1).
521. Luxembourg Accords at pt. a(2).
522. In its Resolution of 9 July 1981 on relations between the European Parliament and the Council at pt. 28(b), Parliament demanded— unsuccessfully — that Member States be required to justify their invocation of important national interests.

Nevertheless, a Member State cannot successfully invoke the Accords unless it can avoid a vote in the Council or ensures that it has enough support to block the measure in question. In 1986 and 1988, the British and German Presidencies, respectively, refused to put agricultural proposals to the vote once the Accords had been invoked. In 1985, the Italian Presidency did put a measure to the vote despite Germany's invocation of the Accords, but it failed to muster the qualified majority needed to enact it. In 1982, by contrast, when the United Kingdom invoked the Accords to prevent the enactment of agricultural legislation in order to force agreement on the unrelated issue of the British contribution to the Community budget, the measure was nevertheless put to the vote and adopted over strenuous British objections. The reason given by the French and other delegations known to favor the Accords for overriding the British veto was that the United Kingdom was abusing the Accords by using them as a form of blackmail.[523]

The present status of the Luxembourg Accords is not entirely clear.[524] They are not part of Community law but, at the very most, a non-binding statement of policy emanating from the Representatives of the Governments of the Member States meeting within the Council.[525] They have been applied, however, consistently, and it is generally accepted that they have survived the SEA.[526] Certainly, their continuing validity was reaffirmed in 1983 by the Council[527] and, as we have seen above, they have been invoked on at least two occasions since the advent of the SEA. The TEU does not contain any provisions that might indicate that the position is now changed. On the other hand, it would seem fair to state that since 1982 the Luxembourg Accords have ceased to be the unsurmountable obstacle to majority decisions that they once were.[528] The failed British veto indicates that they cannot be used in order to stall progress on unrelated issues, and the 1987 change in the Council's Rules of Procedure giving Member States and the Commission the right to call for a vote

523. *See Europe*, Nr. 3049, January 5, 1982. Traditionally, France, the United Kingdom, Denmark, Greece, Ireland and Portugal have supported the use of the Accords, but in 1982 only Greece and Denmark backed the British position.

524. On the issue of the Luxembourg Accords, *see* Freestone and Davidson, *Institutional Framework of the European Communites* at pp. 68-69; Hartley, *Foundations of European Community Law* at pp. 18-20; Kapteyn and Themaat, *Introduction to the Law of the European Communities* at p.206 and pp. 248-251; and Martin Vasey, "Decision-making in the Agriculture Council and the Luxembourg Compromise", (1988) 25 C.M.L Rev. 725.

525. *See* Kapteyn and Themaat, *Introduction to the Law of the European Communities* at p.206. It has been argued that the Accords are invalid and contravene the Court of Justice's ruling in *United Kingdom* v. *Council*, 68/86, [1988] E.C.R. 855 at 900 that it is not open to the Member States to change the voting provisions of the Treaties without a formal amendment — *see The Oxford Encyclopaedia of European Community Law*, Oxford, 1990, at p. 366 and P. Pescatore in "Some Critical Remarks on the "Single European Act", (1987), 24 C.M.L.Rev. 9 at 13. However, as the Accords are little more than a statement of disagreement and thus non-binding, it is difficult to see how, as a document, they can contravene the Treaties.

526. *See* Vasey, "Luxembourg Compromise" at p. 727; Freestone and Davidson, *Institutional Framework of the European Communites* at p. 69 and p. 103; Hartley, *Foundations of European Community Law* at p. 20; *The Oxford Encyclopaedia of European Community Law* at p. 367; and Van Hamme, "The Cooperation Procedure" at p.149.

527. Solemn Declaration on European Union of the Council, E.C. Bulletin (1983) at para. 2.3.6.

528. *See* Van Hamme, "The Cooperation Procedure" at p. 149; Vasey, "Luxembourg Compromise" at pp. 731-732; and Noël, *Working Together* at p. 27.

means that the Presidency can now be restrained from abetting an inappropriate use of the Accords. Moreover, despite the views to the contrary of some Member States, the Accords probably cannot be invoked during the Cooperation (or Co-decision) Procedures. Certainly, this is the view of the British House of Commons, which has nevertheless always been a fervent advocate of the Accords.[529] In fact, the disregard of the British attempt at a veto in 1982 now appears as a watershed, and over the next few years the Luxembourg Accords will probably complete their gentle slide into constitutional oblivion. This would certainly accord with the greater acceptance within the Community as a whole of majority decision-making

3. THE COUNCIL AS A COMMUNITY INSTITUTION

Although the Council is the focal point of the national interests of the Member States and serves to preserve the preeminence of national Governments over the Community institutions, it is nevertheless itself a Community institution that is supposed to act in the interests of the Community.[530] For this reason, the Treaty provisions and the Rules of Procedure speak of *members* rather than *Member States* when referring to the composition the Council.[531] Several factors combine to help the Council in the fulfillment of its somewhat unlikely role.

In the first place, there is the influence of the Commission on the Council's deliberations. The Commission acts as a watchdog for the Community's interests and ensures that no action is taken by the Council that undermines them. In particular, it ensures the consistency of Community legislation in the face of the compromises and shifting political allegiances within the Council. The Commission also plays the role of honest broker. It mediates between the Council and Parliament and, together with the Presidency, elaborates acceptable compromises in order to secure the passage of legislation through the Council. The Commission may also use its powers to prevent measures being taken that isolate any Member State(s), although it is less likely these days to frustrate majority decisions on this ground alone.

The Commission owes its influence over the Council to the various prerogatives that it is given under the Treaties and which have been discussed earlier.[532] Essentially, these impel the Council to follow the Commission's lead, unless it can muster the unanimity needed to amend a proposal unilaterally. Despite some views to the contrary,[533] this rule also applies where the Council modifies a Commission

529. It is also the view of R. Dehousse in "1992 and Beyond: The Institutional Dimension of the Internal Market Program", (1989-90), *Legal Issues of European Economic Integration*, 109 at p. 121. In the case of Co-decision, which Dehousse obviously does not deal with, it is noteworthy that the EC Treaty provides for unanimous voting where important national interests are most likely to be at stake, namely culture (**art. 128(5)**) and multiannual R&D programs (**art. 130i(1)**). This could be taken as an implicit indication that the Accords cannot be invoked during the Co-decision Procedure.

530. Arts. 145 (EEC); 115(EAEC); 26 (ECSC). As Kapteyn and Themaat point out in *Introduction to the Law of the European Communities* at p. 104, the Council's decisions are Community acts and not international agreements.

531. *See e.g.* arts. 148(1) (EEC); 118(1) (EAEC); **147 (EC)**; 4 (ROPCo).

532. *See supra* at pp. 24-27.

533. *See* the discussion in Bieber, "Legislative Procedure" at pp. 718-719.

proposal in order to reach a Common Position. Even where the Council is able to act by unanimity, it cannot unilaterally alter the substance of a proposal[534] and the Commission can always forestall Council action by withdrawing its proposal.[535]

The Commission exercises most influence when the Council acts by a simple or qualified majority. Where a decision requires unanimity, there will necessarily be the requisite consensus in the Council to amend the Commission's proposal unilaterally. Furthermore, in this situation, individual Member States have a veto power that enables them to protect their own interests. Thus, the decrease in unanimous voting in favor of a qualified majority clearly enhances the Commission's influence over the Council and contributes towards making the latter more Community-oriented.

It is not entirely clear how the Co-decision Procedure will affect this relationship between the Commission and the Council. The provision for a direct dialogue between Parliament and the Council in the second round, together with the fact that the Council may by a qualified majority adopt a text in agreement with Parliament that differs from the Commission's proposal, certainly reduces the influence of the Commission. It could even be argued that the Conciliation Committee Procedure gives Parliament and the Council the right to deviate from the substance of the Commission's proposal, as they are empowered to do all that is possible to reconcile their respective positions.[536] On the other hand, there is specific provision for the Commission to act as mediator during this conciliation procedure,[537] and there is no reason to conclude that the Commission will lose its right to withdraw the proposal where it cannot accept the joint text of Parliament and the Council.

It is to be assumed that, in any case, Parliament's more influential role in the Co-decision Procedure will itself encourage a Community orientation on the part of the Council. Indeed, the increase in Parliament's influence under both the Cooperation and Co-decision Procedures must be considered another factor operating in favor of the Community interest within the Council.[538] It also, somewhat paradoxically, strengthens the Commission's mediating role. The Council relies on the Commission under the Cooperation (and Co-decision) Procedures to secure Parliament's approval of its Common Position without unacceptable amendments and not to support them if if they are adopted. The Commission, of course, is in a position to exact a price for this cooperation.

Finally, there is the 1992 process, which has had a great impact on the orientation of the Council. Prior to this re-launching of the process of economic integration, which was the result of the 1985 Commission White Paper, the Community had lost its impetus and slid into an impasse in which national interests were able to dominate. The 1992 initiative, put together and orchestrated by the Commission, succeeded in overcoming this paralysis and has even set the Community on the road to economic, monetary and political union as mapped out in the TEU. The Community's development has now acquired a dynamism of its own, and the Council has little

534. *See supra* at p. 26.

535. It did this in 1988 with its amended proposal on a general right of residence for Community nationals (OJ C 171/1985).

536. **Art. 189b(4) (EC)**.

537. **Art. 189b(4) (EC)**.

538. For a discussion of this increased influence, *see supra* at pp. 39-41.

choice but to follow the Commission's lead in enacting the legislation needed to keep it going. National interests still play a role in the Council's discussions, but they are able less and less to determine the outcome. Swept up into the irreversible process of creating the internal market, the Council has been forced to act more and more as a Community institution. It can apply the brakes, but it cannot change the direction.

4. THE COUNCIL'S FIRST READING

Although the influences that bear on the Council's deliberations in the first round may differ according to whether it is acting under the Cooperation (or Co-decision) Procedure or the traditional procedure, the actual legislative process is the same. Thus, except where the contrary is stated, the following discussion applies to both the adoption of a Common Position and the definitive enactment of legislation. The Council will also follow the normal procedures when it acts under the Social Agreement or **Article K.4 (TEU)** on home and justice affairs.

The Commission's proposal is sent to the President of the Council, who hands it over to the Council's General Secretariat.[539] Working in collaboration with COREPER, the Presidency assigns the proposal to an appropriate Working Party or standing committee. Occasionally, if no Working Party exists that is competent to deal with the proposal, COREPER creates an ad hoc group at the request of the Presidency. This group may become in time one of the permanent Working Parties. The General Secretariat appoints an official or officials from the relevant DG to pilot the proposal through the Council.

The Working Party (or committee) holds various meetings in order to put together an agreement on the proposal from a technical standpoint. The Working Party is concerned primarily with the effectiveness of the proposal, but this necessarily involves political considerations as well. It will also come to involve an examination of the subsidiarity aspect of the proposal once the TEU enters into force.[540] Although the representatives of the various Member States on the Working Party cannot bind their respective Governments, they are aware of what is likely to be acceptable and agreement can be reached on this basis.

Working Parties often commence their work before Parliament or ECOSOC have delivered their opinions. In the case of the Machine Safety proposal, for example, the first meeting of the Working Party took place in March 1988 while it was not until November 1988 that Parliament completed its First Reading. Technically, this is not an infringement of the Treaties, which only require the Council of Ministers to obtain these opinions before making a final decision. Nevertheless, to the extent that what is agreed in a Working Party is accepted without further ado by

539. In the case of the ending of production quotas in the ECSC and, later, home and justice affairs in the European Union, the proposal may emanate from a Member State — *see* arts. 58(3) (ECSC); **K.3(2) (TEU)**. The European Parliament makes the proposal on its own voting procedure — *see* arts. 138(3) (EEC): 108(3) (EAEC); 21(3) (ECSC).

540. *See Edinburgh Summit Conclusions*, Annex 1 to Part A, p. 12.

the Ministers and forms part of the final decision, there would appear to be a violation of the spirit of the Treaties.

Where a Working Party is in agreement on a proposal, it submits it to COREPER for the latter's approval. If the Working Party reaches the conclusion that full agreement at its level is not possible, it submits what it has agreed together with the points of disagreement. Working Parties will nearly always make some changes to the Commission's original proposals, to which the Commission usually agrees, particularly as its own officials participate in the sessions.

Although the operative modalities are still to be established, it would seem that at this stage the Monetary Committee and the CCJHA will also submit to COREPER any preparatory work that they might have carried out. As the activities of these two bodies are not allowed to prejudice the operations of COREPER, it is to be assumed that the latter will have the right to deal with these submissions at its discretion.

COREPER is concerned primarily with the political aspects of a proposal, and its role is to secure the requisite political agreement among the Member States in order to permit the Council to act or at least make progress. Thus, it reviews any agreements reached at Working Party level for their political ramifications and seeks to establish a political consensus on any outstanding points of contention. It will also have to consider the subsidiarity aspect of proposals once **Article 3b (EC)** is in effect.[541]

When there is unanimous agreement at COREPER on a proposal, it is submitted to the Presidency for inclusion in the next Council meeting as an "A" item. Otherwise, the proposal is submitted to the Presidency as a "B" item. COREPER normally retains a dossier until it has reached sufficient agreement to warrant the assumption that the Council will be able to make at least significant progress on the proposal. However, it is ultimately the President of the Council who decides which items are placed on the Council's agenda and how they are categorized.[542]

Where COREPER finds it difficult to achieve a sufficient consensus on a proposal, it will often refer the dossier back to the Working Party or committee. In this case, it will usually give some general guidelines of how the Working Party should proceed. More rarely, COREPER may set up its own ad hoc group to try to break the deadlock. If agreement on important parts of the proposal remains elusive, COREPER may, with the approval of the Presidency, set the proposal aside. Alternatively, the Presidency may decide nonetheless to include the matter as a "B" item for discussion by the Council.

When COREPER submits a proposal to the Council in a form that departs from the opinion of Parliament, the latter may initiate the Conciliation Procedure, either unilaterally or at the Council's request.[543] There is also an agreement between the Council and Parliament dating from 1971 that in this situation the President of the Council may contact the President of the European Parliament for an exchange of views.[544] Often the Chairman and/or the Rapporteur of the parliamentary committee

541. *See Edinburgh Summit Conclusions*, Annex 1 to Part A, p. 12. But *note* the comments in fnn. 169 and 466.

542. Art. 2 (ROPCo). But *see supra* at pp. 67-68 for the rights of Member States and the Commission in this respect.

543. *See* the discussion of the Conciliation Procedure *supra* at pp. 54-56.

544. *See* the note to pt. 5 of Parliament's Resolution of 16 February 1989 on the conciliation procedure.

concerned accompany the President of the Parliament. It is incumbent on the President of the Council to report on this exchange of views to the Council when it considers the proposal.

The advantage of informal consultation is that it can be used for all types of legislation, which is not the case for the Conciliation Procedure. It is also less cumbersome and in many instances can obviate the need for conciliation. Unfortunately, it has for no apparent reason fallen into disuse, but Parliament has called for its reactivation.[545] Parliament has also insisted on the Council keeping it properly informed about the progress of legislation through the Council so that it can react to any divergences of opinion.[546]

It is rare that COREPER submits a proposal to the Council without Parliament or any other body that must be consulted first giving their opinions. This does happen, however, and the result is that the consultation mandated by the Treaties is often rendered nugatory. The incident concerning the comitology procedure in the Second Banking Directive is an illustration.[547] Once again, this is a clear breach of the spirit of the Treaties.

As we have seen, Council agendas are divided into "A" and "B" items.[548] "A" items are destined for approval without discussion, although Member States do have the right to express an opinion on them and have it recorded in the minutes of the Council meeting. If a discussion ensues or if a Member State so requests, an "A" item is withdrawn unless a majority of the Council wish to proceed with it.[549] A majority may use this rule where there is the requisite support for Council action and the minority is considered obstructionist. "A" items that result in the adoption of a Common Position or a legislative act are sent to the jurists/linguists before the Council action is finalized. This latter group vets the text to ensure that it is legally correct and consistent in all nine of the Community official languages.[550] As a result, the official date of legislation and Common Positions is invariably later than that of the actual agreement in the Council.

"B" items are those that are set down for discussion by the Council. There may sometimes be a chance for an agreement, but often these are items on which only a modest progress is expected. On occasion, "B" items are included just to allow the Member States to stake out their bargaining positions. It is with respect to "B" items that the Council Presidency and the Commission must cooperate to try and secure the necessary consensus. If this proves impossible, the item is sent back to COREPER (and probably via COREPER to a Working Party) or sometimes referred to a special ad hoc group set up by the Council. The Spanish Presidency, for example, set up such a group in 1989 to examine the thorny issue of the removal of tax

545. Resolution of 16 February 1989 on the conciliation procedure at pt. 5.
546. Resolution of 16 February 1989 on the conciliation procedure at pt. 10 and Resolution of 9 July, 1981 on the right of legislative initiative at pt. 7.
547. *See supra* at p. 52.
548. Art. 2(6) (ROPCo).
549. Art. 2(7) (ROPCo).
550. The official languages of the Community are Danish, Dutch, English, French, German, Greek, Italian, Portuguese and Spanish. Gaelic is not one of the official languages although some texts are translated into it. Kapteyn and Themaat discuss the Community's linguistic régime in *Introduction to the Law of the European Communities* at pp. 63-65.

barriers after all other attempts to find a compromise solution had failed. The ad hoc groups may report directly to the Council or to COREPER. Certain items may be set aside by the Presidency to be taken up again when circumstances are more favorable. Thus, two Commission proposals on corporate taxation that first came before the Council in 1969 were finally enacted into legislation in 1990.[551]

"B" items on which the Council has managed to reach agreement are invariably sent back to COREPER for final drafting. Thus, EcoFin reached political agreement on a Common Position for a Second Banking Directive on June 19, 1989 and send the dossier back to COREPER. The latter body, working in conjunction with the Working Party, put together the final version, which was submitted as an "A" item to EcoFin for its meeting on July 10, 1989, when the Common Position was formally adopted.

The Council will have to include in all its deliberations an examination of the compatibility of a measure with **Article 3b (EC)** once it comes into effect.[552] The European Council has stressed that this examination should be part of the Council's overall consideration of a dossier and should not give rise to a system of preliminary or parallel decision-making.[553] Much responsibility will devolve upon COREPER for making sure that this does not happen.

As has been emphasized previously, the Council cannot act without first receiving the opinion of Parliament and ECOSOC if this is mandated by the Treaties, although neither body can hold up Council action indefinitely. On occasion, the Council agrees prematurely on a measure but does not formally take action until consultation has taken place. This practice would seem to constitute a clear violation of the spirit of the Treaties, but it has been sanctioned by the Court of Justice, which is even prepared to accept a retroactive consultation.[554]

Legislation enacted by the Council on the first round under the traditional procedure takes effect according to the Treaty Articles without any further involvement of other Community bodies.[555] A Common Position, on the other hand, must be communicated to Parliament together with a statement of reasons for both the Council's and the Commission's position.[556] At first, the Council produced very sketchy statements, which caused President Plumb of the European Parliament to make a formal complaint. He demanded that "[as] a minimum, the Council should provide a specific and explained reaction to each of Parliament's amendments."[557] The Council has now improved and, without acceding completely to Parliament's wishes, normally gives a reasonably comprehensive explanation of its position.[558]

Once the TEU in force, the Council's explanation of its Common Position will have to include a reference to its views on the observance of the subsidiarity provi-

551. Council Directives 90/434 and 90/435 (OJ L 225/1990).
552. But *note* the comments in fnn. 169 and 466.
553. *Edinburgh Summit Conclusions*, Annex 1 to Part A, p. 11.
554. *Tunnel Refineries*, 114/81, at 3210
555. Arts. 189, 191 (EEC); 161, 163 (EAEC); 14, 15 (ECSC). On occasion, there may be need for the Member States to ratify the act — *see* Table 1.
556. Arts. 149(2)(b) (EEC); **189c(b), 189b(2) (EC)**
557. OJ C 318/1987, p. 41. *See also* OJ C 345/1975 at p. 59.
558. *See, e.g.*, the statement accompanying the Common Position on the Second Non-Life Insurance Directive in Co. Doc. 4676/88.

sions of **Article 3b (EC)**, in particular where it has partially or totally rejected parts of the Commission's proposal for non-compliance with this Article.[559] Presumably, the Commission will likewise have to inform Parliament of its position where it has agreed to drop parliamentary amendments from the text of the Common Position because of problems with **Article 3b**.[560]

The Common Position supplants the Commission's proposal as the basis for the discussions and compromises leading up to the measure's final enactment. In most cases, however, it is elaborated in collaboration with the Commission and is usually the result of amendments officially sanctioned by the latter. The Commission retains, of course, its control of the legislative process and can still end it by withdrawing the proposal on which the Common Position is based.[561] It can also submit at any time an amended proposal, but this would destroy the Common Position and perhaps even require re-consultation of Parliament. So far, the Commission has never made use of its right to amend or withdraw after the Council has adopted a Common Position. Parliament, in turn, can amend the Common Position but cannot alter its substance,[562] although it is not clear whether a similar limitation applies to the elaboration of a joint text with the Council under the Co-decision Procedure.[563]

559. *Edinburgh Summit Conclusions*, Annex 1 to Part A, p. 12.

560. The European Council had nothing to say on this point at its Edinburgh meeting.

561. Some Council jurists dispute the Commission's right to withdraw or amend its proposal after a Common Position has been reached — *see supra* at pp. 25-26.

562. Rule 70(1)(a),(b) (ROPParl).

563. *See infra* at p. 102.

Chapter V. Stage 4: The Second Round

1. THE SECOND READING BY THE EUROPEAN PARLIAMENT

1.1. Role of Parliament

In its Second Reading, Parliament's role is to approve, amend or reject the Council's Common Position.[564] If Parliament does not act within three months, it is deemed to have approved the Common Position.[565] This time limit is calculated from the day on which the President of the European Parliament announces the communication of the Common Position to the plenary session.[566] It may be extended to four months by agreement with the Council.[567]

1.2. Co-decision and Cooperation

Parliament has a Second Reading under both the Cooperation and Co-decision Procedures. It operates in largely the same way for both procedures, but there are nevertheless important differences in the Co-decision Procedure that will affect Parliament's influence on the legislative process.

In the first place, a rejection by Parliament of the Common Position under the Co-decision Procedure cannot be overridden by the Council and will end the legislative process.[568] To avoid this outcome, the Council has the option of convening the Conciliation Committee in order to explain its position further to Parliament and to overcome the latter's opposition. Where this happens, the time limit for Parliament to complete its Second Reading is extended automatically to five months.[569]

Clearly, this power of veto will strengthen Parliament's position but perhaps less than might at first appear to be the case. Although the Council can override Parliament's rejection of the Common Position under the Cooperation Procedure, this must be done by unanimity even where the Council is supported by the Commission.[570] As many Common Positions are reached with some difficulty, there may not be the necessary consensus within the Council to overturn a parliamentary

564. Arts. 149(2)(b),(c) (EEC): **189b(2)(a)-(d), 189c(b),(c) (EC)**; Rule 48(2) (ROPParl).
565. Arts. 149(2)(b) (EEC): **189b(2)(b), 189c(b) (EC)**; Rule 49 (ROPParl). Parliament had suggested that its failure to approve the Common Position should instead lead to a meeting of the Conciliation Committee — *see* art. 188b(e) (EP Draft Treaty).
566. Rule 45(1) (ROPParl).
567. Arts. 149(2)(g) (EEC); **189b(7), 189c(g) (EC)**; Rule 46(1) (ROPParl).
568. **Art. 189b(2)(c) (EC)**.
569. **Art. 189b(7) (EC)**.
570. Arts. 149(2)(c) (EEC); **189c(c) (EC)**.

veto. Moreover, some Member States may not be willing to push through legislation in these circumstances. In addition, the Commission, which is sensitive to the wishes of Parliament and can even be forced to resign en bloc by a parliamentary vote of censure,[571] might withdraw a proposal rather than allow the Council to proceed. Parliament thus has a *de facto* power of veto even under the Cooperation Procedure.

The significance of the *de iure* power of veto bestowed by Co-decision is also reduced by the fact that outright rejection by Parliament of the Common Position at its Second Reading is very rare. It has, in fact, only happened once so far in October 1988, when Parliament rejected the Common Position on protection against occupational health risks from benzene. This is because Parliament's primary concern is that the legislation necessary to achieve European integration be enacted, which the use of its veto power would prevent. It matters little that this power be *de facto* or *de iure*. The Co-decision Procedure does have the advantage, however, of providing for direct contact between Parliament and the Council in order to avoid this outcome from which neither party gains.

A second difference concerns Parliament's power of amendment. Both procedures give Parliament the right to re-introduce at Second Reading its earlier amendments that were not incorporated into the Common Position as well as to propose new amendments to those parts of the text that differ from or were not included in the proposal as approved at Parliament's First Reading.[572] However, whereas the Council may disregard this second set of parliamentary amendments under the Cooperation Procedure,[573] it will be obliged under Co-decision either to accept them or to work out with Parliament a mutually acceptable alternative text if it wishes to enact the legislation.[574]

There is no doubt that Parliament will have a greater say in the the final legislative text under Co-decision, but, again, one must be careful when making the comparison with the Cooperative Procedure. Although only a minority of Parliament's second set of amendments are accepted by the Council on average under the latter procedure, these amendments must be added to those already accepted from the First Reading. It is also probable that Parliament will encounter the same difficulty under Co-decision in persuading the Council to take on amendments of which it disapproves and that, if the legislation is to be enacted at all, a compromise will have to be reached that falls short of Parliament's wishes. The advantage with the Co-decision Procedure is that there is explicit provision for Parliament and the Council to meet and work out such a compromise, whereas, under the Cooperation Procedure, the rules are more hazy and less effective.

Even though there may be limits to the increase in Parliament's influence under Co-decision, this new procedure will nevertheless bring about one radical change. Under it, Parliament acquires a legislative function for the first time as its approval is needed for the Common Position to be enacted into Community legislation. This change will have considerable impact in the second round on both the Commission's influence and the Council's freedom of action, as we shall see

571. Art. 144 (EEC).
572. Arts. 149(2)(c) (EEC); **189b (2)(d), 189c(c) (EC)**; Rule 51(2)(a),(c) (ROPParl).
573. Arts. 149(2)(d),(e) (EEC); **189c(d),(e) (EC)**.
574. **Art. 189b(2)-(5) (EC)**.

1.3. Procedure at Parliament's Second Reading

Initial Steps

The announcement to Parliament by its President that the Common Position has been received opens the Second Reading.[575] Before making this announcement, the President examines the accompanying statements from the Council and the Commission to ascertain whether they fully explain the respective positions of these institutions in accordance with Articles 149(2)(b) of the EEC Treaty.[576] Ideally, the Council's statement should explain its attitude towards both Parliament's amendments and the Commission's proposal. As has already been mentioned, there were problems with the Council's initial efforts but these seem to have been more or less resolved. Parliament reserves the right, however, to challenge the validity of legislation where it considers that the Treaty Articles have not been properly followed. The President of Parliament is also obliged to make a prior determination, in cooperation with the Chairman of the responsible parliamentary committee, whether the text received from the Council falls within Parliament's rules for re-consultation.[577] If so, the President must seek the Council's agreement to another First Reading or, where possible, effect changes to the Common Position that bring it more into line with the proposal as approved by Parliament at its First Reading.

The Committee Stage

To save time, a Common Position is deemed on the day of its communication to Parliament to have been referred automatically to the responsible committee and any other committee that was asked for its opinion.[578] The same Rapporteur is normally used,[579] and the Common Position has to be considered at the first meeting of the responsible committee following this automatic referral.[580] Opinions from other committees will only be considered if they meet this deadline.

The parliamentary rules provide for a simple procedure at the committee stage of the Second Reading.[581] Only members of the responsible committee may table amendments,[582] although any MEP may table a proposal for the committee to reject the Common Position.[583] Amendments put forward by committee members are only

575. Rule 45(1) (ROPParl).
576. Rule 45(1) (ROPParl). The same examination will be made under **Articles 189b(2)** and **189c(b)** of the EC Treaty. Once the TEU is in force, these statements will also have to refer to the subsidiarity aspect of the legislation.
577. Note to Rule 45(1) (ROPParl). Parliament's rules for re-consultation are found in Rule 42 (ROPParl) and are discussed *supra* at pp. 53-54.
578. Rule 47(1) (ROPParl).
579. Rule 47(3) (ROPParl).
580. Rule 47(2) (ROPParl).
581. These are contained in a single Rule, 47 (ROPParl). Rules 116, 117 and 120 (ROPParl) do not apply at Second Reading.
582. Rule 47(4) (ROPParl).
583. Rules 47(4), 50(1) (ROPParl).

admissible if they seek to re-introduce amendments from Parliament's First Reading or to amend new parts of the text.[584] Where it appears to the responsible committee that there is a significant divergence from the views of the Council, it may initiate discussions with the latter under Rule 47(5) in order to reach a compromise.[585] Amendments to the Common Position arising from these discussions are also admissible.[586] The Rapporteur may draw up a draft recommendation for the responsible committee, but this is not obligatory under the rules.

At its meeting, the responsible committee considers any motion for rejection of the Common Position, any amendments tabled by its members, the draft recommendation of the Rapporteur if there is one and, lastly, any opinions it has received from other committees. It votes first on the motion to reject the Common Position.[587] If there is no such motion or if it is not accepted, the committee then votes separately on any amendments that have been tabled and finally on the Common Position as amended. All decisions of the committee are made by a majority of the votes cast.[588] The committee's ultimate decision may be to reject the Common Position, which is very rare; to accept it without amendments, which is a little unusual; or to accept it with amendments. The decision, together with any amendments and a short justification, is contained in a Recommendation that is submitted to the full Parliament. Parliament votes on the decision but not on the Recommendation as such.[589]

Theoretically, Rule 36(3) applies to Second Readings, which means that the legal base of a Common Position can be challenged by the responsible committee using the same procedure as at the First Reading.[590] In practice, this rarely happens as most disputes over the legal base of a Commission proposal involve the replacement of the Cooperation (or Co-decision) Procedures by the traditional one-step procedure.[591] As a result, the measure does not come before Parliament for a Second Reading.

The Plenary Session of Parliament

The Common Position and the Recommendation of the responsible committee containing its suggested amendments, if there are any, must be considered by the full

584. Rules 47(4), 51(2)(a)(c) (ROPParl).

585. The Council normally cooperates here although the procedure is based solely on the Parliament's Rules of Procedure. The discussions take place between the Rapporteur and/or the Chairman of the responsible committee and the President of the specialized Council — *see* Resolution of 9 July 1981 on relations between the European Parliament and the Council at pt. 5.

586. Rules 47(4), 51(2)(b) (ROPParl).

587. The rules for voting in the responsible committee are set out in Rule 90(2) (ROPParl), which applies to committees by virtue of Rule 123(4) (ROPParl).

588. Rule 47(4) (ROPParl).

589. Note to Rule 48(1) (ROPParl).

590. *See supra* at pp. 47-48. *Note also* the comments in fn. 319.

591. *See* Council Directive 90/219 (OJ L 117/1990) on the contained use of genetically modified micro-organisms, where the Council replaced Article 100A (EEC: Cooperation Procedure) with Article 130S (EEC: traditional procedure) and thus obviated the need for a Second Reading by Parliament. Parliament nevertheless insisted on giving a supplementary opinion (OJ C 198/1988), but the Council took no account of it.

Parliament before the expiry of the time limit of three (or four) months.[592] Additional amendments may be tabled for Parliament's direct consideration by a committee, a political group or at least twenty-three MEPs.[593] The same rules govern the admissibility of these amendments as at the committee stage [594] They are considered immediately without being referred back to the responsible committee as at the First Reading.[595] Any MEP may table a proposal for Parliament to reject the Common Position.[596]

Where the responsible committee has submitted a Recommendation approving the Common Position as it stands and no other amendments or motion for rejection have been placed before Parliament, the Common Position may be approved without further ado by a majority of votes cast.[597] Alternatively, the President of Parliament may simply declare the Common Position approved without calling for a vote.[598] The latter is the usual procedure where the responsible committee fails to meet the deadline or decides not to submit a Recommendation as long as no other proposals concerning the Common Position have been tabled within the time limit for Parliament's direct consideration. This is because a failure by Parliament to act within the time limit is the equivalent to an approval of the Common Position under both the Cooperation and Co-decision Procedures.[599] Many non-controversial or routine matters are approved in this tacit way by Parliament in order to save time. To prevent approval of a Common Position by default, referrals back to committee are not allowed at Second Reading.[600]

A motion to reject the Common Position is considered before any amendments and requires the support of an absolute majority of MEPs (i.e. at least 260 votes) to be adopted.[601] Under the Cooperation Procedure, the President of Parliament must request the Commission to withdraw its proposal if the Common Position is rejected.[602] Although the Council may not often be able to muster the unanimous vote needed to override Parliament's rejection, withdrawal of the proposal is preferred by Parliament as it ensures that the Common Position will not be enacted into law. The Commission, however, is not obliged to accede to Parliament's request. In the one case that Parliament did reject the Common Position in 1988, the benzene proposal was not withdrawn by the Commission.

Under Co-decision, there will be no need for Parliament to request withdrawal of the proposal as Parliament's rejection ends the legislative process and prevents

592. Rule 48(1) (ROPParl).

593. Rule 51(1) (ROPParl). The figure of twenty-three MEPs may change with the increase in the overall number of MEPs. Where a compromise is reached with the Council pursuant to Rule 47(5) *after* the responsible committee has submitted its Recommendation to Parliament, the committee is able to table the compromise amendment(s) under Rule 51(1).

594. Rule 51(2) (ROPParl). *See supra* at pp. 85-86.

595. Pursuant to Rule 44(3) (ROPParl), Rule 71 does not apply to Second Readings.

596. Rule 50(1) (ROPParl)

597. Arts. 149(2)(b) (EEC); **189b(2)(a), 189c(b) (EC)**; Rules 49, 90(2)(a), 90(4) (ROPParl).

598. Rules 49, 90(2)(a) (ROPParl).

599. Arts 149(2)(b) (EEC); **189b(2)(b), 189c(b) (EC)**. Parliament had suggested instead that the Conciliation Committee should meet where it fails to act — *see* art. 188b(e) (EP Draft Treaty).

600. Pursuant to Rule 44(3) (ROPParl), Rule 103 does not apply at the Second Reading.

601. Arts.149(2)(c) (EEC); **189b(2)(c), 189c(c) (EC)**; Rules 50(1), 90(2)(b) (ROPParl).

602. Rule 50(3) (ROPParl).

the Council from adopting the act in question.[603] However, in this case, Parliament will not proceed immediately to reject the Common Position but first indicate to the Council, by an absolute majority of MEPs,[604] its intention to do so. The Council will then have the option of convening the Conciliation Committee, which consists of the twelve members of the Council or their representatives and an equal number of representatives from Parliament.[605] The Commission will take part in the proceedings of the Committee and help to bring about agreement between Parliament and the Council.

The Council explains to the Conciliation Committee why it adopted the Common Position in its actual form. Although not expressly provided for in **Article 189b(2)(c) (EC)**, there is nonetheless likely to be some discussion and even negotiation between the two groups. The representatives of Parliament report back on the outcome of the Committee meeting and, if Parliament feels that the Common Position can be salvaged, it will propose the necessary amendments to render it acceptable. Sometimes, these amendments will doubtless represent a compromise that has already been reached with the Council in the Conciliation Committee. It is only where the positions of Parliament and the Council remain irreconcilable that Parliament is likely to carry through its rejection of the Common Position, again by an absolute majority. This will probably be as unusual an event under Co-decision as under the Cooperation Procedure. It should be noted that **Article 189(2)(c)** does not provide for Parliament to change its mind and accept the Common Position as a result of conciliation, but this course of action will surely be open to it.

Parliament's time limit for concluding its Second Reading will be automatically extended to five months when the Conciliation Committee is convened in this way.[606] Presumably, if Parliament were to allow the conciliation process to drag on beyond this time limit, the Common Position would be considered adopted by default. It is unlikely, however, that Parliament will permit this to happen.

Where the responsible committee's recommendation is accepted that the Common Position be approved as amended, Parliament considers all the proposed amendments to it.[607] These also require for adoption the support of an absolute majority of MEPs.[608] Where the Common Position is amended, the final vote approving the text as amended is postponed until the Commission has indicated its attitude towards Parliament's amendments to the Rapporteur of the responsible committee.[609] This strategy is crucial in the Cooperation Procedure, but it may also be used in Co-decision.

Under the Cooperation Procedure, the Commission submits a Re-examined Proposal to the Council. As the Council needs to act by unanimity if it wishes to

603. **Art. 189b(2)(c) (EC)**.
604. Parliament had proposed that it should be able to reject the Common Position and invoke the Conciliation Committee by a simple majority of votes cast — *see* art. 188b(e) (EP Draft Treaty).
605. **Art. 189b(2)c), (4) (EC)**.
606. **Art. 189b(7) (EC)**.
607. Rule 90(2)(c) (ROPParl).
608. Arts. 149(2)(c) (EEC); **189b(2)(d), 189c(c) (EC)**; Rule 51(3) (ROPParl). Parliament had suggested that it be able to reject the Common Position in these circumstances and invoke the Conciliation Committee by a simple majority of votes cast — *see* art. 188b(e) (EP Draft Treaty).
609. Rules 50(2), 90(2)(d), 51(4) (ROPParl).

deviate from this Proposal,[610] which is often difficult to achieve, it is very important for Parliament to ensure that the Commission incorporates its amendments into the Re-examined Proposal. This way, it is both easier for the Council to adopt them and more difficult for it to leave them out of the final text. Under Co-decision, Parliament will rely less on the Commission as the Council cannot unilaterally enact legislation that does not include all of Parliament's amendments.[611] Instead, the Conciliation Committee is convened to elaborate, if possible, a compromise text. Nevertheless, even under this procedure, the Commission's support will still be important. It permits the Council to enact the Common Position as amended by Parliament straightaway by a qualified majority, whereas it would need to act by unanimity if it wished at this initial stage to include amendments on which the Commission has delivered a negative opinion.[612] It is only later in the Conciliation Committee that the Council will be able to adopt by a qualified majority parliamentary amendments rejected by the Commission.[613] However, by this time, the legislative process may have been delayed and perhaps even irrevocably compromised.

If the Rapporteur is not satisfied with the Commission's response to Parliament's second set of amendments, he or she may propose that Parliament reject the Common Position instead.[614] This is unlikely to happen under Co-decision because a text that excludes any of Parliament's second-round amendments cannot in any case be enacted into law without its approval. Rejection of the Common Position in these circumstances is thus linked exclusively to the Cooperation Procedure, and it will be followed by a request for withdrawal of the proposal.[615] Such fundamental disagreement between Parliament and the Commission over the former's amendments is infrequent, as the Commission normally seeks to accommodate Parliament. It does, however have to gauge the reaction of the Council to Parliament's amendments as well as considering their effect on the overall thrust of the proposal and, once the TEU is in force, the subsidiarity issue.[616] Essentially, the Commission has the delicate task of finding a common ground between the Council and Parliament while at the same time safeguarding the Community interest and making sure that the Treaties are respected. On average, the Commission accepts about half of the amendments adopted by Parliament at its Second Reading under the Cooperation Procedure. It will be interesting to see how the Commission will react under Co-decision.

The fact that Parliament fails to muster a sufficient majority either to reject or amend the Common Position does not always mean that there is the simple majority of votes needed to approve it. If, for example, out of 400 votes cast, 250 are in favor of rejecting the Common Position, this is not enough to carry the motion but neither are the remaining 150 votes sufficient to approve the Common Position. In this situation, Parliament is stalemated and the Common Position passes by default.[617]

---

610. Arts. 149(2)(d),(e) (EEC); **189c(d),(e) (EC)**.
611. **Art. 189b(3)-(6) (EC)**.
612. **Art. 189b(3) (EC)**.
613. **Art. 189a(1) (EC)**.
614. Rule 50(2) (ROPParl).
615. Rule 50(3) (ROPParl).
616. *See* the comments in fn 450.
617. Arts. 149(2)(b) (EEC); **189b(2)(b), 189c(b) (EC)**: Rule 49 (ROPParl). This could not happen under Article 188b(e) of the EP Draft Treaty, as, in this situation, the Conciliation Committee would meet.

Parliament's Second Reading is terminated when the Common Position is rejected, amended or approved with or without a vote.[618] Parliament's decision containing a short statement of the result of its Second Reading and, where appropriate, its proposed amendments are sent to the Council and the Commission with a covering letter from its President.[619] Where a Common Position is rejected under the Cooperation Procedure and the proposal is withdrawn by the Commission, the President of Parliament informs the Council that the legislative process has come to an end.[620] Presumably this will also happen when a Common Position is rejected under the Co-decision Procedure.

1.4. Follow-Up Procedures

Theoretically, the responsible committee can again request that Parliament vote for the withdrawal of the proposal, the opening of the Conciliation Procedure or re-consultation where it is not satisfied with subsequent legislative developments after Parliament's approval of the Common Position with amendments. In practice, Parliament's freedom of action is much more restricted this time round. In the case of Co-decision, the Conciliation Committee Procedure will be used instead of these procedures.

Cooperation Procedure

Where Parliament is reacting to the Commission's failure to incorporate its amendments into the Re-examined Proposal, any motion for withdrawal of the proposal requires for adoption a majority of current MEPs as opposed to the simple majority of votes cast that suffices at the First Reading.[621] However, where the problem is the intention of the Council to reject parliamentary amendments contained within the Re-examined Proposal, Parliament can still call for withdrawal by a simple majority.[622] In fact, Parliament is unlikely to request withdrawal in either of these situations unless amendments are at stake to which it attaches particular importance.

Although not excluded by the parliamentary rules,[623] the use of the Conciliation Procedure is not feasible after Parliament's Second Reading because of the time limit of three (or four) months that is set down for the Council to make its final decision.[624] In most cases, it is not until COREPER has finalized its recommendation to

---

618. Rule 48(2) (ROPParl).
619. *See* the communication of the Second Reading of the Broadcasting Directive in OJ C 158/1988 at p. 138.
620. Rule 50(4) (ROPParl).
621. Rule 52(2) (ROPParl). *Compare* Rule 41(4), which applies at the First Reading. *See also* Rule 44(4) (ROPParl).
622. In these circumstances, Rule 41(4) (ROPParl) also applies to the Second Reading as it is no longer excluded by virtue of Rule 44(4).
623. Rules 41 and 43 are not excluded by Rule 44(3),(4) (ROPParl.).
624. Arts. 149(2)(f),(g) (EEC); **189c(f)(g) (EC)**. Bieber, "Legislative Procedure" takes this view at p. 721.

the Council that the divergence with Parliament becomes apparent, by which time it is too late to start the process. It is doubtless for this reason that Parliament does not advocate the use of the Conciliation Procedure after its Second Reading in its resolution of February 16, 1989.[625] In any case, by authorizing direct negotiations between the responsible committee and the Council, Rule 47(5) of the parliamentary rules establishes an alternative conciliation procedure for the second round of the Cooperation Procedure. It lacks, however, the official sanction of the Treaty and does not even set out how this dialogue with the Council is to be conducted.[626] It is certainly no substitute for the Conciliation Committee Procedure, although it is conceivable that the Rule could be invoked under Co-decision for minor problems. There is also nothing to prevent an exchange of views between the Presidents of the Council and Parliament under either Co-decision or the Cooperation Procedure, should the 1971 Agreement be reactivated.[627]

Re-consultation of Parliament in the form of a new Second Reading is also not excluded by the parliamentary rules[628] but is even more improbable than the use of the Conciliation Procedure. An important point to note is that the Re-examined Proposal which the Commission submits to the Council either incorporates Parliament's amendments or not; it cannot contain any new material as this would constitute an amended proposal and destroy the Common Position.[629] Thus, the only ground on which Parliament could call for re-consultation under Rule 42 would be that the Council intends to amend the Re-examined Proposal substantially, by which time there would be little time for re-consultation. The Council must act on the Re-examined Proposal within three months, extended to four if Parliament agrees.[630] If it were forced to re-consult Parliament, then there is a good chance that it would miss this deadline and the proposal would be deemed not to have been adopted.[631]

Co-decision Procedure

Under Co-decision, the President of the Council will be obliged to convene a meeting of the Conciliation Committee if the Council is unable to adopt a legislative act incorporating all of Parliament's amendments to the Common Position. Although the language of **Article 189b(3) (EC)** suggests that the Committee need not meet if the President of Parliament does not agree to its convocation, such lack of cooperation is unlikely as it is in Parliament's interest to find an acceptable text for final adoption as legislation.

625. Resolution of 16 February 1989 on the conciliation procedure.
626. The dialogue in fact takes place between the Rapporteur and/or the Chairman of the responsible committee and the President of the specialized Council — *see* Resolution of 9 July 1981 on relations between the European Parliament and the Council at pt. 5.
627. This Agreement is discussed *supra* at pp. 79-80.
628. Rules 41(4) and 42 (ROPParl) apply to the Second Reading — *see* Rule 44(3) (ROPParl).
629. This would seem to be the clear intent of Articles 149(2)(d) (EEC) and **189c(d) (EC)**. *See infra* at p. 96.
630. Arts. 149(2)(f),(g) (EEC); **189c(f),(g) (EC)**.
631. But *see* the discussion on the binding nature of these deadlines *infra* at pp. 107-108.

This Conciliation Committee Procedure forms part of the Council's second round and is considered later. It suffices to note in the context of Parliament's role that the Committee operates in similar fashion to the 1975 Conciliation Procedure,[632] and that, in both cases, the Commission is given the right to participate in the discussions in order to "take all the necessary initiatives with a view to reconciling the positions of the European Parliament and the Council."[633] The Conciliation Committee Procedure, however, has the advantage of being set down in the Treaty in a series of detailed provisions.[634]. It also has general application and is not limited, like the Conciliation Procedure, to legislative acts with appreciable financial implications. Nor will its use in any way limit Parliament's right to pursue other options or demand re-consultation.

2. SUPPLEMENTARY OPINIONS

2.1. ECOSOC

The Cooperation and Co-decision Procedures do not provide for a second consultation of ECOSOC, but the Committee sometimes now delivers a supplementary Opinion on the Council's Common Position. This way, the Committee seeks to be heard in the second round of the procedure and to influence the final outcome.

This supplementary Opinion is drawn up under Article 23 of ECOSOC's Rules of Procedure, which empowers the Chairman of the Committee to request it in exceptional circumstances from the Section that drew up the original Opinion. The Chairman may also act in response to a request from this Section. The procedure used for producing the supplementary Opinion is identical to that employed by ECOSOC to draw up the original Opinion, and the same Section is put in charge.

2.2. Other Advisory Bodies

There is nothing in the original Treaties or the TEU to prevent COR, the EMI, the Court of Auditors, the Monetary Committee or the CCJHA from giving own-initiative opinions on the Council's Common Position. It is not done at present, however, but it will be interesting to see whether COR follows ECOSOC's lead and gives supplementary opinions where regional interests are involved.

3. THE COMMISSION'S REACTION

3.1. Role of the Commission

The Commission's role in the second round of the Cooperation Procedure is to react

632. The Conciliation Procedure and its shortcomings are described *supra* at pp. 54-56.
633. **Art. 189b(4) (EC)**.
634. **Art. 189b(4)-(6) (EC)**.

to Parliament's Second Reading, unless the Common Position is approved without amendments, in which case its role is much reduced. Where Parliament requests withdrawal of a proposal either upon rejection of the Common Position at its Second Reading or subsequently, the Commission must decide whether to accede to the request or not. If Parliament amends the Common Position, the Commission has to decide which amendments to endorse, if any.

Under the Cooperation Procedure, the Commission exercises considerable influence over the outcome of the legislative process in the second round. It alone can definitively prevent the Council from enacting the Common Position into law by withdrawing the proposal on which it is based. It is also the Commission which determines to a great extent the final text of the legislation by virtue of the Council's need to muster a unanimous vote if it wishes to modify the Re-examined Proposal.

Under Co-decision, the Commission's role is reduced. Parliament itself will be able to prevent the enactment of the Common Position into law and, even more significantly, it will negotiate a compromise text directly with the Council in the event that any of its amendments to the Common Position are not accepted. The Commission will, however, participate in these negotiations and retain its right to withdraw its proposal in order to prevent adoption of an act that it judges inacceptable. Thus, during the second round of both the Co-decision and the Cooperative Procedures, the Commission continues to play its traditional roles of mediator between Parliament and the Council and watchdog of the Community interest.

3.2. Rejection of the Common Position by Parliament

Cooperation Procedure

If Parliament rejects the Common Position under the Cooperation Procedure, its President is bound to request the Commission to withdraw its proposal.[635] The final decision belongs to the Commission as it is responsible for initiating the proposal and it alone can withdraw it. It is likely, however, to pay attention to a request that is supported by an absolute majority of MEPs in order to retain Parliament's good will and perhaps even to avoid a vote of censure. Parliament has in fact only rejected the Common Position once.[636] The Commission did not withdraw the proposal, but in this case neither did the Council override Parliament's rejection.

Parliament may also request withdrawal of a proposal subsequent to approving the Common Position where it finds itself in strong disagreement with the Commission or the Council.[637] This has never happened, but the Commission would probably be more reluctant to accede to the request at this late stage unless it feared for its relationship with Parliament or also disapproved of the form in which the Council intended to enact the legislation. Under the TEU, of course, the Commission would be obliged to act if it considered that the Council's intended text contra-

635. Rule 50(1)-(3) (ROPParl.).

636. In October 1988, Parliament rejected at its Second Reading the proposed Directive on the protection of workers exposed to benzene at work.

637. *See* Rules 41(4), 44(4), 52(2) (ROPParl.) *See also supra* at p. 90

vened **Article 3b (EC)**. However, as subsidiarity is an issue more dear to the Council than the Commission, this situation is not likely to arise very often.

Although the Common Position forms the basis for discussion during the second round of the legislative procedure, it is nonetheless based on the Commission's proposal and cannot exist independently of it. Withdrawal of the proposal, therefore, destroys the Common Position and terminates the legislative process. For this reason, no Re-examined Proposal would be submitted if the Commission were to withdraw a proposal at this stage, which it has not yet done. The Commission could, of course, choose instead to amend its proposal, which would then have to be re-submitted to the Council for a new Common Position. There might also have to be another First Reading by Parliament.[638]

Co-decision Procedure

If Parliament rejects the Common Position under the Co-decision Procedure, the Council will have the option of acquiescing in this decision, in which case the Commission has no role to play, or of convening the Conciliation Committee.[639] The Commission will participate in the meeting of the Committee and play its normal mediating role if any negotiations take place between Parliament and the Council. This is, however, a subordinate role, and the final decision on the fate of the Common Position is transferred to Parliament.

3.3. Approval of the Common Position by Parliament with Amendments

The Commission's reaction to the amendments emanating from Parliament's Second Reading is determined by various factors, which are often in conflict and which may differ according to whether the Cooperation or Co-decision Procedure is used.

The Commission is always under pressure to reach an accommodation with Parliament. Under the Cooperation Procedure, it courts the possibility of rejection of the Common Position if it does not incorporate Parliament's amendments into the Re-examined Proposal. Under Co-decision, the Commission may lose control of the legislative process if its negative attitude thwarts adoption by the Council of the Common Position as amended and the text is referred to the Conciliation Committee. In extreme cases, the Commission could, under either procedure, face a vote of censure by Parliament.

The Commission is particularly susceptible to this pressure from Parliament because of the wide pan-European support in Parliament that its proposed amendments necessarily command. On the other hand, it must take into consideration the political realities existing in the Council. If the Common Position as amended is to be enacted into legislation, a qualified majority has to be preserved whether the Cooperation or, in the future, the Co-decision Procedure is being used. This need not

638. Parliament's rules for re-consultation are found in Rule 42 (ROPParl) and are discussed *supra* at pp. 53-54.

639. The operation of the Conciliation Committee in this situation is described *supra* at p. 88.

be the same qualified majority that adopted the Common Position, but it is rare that the Commission is able to exploit parliamentary amendments to gain the support of dissenting Member States. It is also rare for all of Parliament's amendments to be acceptable to a qualified majority of the Council, which situation is unlikely to change under Co-decision. Thus, under both procedures, the Commission is forced to mediate between Parliament and the Council, while at the same time safeguarding the Community interest as a whole and the integrity of the Treaties, including **Article 3b (EC)** when it comes into force.[640] On occasion, it may still feel obliged to protect the vital interests of a minority Member State as well.

The Cooperation Procedure and the Commission's Re-examined Proposal

The reaction of the Commission to Parliament's amendments under the Cooperation Procedure is contained in its Re-examined Proposal, which sets out the amendments to the Common Position that it has accepted. A supplementary document containing the amendments rejected by the Commission together with an explanation of these rejections is also submitted to the Council.[641] The Council may enact the Common Position as amended by the Re-examined Proposal by a qualified majority,[642] but it requires unanimity for the Council to adopt the parliamentary amendments that have been rejected by the Commission or to depart in any other way from the Re-examined Proposal.[643] As unanimity is not always easy for the Council to achieve, it often has to accept the Re-examined Proposal or persuade the Commission to modify it.[644] Either way, the Commission exercises considerable influence.

The Commission only has one month in which to submit its Re-examined Proposal, and there is no provision in the Treaty for extending the time limit.[645] This deadline leaves the Commission little time for manoeuvre. It must try to accommodate Parliament's position in order to complete the latter's Second Reading, but it then often has to adapt the Re-examined Proposal to meet the Council's wishes to ensure final passage of the legislation. This leaves the Commission with what can be the difficult task of reconciling Parliament to the changes required by the Council or even fending off a call for withdrawal of the proposal.

The advantage of the Cooperation Procedure for the Commission is that it retains considerable control over the second round of the legislative procedure. It is true that the parliamentary rules provide for direct contact between the responsible

640. *See* the comments in fn 450.

641. Arts. 149(2)(d) (EEC); **189c(d) (EC)**. The list of rejected amendments and the accompanying explanation may be contained in the Re-examined Proposal itself where the Commission decides not to accept any of Parliament's amendments — *see* OJ C 154/1989, at p.4.

642. Arts. 149(2)(c) (EEC); **189c(e) (EC)**.

643. Arts. 149(2)(d)(e) (EEC); **189c(d)(e) (EC)**.

644. There may be a legal problem in the Commission modifying the Common Position in this way— *see infra* at pp. 96-97.

645. Articles 149(2)(g) (EEC) and **189c(g) (EC)** only refer to extending the time limits with respect to the Council and the European Parliament. Note, however, that Rule 46 (ROPParl) provides for extending the Commission's deadline as well. On this topic, *see* van Hamme, "The Cooperation Procedure" at p. 138.

committee and Parliament and that in some cases the 1975 Conciliation Procedure may be invoked, but neither of these possibilities have been exploited enough to undermine the Commission's central role. It is not even clear whether the Conciliation Procedure will survive the TEU.

It is important to distinguish between a Re-examined Proposal and an amended proposal. The Common Position of the Council supplants the Commission's proposal (amended or not) as the basis for the discussions leading up to the final enactment of legislation, and the Commission's Re-examined Proposal serves only as a filter for Parliament's reaction to the Council's legislative intentions. The Commission cannot put forward any new material at this stage. This is clear from the wording of Article 149(2)(d) of the EEC Treaty,[646] which limits the Commission's role in preparing its Re-examined Proposal to "taking into account the amendments proposed by the European Parliament". It is also noteworthy that the Commission's amending power is contained in another paragraph that is quite separate from the one which defines its particular role in the second round of the Cooperation Procedure.[647]

This distinction between an amended proposal and a Re-examined Proposal also accords with the inner logic of the Cooperation Procedure. The Common Position is the Council's legislative intention, which is laid before Parliament for its scrutiny and comments before being enacted into legislation. If the Commission were allowed to introduce exogenous material into the Common Position after Parliament's Second Reading, it would no longer be the Council's intentions that Parliament had scrutinized and the whole point of its Second Reading would have been lost.

There is, of course, nothing under either the Cooperation (or Co-decision) Procedures to prevent the Commission from amending its proposal at any time, including during and after Parliament's Second Reading.[648] However, an amended proposal at this late date would nullify the Common Position and require a new one to be adopted on the basis of the Commission's new text. This in turn would have to be re-submitted to Parliament for another Second Reading. Moreover, if the amended proposal were to contain substantial modifications or be undertaken after the nature of the problem at issue had fundamentally changed, another First Reading by Parliament might have to take place as well.[649]

So far, however, the Commission has never formally submitted an amended proposal subsequent to the adoption of a Common Position by the Council. However, the Commission frequently cooperates with the Council during the second round of the Cooperation Procedure by sanctioning the inclusion of new material in the final legislative act. This permits the Council to act by a qualified majority, but

646. **Art. 189c(d) (EC)**.

647. *Compare* Article 149(2)(d) with Article 149(3) (EEC) and **Article 189c(d)** with **Article 189a(2) (EC)**.

648. This view is contested by some Council jurists, but their argument that the right to amend a proposal is inconsistent with the limitations placed on the Commission when drawing up a Re-examined Proposal ignores the fact that the amended proposal has to go through the Council and Parliament again. It cannot be used as a stratagem to enable the Commission to circumvent the restrictions surrounding the Re-examined Proposal.

649. Rule 42 (ROPParl). *See also supra* at pp. 53-54.

in putting forward these alterations to the Common Position, the Commission could be seen as making an amended proposal under Article 149(3) (EEC).[650] Suggestions put forward by the Commission for modifying the Common Position where there is no Re-examined Proposal could similarly be considered an amended proposal. In principle, the result in both cases would be to destroy the existing Common Position and require the Council to adopt a new one. One and perhaps even two Readings by Parliament would then be required. However, this may be an excessively legalistic view; it is difficult to envisage the Court of Justice accepting the notion that the Common Position has ceased to exist when the Council has just demonstrated the contrary by enacting it into legislation. This problem does not exist under the Co-decision Procedure as new material can only be added to the Common Position by Parliament and the Council acting within the Conciliation Committee.

The Co-decision Procedure

The Commission will not issue a Re-examined Proposal under Co-decision. Instead, it will deliver an opinion to the Council on Parliament's amendments to the Common Position.[651] No time limit is set for the Commission to react, but presumably it will not be able to delay the Council's decision indefinitely, particularly as the latter is subject to a time limit of three (or four) months from the time it receives the amendments from Parliament.

Initially, the Council will need to act by unanimity if it wishes to adopt parliamentary amendments on which the Commission has delivered a negative opinion,[652] but later, in the Conciliation Committee, it can agree on a compromise text that includes these amendments by a qualified majority.[653] Another significant difference in Co-decision is that the Commission and the Council cannot change the Common Position unless Parliament agrees.[654]

The crucial time for the Commission under Co-decision becomes Parliament's Second Reading itself. Once amendments to the Common Position have been adopted by Parliament, they must either be incorporated into the final legislation or the Conciliation Committee will be convened.[655] To avoid this development, which will be time-consuming, may not succeed and which will reduce its say in the final outcome, the Commission will have to try to secure passage of the Common Position through Parliament in a form that it can accept and which will command a qualified majority in the Council.

Once Parliament's Second Reading is over, the Commission's influence will decline. Its attitude towards Parliament's amendments is no longer so decisive as it is now Parliament and not the Commission with which the Council must ultimately reach accommodation. Where the Council cannot muster the unanimity or qualified

650. **Art. 189a(2) (EC)**.
651. **Art. 189b(2)(d) (EC)**.
652. **Art. 189b(3) (EC)**.
653. **Arts. 189a(1), 189b(4),(5) (EC)**.
654. This is the effect of **Article 189b(3),(4) (EC)**.
655. **Art. 189b(3) (EC)**.

majority needed to adopt parliamentary amendments, depending on whether they have been rejected or accepted, respectively, by the Commission, it must meet with Parliament's representatives in the Conciliation Committee and try to agree on a compromise text. It must do likewise if it wishes to change the Common Position. If the Conciliation Committee does not reach agreement, the Council may confirm its original Common Position with or without amendments adopted by Parliament at its Second Reading. If Parliament does not reject this text anew by an absolute majority of MEPs, it will become law.

Although the Commission will still have influence under Co-decision and participate in the Conciliation Committee Procedure as mediator between Parliament and the Council, it will no longer be the latter's chief protagonist. Nevertheless, it retains its right to withdraw the proposal, which gives it a power of veto in case it finds the compromise text unacceptable. It could also sabotage the conciliation process by introducing an amended proposal, but this would profoundly irritate the other two institutions and probably redound upon the Commission.

3.4. Approval of the Common Position by Parliament Without Amendments

When Parliament approves a Common Position without amendments, the Commission normally has no further role to play as the parliamentary decision is conveyed directly to the Council, which normally proceeds to enact the Common Position into legislation within three or four months.[656] There is no Re-examined Proposal. However, assuming that it is possible for the qualified majority in the Council to fall apart, the Commission would have to help salvage the legislation.[657]

Under the Cooperation Procedure, the Commission would play a major role in this salvage operation. It would consult with the members of the Council and might have to submit a modified version of the Common Position in order to build up a new qualified majority.[658] Under the Co-decision Procedure, the Commission would not be able to do this. If the Council is indeed free not to adopt the Common Position after it has been approved by Parliament, it will be the Conciliation Committee that works out a new compromise text, although the Commission would be present to facilitate agreement between the other two institutions.[659]

It is highly unlikely that the Commission would ever withdraw its proposal or submit a formal amended proposal after Parliament has approved the Common Position, although theoretically it would be entitled to do so. If it had not approved of the Common Position adopted by the Council, the Commission would presumably have acted before Parliament's Second Reading.

656. Arts. 149(2)(b) (EEC); **189b(2)(a),(b), 189c(b) (EC)** — *see also infra* at p. 101.
657. The possibility of the Council not enacting into legislation a Common Position approved by Parliament is discussed *infra* at pp. 101-103.
658. There may be a legal problem in the Commission modifying the Common Position in this way—*see supra* at pp. 96-97.
659. **Arts. 189b(3)—(5) (EC)**. *See also infra* at pp. 102-103.

3.5. Operation of the Commission

The Commission now reaches its decision collectively on how to react to Parliament's Second Reading. The parliamentary amendments or any request for withdrawal of the proposal are dealt with first by the inter-cabinet committee for parliamentary affairs. If no agreement on a common approach is reached at this level, the dossier is referred to the weekly meeting of the chefs de cabinet. Where agreement is still not forthcoming, the Commissioners have to make a collective decision at their own weekly meeting. The Commission official or officials responsible for the dossier participate in the discussion at each level.

4. THE COUNCIL'S SECOND READING AND FINAL DISPOSITION

4.1. Role of the Council

The Council retains its legislative primacy under the Cooperation Procedure. Although Parliament and the Commission exercise an influence on the process to varying degrees, it is nevertheless the Council that ultimately determines whether and in what form the Common Position is enacted into legislation.[660]

The Co-decision Procedure will eliminate this legislative primacy almost completely. The role of the Commission may be reduced, but Parliament will now share in the Council's legislative authority.[661] It will no longer be possible for the Council to adopt a legislative act without Parliament's approval, and the latter is given an equal role with the Council in working out an alternative text where there is disagreement between the two institutions over the final form of the legislation. The Council will, however, retain some advantage. If no compromise text is agreed upon with Parliament, it has the right to confirm its original Common Position, with or without parliamentary amendments, and this act will become law unless Parliament rejects it anew by an absolute majority of MEPs.[662] Parliament has criticized this provision, arguing that it forces Parliament into a third reading and put the onus on it of holding up the progress of the Community.[663] It is also conceivable that, by this stage, enough MEPs may decide not to pursue the conflict with the Council to secure passage of the legislation by default.

As far as the Council's voting procedures during the second round of the Cooperation Procedure are concerned, the Treaty provides that it can act by a qualified majority whenever it adopts the Commission's Re-examined Proposal.[664] Where the Council departs from this Re-examined Proposal in any way or enacts the Common Position into legislation despite Parliament's rejection of it, it must act by

660. Arts. 149(2)(d),(e) (EEC); **189c(d),(e) (EC)**.
661. **Art. 189b(2)-(6) (EC)**.
662. **Art. 189b(6) (EC)**.
663. Resolution of 11 July 1990 on the Intergovernmental Conference in the context of Parliament's strategy for European Union at pt. 32.
664. Arts. 149(2)(e) (EEC); **189c(e) (EC)**.

unanimity.[665] Article 149(2)(b) of the EEC Treaty[666] is silent on the Council's voting procedure following Parliament's approval of the Common Position without amendments, but the individual Articles providing for use of the Cooperation Procedure state that it acts by a qualified majority.[667]

Under Co-decision, the Council will act by a qualified majority throughout the second round except in two circumstances. It must operate by unanimity where it wishes to adopt an act that contains parliamentary amendments rejected by the Commission straightaway without involving the Conciliation Commission.[668] It must operate by unanimity throughout *all* the procedures of the second round where it is acting pursuant to **Articles 128(5)** and **130i(1) (EC)**.

The Treaty is silent with respect to the composition of these qualified majorities, but Council practice suggests that the composition need not be the same for both the initial adoption of the Common Position and its subsequent enactment into legislation.[669] In the case of the Broadcasting Directive (Council Directive 89/552), for example, the qualified majority which adopted the Common Position differed from that which enacted the final legislative text on October 3, 1989.

Under both the Cooperation and Co-decision Procedures, the Council has to enact the legislation by the requisite majority. The Commission proposed that a text on which Parliament and the Commission are agreed should be considered adopted unless the Council rejects it by a simple majority,[670] but this idea was not taken up in the TEU.

In the discussion that follows, two issues recur. These concern the discretion that the Council enjoys when enacting the Common Position into law and the time limits within which it must operate. The Co-decision Procedure will largely resolve both of them, but there is at present uncertainty under the Cooperation Procedure. By contrast, it is now generally accepted that, where the Commission withdraws a proposal, the legislative process is ended and the Council can no longer act at all.[671]

4.2. Approval of the Common Position by Parliament without Amendments

Wording of the Treaties

When Parliament approves the Common Position without amendments under its Rule 49 with or without a vote, Article 149(2)(b) of the EEC Treaty[672] states that "the Council *shall* definitively adopt the act in question *in accordance with the com-*

665. Arts. 149(2)(c),(d),(e) (EEC); **189c(c),(d),(e) (EC)**.
666. **Art. 189c(b) (EC)**.
667. *See* Table 2.
668. **Art. 189b(3) (EC)**.
669. Interrogated on this point, a Council jurist rather snootily remarked that it was obvious that the composition need not be the same. With all respect, however, the language is *not* clear in Articles 149(2) (EEC) and **189b and 189c (EC)**, and the argument that different qualified majorities make it easier to pass legislation and are therefore unfair on the minority is not without some merit.
670. Commission Opinion of 21 October 1990 at pt. III, 1.
671. Rule 50(4) (ROPParl). But *see supra* at pp. 25-26.
672. **Art. 189c(b) (EC)**.

mon position " (emphasis added). **Article 189b(2)(a) (EC)** reads "that" rather than "the" common position and **Article 189b(2)(c) (EC)** omits the word "definitively" and refers to "its" common position. However, it is difficult to see any substantive difference between these various wordings.

Time Limit for the Council to Act

Under the Cooperation Procedure, the Council has no time limit in which to enact a Common Position approved by Parliament into law,[673] although in practice it has always acted within three or four months of receiving the official communication from Parliament of its approval of the Common Position. The situation may differ under the Co-decision Procedure if the Conciliation Committee Procedure applies,[674] in which case the Council will have three months to act before the procedure is invoked. This period can be extended to four months if Parliament agrees.[675] The Conciliation Procedure itself lasts between twelve and twenty-four weeks.[676]

The Council's Obligation to Act

The words from Article 149(2)(b) (EEC) that are set out above in italics are what causes the real controversy. First of all, the language suggests quite strongly that the Council is *obliged* to enact the legislation under the Cooperation Procedure where Parliament has approved the Common Position without amendments. This is certainly the view of the latter, whose Rules of Procedure provide for the President of Parliament to bring an action on its behalf against the Council under Article 175 of the EEC Treaty if the Common Position is not enacted in these circumstances.[677] Academic opinion, on the other hand, is divided.[678]

The absence of any time limit for the Council's action under Article 149(2)(b) (EEC),[679] after which the Cooperation Procedure would be deemed to have ended inconclusively, implicitly favors Parliament's view that rejection is not a choice open to the Council. One must also consider the nature of the Cooperation Procedure, which calls for the Council to lay its legislative intentions before Parliament in the form of a Common Position before enacting them into law. It would seem to contradict the intrinsic logic of this process if the Council were free to abandon its intentions once Parliament had approved them. Against these arguments and the wording of the Treaty stands only the traditional role of the Council as the final arbiter of the legislative process. Despite the absence of any Treaty provision to sup-

673. *See* arts. 149(2)(b),(f) (EEC); **189c(b),(f) (EC)**.
674. **Art. 189b(3) (EC)**. *See infra* at pp. 102-103.
675. **Art. 189b(3),(7) (EC)**.
676. **Art. 189b (4)-(6) (EC)**.
677. Rule 54 (ROPParl). Article 175 (EEC) provides for court action against the Council where, in violation of the Treaty (*e.g.* Article 149(2)(b)), it fails to act.
678. Van Hamme in "The Cooperation Procedure" at p. 133 maintains that the Council must act. *Contra* Bieber, "Legislative Procedure" at p. 723.
679. **Art. 189c(b) (EC)**.

port it, the view persists that the Council cannot be forced to act. Whether going through with its own stated legislative intentions is the same as being forced to act is open to question. It is also doubtful whether the Court of Justice would now accept such predominance for the Council without unequivocal support from the Treaty.

It is improbable that the controversy will persist with the Co-decision Procedure although the Treaty provisions are identical in substance. The fact that Parliament will share in the Council's legislative authority adds weight to the argument that the Council is obliged to act. It is also possible that a failure by the Council to enact legislation in these circumstances will be covered by **Article 189b(3) (EC)**, in which case the Conciliation Committee would be convened. Although the first sentence of **Article 189b(3)** seems to restrict the Article's application to where Parliament has amended the Common Position, the second sentence states generally that the Committee shall be convened whenever "the Council does not approve the act in question." Assuming that **Article 189b(3)** will apply where the Council fails to enact legislation following Parliament's approval of the Common Position, the following procedure would be followed.[680]

The Conciliation Committee, consisting of the twelve members of the Council (i.e. Ministers of the national Governments) or their representatives and twelve MEPs, would be called into session immediately upon the expiry of three (or four) months from the day on which the Council received notification of Parliament's approval. The Committee has six (or eight) weeks in which to agree upon on a new text. The text requires for its joint adoption a qualified majority among the representatives of the Council and a simple majority among the MEPs. The Commission participates in the discussions of the Committee and is empowered to assist the parties in reaching agreement. It does not, however, have any vote and its approbation is not needed for the Council to act by a qualified majority.[681] Furthermore, as the essence of the Conciliation Committee Procedure is a dialogue between Parliament and the Council, it may well be that the joint text can deviate from the substance of the Commission's proposal.[682]

Where the Conciliation Committee agrees upon a joint text, this must be approved within six (or eight) weeks by a qualified majority in the Council and by a majority of votes cast in Parliament.[683] Once approved by the two institutions, the text becomes a legislative act. On the other hand, failure by either institution to approve the text within the time limit will end the legislative process.

Where the Conciliation Committee fails to agree on a joint text within six (or eight) weeks, the legislative process is similarly brought to an end unless the Council decides within six (or eight) weeks of this failure to confirm its Common Position.[684] It will then be up to Parliament to reject this Common Position anew by an absolute majority of MEPs within six (or eight) weeks from its re-confirmation,

680. The Conciliation Committee procedure is set out in **Article 189b (4)-(6) (EC)**. The time limits of three months and six weeks can be extended to four months and eight weeks, respectively, if the Council and Parliament so agree — *see* **Art. 189b(7) (EC)**.

681. **Art. 189a(1) (EC)**.

682. Amendments to Commission proposals are not normally permitted to alter the substance of the proposal — *see supra* at p. 26.

683. **Art. 189b(5) (EC)**.

684. **Art. 189b(6) (EC)**.

otherwise it becomes law. This option is not open to the Council where the Committee's joint text has failed to secure the necessary approvals. It is somewhat unlikely, however, that the Council would act in this rather inconsistent fashion unless, for some reason, it had proved possible to build a new consensus in favor of the original Common Position. Where this does happen, it is likely that Parliament would approve the Common Position, given that it already would have done so once before.

An important point to note about the Conciliation Committee Procedure is that it does not oblige the Council to act. For this reason, it would not be appropriate to this situation if the Court of Justice were to rule that, under **Article 189b(2)(a)** and **(b) (EC)**, the Council is required to enact into legislation a Common Position approved by Parliament.

The Council's Freedom of Action

The issue of whether the Council has the right to enact legislation in a form that differs from the Common Position as approved by Parliament is resolved in the context of the Co-decision Procedure. Although **Article 189b(2) (EC)** does not expressly prohibit such action, acts must be adopted under this procedure *jointly* by Parliament and the Council and signed by the Presidents of both institutions.[685] This will not leave the Council any possibility of changing unilaterally the final form of the legislation.

As far as the Cooperation Procedure is concerned, the language of Article 149(2)(b) (EEC)[686] and the intrinsic logic of the procedure also indicate that the Council cannot unilaterally change the final form of the legislation. Even if one does not accept that the Treaty obliges the Council to act, it would still appear to circumscribe the Council's freedom where it does decide to act. The imperative "shall" must surely be read as applying at least to adopting the act "in accordance with the common position," otherwise it is totally redundant. It also makes no sense within the context of the Cooperation Procedure to have Parliament vet the Council's legislative intentions, only to permit the latter to change them subsequently at will. In this case it would not have been the Council's real intentions that Parliament scrutinized, and the role of its Second Reading in the legislative process is undermined. For both these reasons, the ruling of the Court of Justice in the *Chemiefarma* case that the Council may unilaterally change in a minor way a text approved by Parliament should not apply to this situation.[687]

Despite these arguments, there is a body of opinion that refuses to limit the Council's freedom of action in this way under the Cooperation Procedure.[688] Apart from the Council's traditional predominance, which may no longer exist, the refusal is also based on Article 149(1) (EEC),[689] which could well be interpreted as giving

685. *See e.g.* **Arts. 190, 191(1) (EC)**.

686. **Art. 189c(b) (EC)**.

687. 41/69, at p. 622 (pt. 31) and p. 691 (pts. 68, 69). *See also* fn. 362.

688. *See* Bieber, "Legislative Procedure" at p. 722. *Contra*, Glaesner, "La procédure de coopération" at p. 77.

689. **Art. 189a(1) (EC)**.

the Council a right of amendment that continues throughout the Cooperation Procedure and applies to all its various scenarios. The Council will, of course, need the Commission to cooperate by submitting amendments unless it can find the necessary consensus to act by unanimity.[690] Unanimity is not easy to achieve, and the Commission may well be wary of abetting what amounts to a circumvention of Parliament and refuse to cooperate. It may even withdraw the proposal, either on its own initiative or at Parliament's request. Furthermore, if the Council is forced to act unilaterally, it cannot alter the substance of the Common Position. Even if it does secure the Commission's support for substantial changes, the Council may be called upon to re-submit the text to Parliament for another Second Reading.[691]

4.3. Rejection of the Common Position by Parliament

Cooperation Procedure

Under the Cooperation Procedure, Parliament's rejection of the Common Position is not final. Assuming that the Commission does not withdraw its proposal, the Council can still enact the Common Position into legislation as long as it can act by unanimity.[692] This is the one instance under the Cooperation Procedure where unanimity is required for Council action even though it is supported by the Commission. In reaching its decision, the Council is subject to a time limit of three months,[693] which presumably runs from the date of the official communication of Parliament's decision to the Council. This time limit may be extended to four months with the agreement of Parliament,[694] but it is unlikely under these circumstances that Parliament would agree! On the sole occasion that Parliament rejected the Common Position, the Council did not override the rejection although the proposal was not withdrawn by the Commission.[695]

The issue of the Council's right to enact the Common Position in an amended form arises again. While such an amendment would still seem to be at odds with the intent behind Parliament's Second Reading under the Cooperation Procedure, it should be noted that the wording of Article 149(2)(c) (EEC)[696] does not contain any limitation on the Council's freedom of action similar to that found in Article 149(2)(b).[697] In addition, there is the right to amend that is granted to the Council by Article 149(1).[698] As the Council must act here by unanimity, it can dispense with

690. There may be a legal problem in the Commission modifying the Common Position in this way—*see supra* at pp. 96-97.

691. But *see supra* at p. 91.

692. Arts. 149(2)(c) (EEC); **189c(c) (EC)**.

693. Arts. 149(2)(f) (EEC); **189c(f) (EC)**.

694. Arts. 149(2)(g) (EEC); **189c(g) (EC)**.

695. In October 1988, Parliament rejected at its Second Reading the proposed Directive on the protection of workers exposed to benzene at work.

696. **Art. 189c(c) (EC)**.

697. **Art. 189c(b) (EC)**.

698. **Art. 189a(1) (EC)**.

the Commission's cooperation, in which case, however, it cannot alter the substance of the Common Position.[699]

Co-decision Procedure

The situation under Co-decision is quite different. Parliament's rejection of the Common Position is final and ends the legislative process.[700] The Council will have the option of convening the Conciliation Committee in order to explain its position further and perhaps negotiate some compromise with Parliament, but it will be up to the latter to decide whether to go through with its rejection, propose amendments or even change its mind and accept the Common Position as is.[701] It is thus Parliament and not the Council that makes the decision in this situation. There will be no room, therefore, for the Council to make unilateral changes to the Common Position.

4.4. Approval of the Common Position by Parliament with Amendments

Cooperation Procedure

Where the Common Position is approved by Parliament with amendments under the Cooperation Procedure, the Council must wait for the Commission to submit its Re-examined Proposal before it can act.[702] The Commission has one month in which to do this.[703] The Council then has three months from the day on which the Presidency receives the Re-examined Proposal to enact it into legislation as it stands by a qualified majority or in a modified form by unanimity.[704] This time limit may be extended to four months with the agreement of Parliament.[705]

The scope of the Council's right to amend the Re-examined Proposal is the subject of some discussion. It has been suggested that in making these modifications, the Council is limited to incorporating parliamentary amendments that the Commission has rejected.[706] Again, the logic of the Cooperation Procedure supports this contention, but the wording of the Treaty suggests otherwise. Apart from the general right of amendment conferred on it by Article 149(1) (EEC),[707] it is significant that the Council is given a specific right both to adopt parliamentary amendments rejected by the Commission[708] and to amend in other ways the Re-examined

699. It may indeed have to forego the Commission's cooperation — *see supra* at pp. 96-97.
700. **Art. 189b(2)(c) (EC)**.
701. This conciliation procedure is described *supra* at pp. 87-88.
702. Arts. 149(2)(d) (EEC); **189c(d) (EC)**.
703. On the Commission's time limit, *see supra* at p. 95. On the general enforceability of time limits, *see infra* at pp. 107-108.
704. Arts. 149(2)(d),(e) (EEC); **189c(d),(e) (EC)**.
705. Arts. 149(2)(g) (EEC); **189c(g) (EC)**.
706. *See* Glaesner, "La procédure de coopération" at p. 77. *Contra*, Bieber, "Legislative Procedure" at p. 722.
707. **Art. 189a(1) (EC)**.
708. Arts. 149(2)(d) (EEC); **189c(d) (EC)**.

Proposal.[709] In both instances it must act by unanimity and it cannot change the substance of the Re-examined Proposal.

Co-decision Procedure

Under Co-decision, the Presidency will receive Parliament's amendments directly and have three months in which to decide whether to accept them or not.[710] This period can be extended to four months with Parliament's agreement.[711] The Council will have to wait, however, for the Commission to deliver its opinion on these amendments, as it has to act by unanimity if it approves amendments on which the Commission has delivered a negative opinion. Presumably, it may operate on the basis of a positive opinion if the Commission fails to respond within a reasonable time. Otherwise, it might find itself running out of time and the Commission would have sabotaged the legislative process. It is, however, unlikely that the Commission will deliberately delay its opinion; if it really wants to prevent adoption of the legislation, it can always withdraw the proposal.

Where the Council accepts all of Parliament's second set of amendments, either by a qualified majority or unanimity, it will enact the Common Position as amended into legislation without delay and submit it for the signature of the President of Parliament.[712] It may not add any new material. If the Council is unable to accept all of Parliament's amendments, it will have to convene a meeting of the Conciliation Committee immediately the stalemate becomes apparent or, at the latest, on the expiry of the three (or four months) set for its second round deliberations.[713]

The Conciliation Committee Procedure has been described in the context of the Council failing to enact a Common Position approved by Parliament.[714] It will operate in exactly the same way here. Once again, the compromise text must be approved by a qualified majority of the Council and an absolute majority of votes cast in Parliament or the legislative process will end without issue. It should be noted that, even where the joint text incorporates parliamentary amendments rejected by the Commission, the Council will still be able to adopt it by a qualified majority.[715] If the Conciliation Committee fails to produce a joint text, the Council can decide within six (or eight) weeks to confirm its original Common Position with or without some of Parliament's second round amendments.[716] It is not clear whether the Council will have to act here by unanimity where it incorporates amendments rejected by the Commission. **Article 189b(6) (EC)** provides only for it to act by a qualified majority, but **Article 189a(1)** does not include this particular act in its exceptions from the unanimity rule. The Council will not be able to add any new material to the Common Position. If Parliament does not reject the Common

709. Arts 149(2)(e) (EEC); **189c(e) (EC)**.
710. **Art. 189b(2)(d),(3) (EC)**.
711. **Art. 189b(7) (EC)**.
712. **Arts. 189b(3), 191(1) (EC)**.
713. **Art. 189b(3) (EC)**.
714. *See supra* at pp. 102-103.
715. **Art. 189a(1) (EC)**.
716. **Art. 189b(6) (EC)**.

Position by an absolute majority of MEPs within six (or eight) weeks of its re-confirmation, it will become law.

4.5. Expiry of the Time Limit without Action by the Council or Parliament

Under the Cooperation Procedure, the Council has a time limit of three months in which to act where Parliament either rejects or amends the Common Position.[717] These deadlines can be extended to four months with the approval of Parliament.[718] There does not appear to be any time limit for the Council's action where Parliament approves the Common Position. The EEC Treaty does not indicate the dates from which these time limits are calculated, but they are easy to extrapolate. Depending on the circumstances, time must run from the day on which either Parliament communicates to the President of the Council its rejection of the Common Position or the Commission submits its Re-examined Proposal.

Under Co-decision, both the Council and Parliament will have a time limit of six weeks to adopt a joint text emanating from the Conciliation Committee.[719] The Council will have the same time in which to confirm its Common Position, with or without amendments, where the Conciliation Committee has failed to agree on a joint text.[720] These time limits, which may be extended to eight weeks by common accord of Parliament and the Council,[721] will run, respectively, from the approval of the joint text by the Conciliation Committee and the expiry of the six weeks laid down for the Committee's work.[722]

If the Council or Parliament fail to act within these time limits, the legislative process is deemed to end without the adoption of the act in question.[723] There is, of course, nothing to prevent the Commission re-submitting its proposal to the Council with or without amendments, but the Council would have to reach a new Common Position and Parliament would have to give another Second Reading. If the Commission substantially altered the proposal or re-submitted it after a significant passage of time or change in circumstances, Parliament might insist also on repeating its First Reading.[724]

Considerable doubt on the binding nature of these time limits must now exist, however, following the Council's enactment of Directive 89/552,[725] the so-called "Television without Frontiers" Directive. The Council received the Re-examined Proposal from the Commission on May 26, 1989, which gave it until August 26, 1989 to act. This deadline was extended by agreement with Parliament to September 26, 1989, but the Directive was not finally enacted until October 3, 1989, which was over a week past the time limit. According to Article 149(2)(f) (EEC),[726] this enact-

717. Arts. 149(2)(f) (EEC); **189c(f) (EC)**.
718. Arts. 149(2)(g) (EEC); **189c(g) (EC)**; Rule 46(2) (ROPParl).
719. **Art. 189b(5) (EC)**.
720. **Art. 189b(6) (EC)**.
721. **Art. 189b(7) (EC)**.
722. **Art. 189b(5),(6) (EC)**.
723. Arts. 149(2)f) (EEC); **189b(5),(6), 189c(f) (EC)**.
724. Rule 42 (ROPParl). *See also supra* at pp. 53-54.
725. OJ L 298/1989
726. **Art. 189c(f) (EC)**.

ment was invalid as the Cooperation Procedure had already come to an end. Presumably, Directive 89/552 could be challenged before the Court of Justice on this ground under Article 173, but it is difficult to imagine the Court striking down such an important piece of legislation that was validly enacted in all other aspects. Yet, unless the Court were to take such a drastic step, the effectiveness of the time limits set down by the Treaty to ensure the progress of legislation through the second round would be seriously undermined.

4.6. Operation of the Council

Cooperation Procedure

Under the Cooperation Procedure, the Council's second round commences once the Presidency receives either the decision of Parliament approving or rejecting the Common Position or the Commission's Re-examined Proposal. The latter is accompanied by the parliamentary amendments that the Commission has rejected together with an explanation. The dossier is turned over to the Council's General Secretariat and brought before COREPER.

COREPER acts more or less in the same manner as for the Council's First Reading. If there is unanimous agreement in the Committee, then the matter will be submitted to the Presidency for inclusion on the Council agenda as an "A" item. Otherwise, it will submitted as a "B" item. Once again, however, it is the Presidency that ultimately decides the Council agenda.[727] Even if there is substantial dissension at COREPER level, it is rare that the Presidency will not bring the matter before the Council of Ministers as a "B" item in a final attempt to reach some compromise agreement. As at its First Reading, the Council may well agree on the general thrust of its final position and send it back to COREPER to work out the details. If substantial amendments to the Common Position are involved which raise new technical problems, the dossier is returned to the Working Party. Otherwise, Working Parties are not frequently used on the Council's Second Reading as the issues are by now political rather than technical in nature. Once COREPER has given its final approval, the dossier is then re-submitted to the Council as a "A" item. All legislation enacted by the Council goes to the jurists/linguists before its formal release.

Theoretically, the Conciliation Procedure is available where COREPER's recommendation to the Council differs from Parliament's opinion at its Second Reading. This will be the case when it proposes that the Council reject parliamentary amendments, particularly those accepted by the Commission, or incorporate new material that Parliament has not vetted. This process is not, however, suited to the second round of the Cooperation Procedure as strict time limits apply (*pace* the Broadcasting Directive).[728] On the other hand, the 1971 Agreement on an exchange of views between the Presidents of Parliament and the Council could serve a useful purpose if it were reactivated. Nothing, however, can prevent the Council from acting on its Second Reading contrary to Parliament's opinion, unless the Commission

727. Art. 2 (ROPCo).

728. *See supra* at pp. 90-91.

withdraws its proposal or the Council fails to muster the necessary support. It is therefore up to the responsible parliamentary committee to establish a close dialogue with the Council in accordance with parliamentary Rule 47(5) in order to ensure that Parliament's views are not spurned.[729]

Co-decision

COREPER will also be involved in preparing the Council's reaction under the Co-decision Procedure, but there will be less work for it to do. Where Parliament approves the Common Position as is or with amendments, COREPER will have to recommend to the Council whether to enact the legislation or which of Parliament's amendments to accept. It will not be able, however, to recommend any unilateral changes to the Common Position. The matter is submitted to the Council as an "A" or "B" item depending on whether there is consensus in COREPER.

If the Conciliation Committee is convened either to explain the Council's position in order to remove the threat of a parliamentary veto or to elaborate a compromise text, COREPER may be called upon to represent the Council. If COREPER participates in drawing up a compromise text, it will submit it to the Council for adoption. Again, this may be as an "A" or "B" item. Even where COREPER is not involved in the work of the Conciliation Committee, it may vet the compromise text before it comes before the Council for final adoption.

729. *See* fn. 585 for a brief discussion of this procedure.

Chapter VI. The Commission As Legislator

1. INTRODUCTION

The Commission enacts legislation of general application under the authority of either the Treaties or the Council.[730] In preparing this legislation, it follows the same basic internal procedures as for drawing up a legislative proposal. However, while the Commission often consults the Council, Parliament, the Member States and European organizations, the fact that it does not usually require their cooperation in order to legislate permits it to rely to a much greater extent on its own services and independent experts. In Parliament's view, it has relied too much on itself.[731] It remains to be be seen whether the Commission's commitment to wider consultation will apply here as well.[732]

2. SECONDARY LEGISLATION OF THE COMMISSION

The Commission's general legislative powers of implementation and application under the EEC Treaty are not subject to any requirement for consultation.[733] The EAEC Treaty, on the other hand, obliges the Commission to consult the Scientific and Technical Committee or ECOSOC,[734] and it must even obtain the approval of the Council before laying down the nature and extent of operating records for ores, source materials and special fissile materials used or produced.[735] The Commission's extensive powers to implement and apply the ECSC Treaty normally require consultation of the Consultative Committee[736] and sometimes of the Council as well.[737] Important legislation must be endorsed by the assent of the Council.[738]

Consultation under the Treaties does not impinge on the Commission's legislative powers. Furthermore, it can set a time limit of not less than ten days for ECOSOC and the Consultative Committee to deliver their opinions,[739] extended to

730. *See supra* at pp. 10-14.
731. *See* Parliament's criticism of the Commission's unilateralism in its Resolution of 13 December 1990 on the powers of the Commission at pt. 4.
732. *See* fn. 153.
733. *See* arts. 33(7), 45(2), 48(3)(d), 90(3) (EEC).
734. *See* arts. 8(1), 9(1) (EAEC).
735. Art. 79 (EAEC)
736. *See* arts. 58(1), 59(5), 59(6), 60(1), 61 (ECSC). Exceptions are Articles 65(2) and 66(3) (ECSC).
737. *See* arts. 60(1), 61 (ECSC).
738. *See* arts. 58(1), 59(5), 66(3), 95 (ECSC).
739. Arts. 198 (EEC); 170 (EAEC); 19 (ECSC).

one month by the TEU for ECOSOC.[740] No equivalent provisions exist for the Scientific and Technical Committee or the Council. In view of its attitude toward Parliament's delaying powers,[741] it is unlikely that the Court of Justice would permit the Scientific and Technical Committee to hold up the Commission unduly. It is unclear whether the Council can be by-passed if it fails to deliver an opinion, but it certainly cannot be forced to consent to any proposed measure. Thus, the Commission may on occasion have to amend its legislative intentions where it needs to obtain the approval or assent of the Council.

3. TERTIARY LEGISLATION OF THE COMMISSION

The greater part of the Commission's general tertiary legislation involves the implementation of Council rules pursuant to Article 145 of the EEC Treaty and is subject to the comitology procedures set out in Council Directive 87/373.[742] There are three types of committees, all of which are composed of representatives from the Member States and chaired by a Commission official, who does not vote. In all cases, the Commission must submit a draft of its proposed legislation to the committee for its opinion.

An advisory committee (Procedure I) delivers its opinion by consensus or majority vote. The Commission is only obliged to take the utmost account of this opinion and to inform the committee of the manner in which it has done so. Failure of an advisory committee to deliver an opinion within the time limit set by its Chairman (a Commission official) dispenses the Commission from taking it into account.

A management committee (Procedure II) delivers its opinion by a qualified majority vote using the same national weighting that is prescribed for the Council.[743] Where this opinion endorses the Commission's proposed legislation or where the committee fails to render an opinion within the time limit set by its Chairman, the Commission can enact its legislation, which applies immediately. In the event of an unfavorable opinion, the Commission can still adopt the measure but it must refer the matter to the Council, which has up to three months in which to enact legislation different from that of the Commission. Failure to do so acts as an endorsement of the Commission's legislation. Depending on the variant used, the Commission may have the choice of suspending the application of its measure during this period (Variant "A") or it may be obliged to do so (Variant "B ").

The procedure in the case of a regulatory committee (Procedure III) differs from that of the management committee in two major aspects. Firstly, failure of a regulatory committee to deliver an opinion has the same effect as a negative opinion. Secondly, the Commission cannot adopt its measure in the face of an unfavorable verdict from the committee but must submit a proposal for the Council to act in its stead. Although this is not mandatory, the proposal will probably incorporate at least

740. **Arts. 198 (EC); 170 (Revised EAEC)**.

741. *See supra* at pp. 38-39

742. OJ L 197/1987, art. 2.

743. *See* art. 148(2) (EEC). Qualified majority voting in the Council is discussed *supra* at pp. 71-72.

some of the suggestions of the regulatory committee. The Council again has up to three months in which to act by a qualified majority (or by unanimity if it wishes to amend the Commission's proposal). If it fails to act, the Commission is free to enact its proposal into legislation itself, but, under Variant "B", the Council can by a simple majority prevent such unilateral action by the Commission.

There has been constant friction between the Community institutions regarding the choice of committee procedure.[744] The Commission, supported by the European Parliament, obviously prefers the advisory committee, although it will accept the management committee as a compromise, while the Council often insists on the regulatory committee.[745] The Declaration on the powers of implementation of the Commission that is appended to the SEA exhorts the Council to use the advisory committee in connection with Article 100A of the EEC Treaty. In fact, the Commission opts exclusively for this procedure in its proposals relating to the completion of the internal market. It also refuses now to propose the use of Variant "B" of Procedure III.[746] The European Parliament has voted for the abolition of regulatory committees.[747]

Prior to the enactment of Council Directive 87/373, the management and regulatory committee procedures were challenged before the Court of Justice as infringing the Treaties. It was alleged that the use of these committees circumvented the legislative procedures set out in the Treaties and also constituted an impingement on the Commission's initiatory power.[748] The Court of Justice has consistently rejected these arguments.[749] As long as the basic elements of a matter are adopted in accordance with the relevant Treaty provision, tertiary implementing legislation can be handled in whichever way the Council authorizes. The use of a management or regulatory committee does not impinge on the Commission's power as long as neither committee can substitute its decision for that of the Commission. Both committees operate, in fact, only so as to ensure the involvement of the Council where there is a difference of opinion between the Member States and the Commission.[750]

Council Directive 87/373, which institutionalizes these committee procedures, was itself challenged by the European Parliament. The Court of Justice disposed of the case by rejecting Parliament's right to bring an action for annulment under Article 173 of the EEC Treaty,[751] but it is unlikely that the court would have departed from its earlier jurisprudence on the issue. In any case, Parliament's complaint about being circumvented is not entirely justified by Commission practice, which is

744. *See e.g.* Parliament's Resolution of 13 December 1990 on the powers of the Commission at pt. 2.

745. *See* the various texts relating to the Second Banking Directive — OJ C 84/1988, Art. 20(2); OJ C 96/1989, Art. 20(2); OJ C 167/1989, Art. 20(2); Council Document 7835/89, Art. 22(2); European Parliament Document A2—427/88/SIN 10, Art. 22(2); OJ L 386/1989, Art. 22(2).

746. Answer of Mr. Delors to Written Question No. 1058/88, OJ C 121/1989. Nevertheless, the Council still insists occasionally on the use of Variant "B".

747. *See* the note to Rule 53 (ROPParl). *See also* art. 155 (EP Draft Treaty). In fact, Parliament would like to see only advisory committees used — *see* Resolution of 17 April 1980 on the relations between the European Parliament and the Commission at pt. 6.

748. *See Einfuhr- und Vorratsstelle* v. *Köster*, 25/70, [1970] E.C.R. 1161 at 1165.

749. *See Köster*, 25/70, at 1170.

750. *See Köster*, 25/70, at 1171.

751. *Parliament* v. *Council*, 302/87, at 5644.

to seek Parliament's opinion on most of its proposed tertiary implementing measures.[752]

Another important part of the Commission's general tertiary legislation relates to block exemptions from the Community's competition rules. It acts here pursuant to detailed rules set down by the Council in one of three regulations enacted under Article 87(2)(b) (EEC).[753] In all three cases, the Commission has to consult the Advisory Committee on Restrictive Practices and Dominant Positions before publishing its draft regulation and again before enacting the block exemption.[754] Thus, the proposed legislation passes through two readings by the committee, although in neither instance is the Commission obliged to follow its opinion.

752. *See* Rule 53 (ROPParl).

753. Council Regulations 19/65 (OJ 36/1965), art. 1; 2821/71 (OJ L 285/71), art. 1; 3976/87 (OJ L 374/87), art. 1.

754. Article 6 of Council Regulations 19/65, 2821/71 and 3976/87.

Chapter VII. Conclusion

1. THE INTERPLAY BETWEEN THE COMMUNITY INSTITUTIONS IN THE ENACTMENT OF COUNCIL LEGISLATION

1.1. The Commission

The Commission's role in the legislative process is to further and defend the interest of the Community. This will include ensuring that the subsidiarity provisions of **Article 3b (EC)** are respected once they enter into force. In performing its role, the Commission has to accommodate the other two legislative institutions in order to secure the timely enactment of its proposals into law.

Before the Commission can bring a new proposal before the Council or submit a text under the Cooperation (and Co-decision) Procedures for final enactment into law, it has to deal with the European Parliament, which has the power to approve, amend or reject. Under the traditional and Cooperation procedures, the Commission is in the dominant position as it cannot be forced to incorporate Parliament's amendments or withdraw a proposal that Parliament has rejected. It is also free to remove parliamentary amendments from a text in order to secure its enactment by the Council. Nevertheless, Parliament can oppose an uncooperative Commission by stalling the legislative process, rejecting a text at its Second Reading or even forcing the collective resignation of the Commission.

In dealing with Parliament, the Commission is inclined to respect its wishes both for tactical reasons and because it represents the democratic principle, being the only Community institution that is directly elected by the peoples of the Community. As a matter of strategy, the Commission also needs to retain Parliament's goodwill so that it will support future proposals, thus making it easier for the Commission to pilot them through the Council without substantial alteration. The Commission is not, however, the pliant instrument of Parliament's will. It must constantly weigh the latter's wishes in the light of the Community interest, the protection of which is its particular responsibility, and their acceptability to a sufficient majority in the Council. These are the grounds on which the Commission will oppose parliamentary amendments or refuse to withdraw a proposal. Once the TEU is in force, the Commission will also have to judge Parliament's amendments against the criteria established by the subsidiarity provisions.

Under Co-decision, the relationship between the two institutions will be more equal. Parliament will not need the Commission to withdraw its proposal in order to end the legislative process, and it will not have to rely on the Commission to adopt and advocate its amendments to the Common Position. In fact, it will now be the Commission that must rely on Parliament to approve a text so that it may be enacted into law. Nevertheless, even under this procedure, the Commission will still be in control during the first round, and its support in the second round will make it easier for the Council to incorporate Parliament's amendments into the final legislative act.

Once a proposal is before the Council, the Commission is faced with a different set of priorities and objections flowing from the national interests of the twelve Member States. Under the traditional and Cooperative procedures, it is almost exclusively the Commission that deals with the Council. It must cooperate with the Council sufficiently to secure enactment of the legislation or adoption of a Common Position without jeopardizing its relationship with Parliament or compromising the Community. It must both judge the reactions of the Council from the perspective of the Community interest and harmonize them with the interests of the electorate as expressed in the parliamentary amendments that it has incorporated into its proposal. This is a difficult task for the Commission as it often caught between these conflicting interests. Its overall strategy tends to center on nudging the Council towards Parliament's views, which are normally more Community-oriented than those of the Council.

The Commission's main weapon against the Council is persuasion. Indeed, this is its only way of inducing the Council to act upon its proposals. Once the legislative process is under way, however, the Commission can seek to pressure the Council by withholding its cooperation and forcing the Council to act unanimously. It can even threaten to change the direction of the process by introducing an amended proposal or to bring it to an end by withdrawing the proposal. Such tactics contain a large element of bluff, as the Community interest normally demands above all that the legislation be enacted. Thus, once it is satisfied that the Council is not going to make any more concessions, the Commission will normally acquiesce. It is only where the proposed Council action is manifestly contrary to the Community interest or where it is likely to involve the Commission in grave difficulties with Parliament that cooperation is withheld or the proposal withdrawn and perhaps replaced by an amended text. In practice, the very number of conflicting interests within the Council that must be reconciled makes it easier for the Commission to fashion a compromise acceptable to itself. It is on those occasions that the Commission is faced with a hostile consensus within the Council that it is less likely to achieve this result.

Under Co-decision, the Commission will no longer be the Council's sole protagonist. It will still work alone with the Council on the adoption of the Common Position, and the Council will rely on it to pilot this Common Position through Parliament's Second Reading without unacceptable amendments. However, once the Second Reading is over, it will be Parliament with which the Council must negotiate if it wishes to overcome a rejection of the Common Position or elaborate an alternative text where it cannot accept all of Parliament's amendments. The Commission will participate in these negotiations, but its approval is not required and it will no longer be able to force the Council to act by unanimity by withholding its cooperation. Parliament and the Council may even be able to change unilaterally the substance of the text during the conciliation procedure. All this clearly reduces the Commission's influence on the outcome of the second round of the Co-decision Procedure, but it cannot be completely disregarded. The Commission's help and expertise in finding compromise formulae will continue to be needed, and it will retain the right to withdraw the proposal and bring the legislative process to an end. Theoretically, it could also submit an amended proposal, which would sabotage the conciliation procedure and take the process back to the first round.

1.2. The European Parliament

The European Parliament is the most volatile of the Community institutions. It is directly elected by universal suffrage in all the Member States and represents the people of the Community in the legislative process. Yet the very breadth of this role means that, unlike the other two institutions, it does not have a dominant perspective. Its members will defend variously the Community interest, national interests, political and social ideals and the concerns of their constituents. On occasion, they are also swayed by self-interest and influenced by lobby groups.

Parliament's influence on the legislative process has increased over the years, but it is still dependent to a very large extent on the Commission. It has no veto under the traditional procedure and, under the Cooperation Procedure, its rejection of the Common Position, which in any case requires an absolute majority of MEPs, can be overridden by the Council acting unanimously. It is only if the Commission is willing to withdraw its proposal that Parliament can be certain that the legislation will not be adopted over its objections. There is also little direct dialogue between the Council and Parliament under these two procedures, and so Parliament must rely on the Commission to be its advocate and insist, where necessary, on retaining parliamentary amendments in the final text. Under the traditional procedure, the Council still tends to ignore Parliament's amendments altogether if they are not supported by the Commission. Even under the Cooperation Procedure, where it is obliged to consider all amendments passed by Parliament, the Council rarely incorporates any into the final legislative act or the Common Position that the Commission has not accepted. All this means that it is crucial for Parliament to have the Commission's cooperation.

Like the Commission in its dealings with the Council, Parliament uses pressure tactics to have its way with the Commission, such as delaying the passage of legislation and threatening on occasion to reject legislation at its Second Reading or even censure the Commission. At the end of the day, however, Parliament will usually cooperate once it realizes that the Commission is not going to move any closer to its point of view. This alliance between Parliament and the Commission is not merely tactical. Both are concerned with the Community interest, although, in the case of Parliament, this is one of many perspectives. However, even where Parliament is swayed by other considerations, such as the environment, social policy priorities or consumer rights, these tend to be European in scope rather than national. As a result, there is a natural affinity between the two institutions that neither has with the Council, and this enables them on most occasions to work together constructively and fruitfully. Parliament's relations with the Council, by contrast, are more strained, and most of its disagreements are with this latter institution.

The Co-decision Procedure will change Parliament's relationship with the Commission. Although it will still need the Commission's cooperation during the first round, Parliament will be able to act independently in the second round. Its rejection of the Common Position ends the legislative process, and its amendments must be accepted by the Council or an alternative text agreed upon by the two institutions. In neither case will the Commission's intervention be necessary. In fact, Parliament will move in the second round of the Co-decision Procedure from a subordinate to a dominant position vis-à-vis the Commission. Nonetheless, it will still be easier for the Council to adopt Parliament's amendments to the Common Position if the Commission supports them, and Parliament will probably need the Commission to help it reach a satisfactory compromise with the Council in the Conciliation Committee. For these reasons, the Co-decision Procedure reduces but does not eliminate Parliament's reliance on the Commission.

Parliament has practically no influence over the Council under the traditional procedure. There is little, if any, dialogue between the two institutions, and the Council is neither bound by Parliament's Opinion nor affected by its rejection of a Commission proposal. The Cooperation Procedure strengthens Parliament's hand somewhat by providing for a Second Reading at which amendments can be re-introduced and the Common Position even rejected. However, there is still little contact between Parliament and the Council. Parliament's second round amendments can also be disregarded, and the Council may unilaterally change the Common Position before it is enacted into law. Nor can Parliament on its own prevent the enactment of a measure that has unanimous support in the Council.

This situation will be altered by the Co-decision Procedure. Under this procedure, the Council loses its legislative supremacy and must make law jointly with Parliament. If Parliament rejects the Common Position, that is the end of the matter unless it changes its mind as a result of its meeting with the Council in the Conciliation Committee. Where the Council is unable to accept Parliament's proposals for the final legislative act, the Conciliation Committee will again meet in an attempt to elaborate a compromise text acceptable to both institutions. Thus, the Council will no longer be able to ignore Parliament's views or unilaterally change the Common Position. It should also be noted that the TEU will give Parliament an additional veto power under the traditional procedure for a few matters. This power will have the same effect as the Co-Decision Procedure in putting Parliament on a much more equal footing with the Council, except that the Conciliation Committee Procedure cannot be used in this case to settle differences between the two institutions.

Despite these changes, Parliament will remain the junior partner in the legislative process even under the TEU. While the Commission and, to a much lesser extent, the Council prefer Parliament's cooperation, they are able ultimately to proceed without it in most cases as neither the veto nor the Co-decision procedures will apply. Even if they do apply, Parliament will normally have to accept a compromise if it wants the legislation to be adopted. In addition, the Council's right under Co-decision to re-confirm the Common Position after failure of the conciliation process gives it a substantial advantage as Parliament may not always be able to muster the absolute majority of MEPs needed to reject it again on a Third Reading. In many cases, therefore, the final text that is enacted into law will probably continue to satisfy primarily the Council and leave Parliament somewhat frustrated.

1.3. The Council

The Council is made up of Ministers from the national Governments of the twelve Member States, who inevitably defend the interests of their respective countries. This defence of national interests is the legitimate role of the Council as long as its members are prepared to accept accommodation rather than insisting on these interests to the exclusion of those of the Community and the Community electorate. The need to pass the legislation required to implement the single market by January 1, 1993, in which all Member States have a stake, the increase in qualified majority voting and the increasing tendency to dispense with consensus have all encouraged a more constructive approach by the Council.

It has also been suggested that the Council may have found it easier to reach a Common Position than enact a final piece of legislation as individual Member States perceive this as a less irrevocable act.[755] The success of the Cooperation Procedure in expediting the passage of Community legislation seems to support this view. The catch for the Member States is that once a Common Position has been agreed, the legislative process is likely to acquire an impetus that is difficult to stop.

The Council's new dynamism has also spilled over into the traditional procedure, and it is now only in a few very sensitive areas, such as taxation, immigration and social policy, that individual members of the Council still insist on their national interests and hold up legislation. It is to be hoped that the Council's responsibility for ensuring that Community legislation conforms to the subsidiarity provisions of **Article 3b (EC)** will not be used as a smokescreen for the recrudescence of a more nationalistic approach.

A crucial role in achieving the necessary accommodations within the Council is played by the Commission, which, together with the Council Presidency, acts as honest broker between the Council members. The Council also relies on the Commission to deal with Parliament's amendments and to pilot its Common Positions through the latter's Second Reading. The Council has the upper hand, however, in its dealings with the Commission.[756] Either alone or, under the TEU, jointly with Parliament, it makes the final decision whether to enact a particular text into law or to adopt a Common Position. In the face of a refusal to act by the Council, the Commission is powerless. Moreover, during conciliation under the Co-decision Procedure, the Council, with Parliament's support, will only need a qualified majority to modify Commission proposals and may even be able to alter their substance. On the other hand, the Commission can always amend or withdraw a proposal and, under the traditional and Cooperation procedures, it can withhold its cooperation and force the Council to act by unanimity. With the increasing need for Community legislation to complete the internal market and perhaps also to achieve Economic and Monetary Union, these strategic ploys constitute a real threat and counterbalance to some extent the Council's preponderance.

The Council has traditionally paid little attention to Parliament and has tended to deal with it through the medium of the Commission. The Cooperation Procedure

755. D. Edward, "The Impact of the Single Act on the Institutions", (1987) 24 *C.M.L.Rev.* 19 at p. 30.
756. On this point, *see* Freestone and Davidson, *Institutional Framework of the European Communities* at p. 56.

did not really change this relationship. It does encourage the Council to adopt more parliamentary amendments, because Parliament now has two opportunities to put them forward and, at least in the first round, the Council has to justify its rejection of them. However, the Council is still under no compulsion to accept Parliament's views. In fact, it continues to concentrate on those first round parliamentary amendments that the Commission has adopted, and it accepts only a minority of the amendments from Parliament's Second Reading. Although it may well be difficult for the Council to find the unanimity necessary to override rejection of its Common Position, Parliament has shown itself reluctant to use this weapon. As well, any increase in Parliament's influence under the Cooperation Procedure must be balanced against the Council's apparent right in some circumstances to adopt provisions in its second round that Parliament has never seen. Thus, except in the few instances where the TEU will give Parliament a power of veto, the Council exercises and will continue to exercise a clear supremacy over it under the traditional and Cooperation procedures.

This supremacy will all but be eliminated by the Co-decision Procedure. Under this procedure, the Council will have to share its legislative power with Parliament and deal with it on the basis of equality. It cannot be forced to act by Parliament and it cannot be by-passed, but the final text of all legislative acts enacted under Co-decision will have to be approved by Parliament and bear the signature of the President of Parliament as well as that of the President of the Council. The Council will now have to persuade Parliament to renounce its rejection of the Common Position as it will no longer be able to override the parliamentary veto by acting unanimously. Where the Council is not prepared to accept Parliament's second round amendments, it will not simply be able to go ahead without them but will have to work out a compromise text with Parliament. The only advantage that the Council will enjoy under Co-decision is its right to re-confirm its Common Position if conciliation fails, which becomes law unless Parliament can again muster an absolute majority of MEPs to vote against it.

2. THE DEMOCRATIC DEFICIT IN THE COMMUNITY

The undemocratic nature of the Community's institutions and legislative process under the original Treaties and the SEA has been widely criticized.[757]

The Council's dominance of the legislative process is the essence of the democ-

757. *See* the European Parliament's Resolution of 17 June 1988 on the democratic deficit in the European Community; Resolution of 14 March 1990 on the Intergovernmental Conference, at pt. F; Resolution of 12 July 1990 on the preparation of the meeting with the national parliaments at pts. A—D. *See too* the Commission's Opinion of 21 October 1990 on the proposal for amendment of the Treaty at pt. III,1 and the Proceedings of the Conference of the Parliaments of the European Community. For an academic discussion of this problem, *see* Kapteyn and Themaat, *Introduction to the Law of the European Communities* at pp. 268-271 and T.C. Hartley, *Foundations of Community Law* at p. 33 and pp.45-47.

ratic deficit in the Community.[758] It is a body made up of ministerial delegates from the Member States who are not directly elected to the position. Thus, its lack of accountability to the European Parliament means that there is no *direct* democratic control of the Community's legislative process. The secrecy of the Council's deliberations further isolates it from public scrutiny.

Criticism has also been directed at the Member States' exclusive right to appoint the Commission, which institution serves as the executive organ of the Community and alone can exercise some control over the Council under the traditional and Cooperation Procedures.[759] The European Parliament, moreover, has long wished to share in the Commission's right of initiative and to have a more effective means of exercising its political control over it.[760]

While it is certainly true that the absence of effective parliamentary control over extensive areas of legislative activity represents a worrisome "decline of democracy in Western Europe",[761] we must nevertheless keep a sense of perspective when considering the Community's pre-Maastricht institutional structure. The criticisms of the Council, for instance, some of which even compare it to the politburos of soviet-style communism, are often too extreme. Its members are after all Ministers in directly-elected governments, and their tenure of office is subject to the will of their national electorates. They are not directly elected to their Community responsibilities, but this is a far cry from the common accusation levelled against them that they form an unelected body. It is also false to claim, as Parliament does,[762] that the Council is not subject to *any* democratic control. Ministers must answer to national parliaments for their conduct of affairs, which includes Community affairs. This certainly does not provide enough scrutiny of the Council's legislation, but it does mean that, in the final analysis, the people have ultimate control over their lawmakers, albeit in a fragmented, national form.

Finally, not too much should be made of the Council's secrecy. It is unavoidable as Ministers must negotiate and compromise in order to reach agreement. Even if the legislative process were opened up to the public, as the European Council now wishes to some degree,[763] these deliberations would merely take place in private beforehand. Besides, the real issue is surely the control and scrutiny of the Council's decisions rather than how it makes them.

---

758. *See* Parliament's Resolution of 17 June 1988 on the democratic deficit at pts. 4 and 15; Resolution of 11 July 1990 on the Intergovernmental Conference, at pt. 21. *See also* Kapteyn and Themaat, *Introduction to the Law of the European Communities* at pp. 268-271 and T.C. Hartley, *Foundations of Community Law* at pp. 45-46

759. *See* fn 127. *See also* pt. 18 of the Proceedings of the Conference of the Parliaments of the European Community. *See also* Kapteyn and Themaat, *Introduction to the Law of the European Communities* at pp. 268-271 and T.C. Hartley, *Foundations of Community Law* at p. 45.

760. *See* its Resolution of 9 July 1981 on the right of legislative initiative at pts. 3,4. *See also* arts. 158,188a (EP Draft Treaty).

761. The European Parliament's Resolution of 12 July 1990 on the preparation of the meeting with the national parliaments, OJ C 231/90, at pt. A.

762. Resolution of 17 June 1988 on the democratic deficit at pt. 4.

763. *See supra* at p. 66. Note that, under the European Council's proposals, the real deliberations would still take place in private.

By contrast, the influence of the European Parliament under this legislative system is often underestimated. It has, in fact, found ways to have more impact that the Treaties would suggest. In particular, its Rules of Procedure exploit the fact that, where its Opinion or First Reading is mandated by the Treaties, this is an essential procedural requirement that must be fulfilled before the Council can act on a proposal. The threat of a rejection of the Common Position at Parliament's Second Reading under the Cooperation Procedure also serves to put pressure on the Commission. Other procedural devices aimed at augmenting Parliament's influence over the legislative process are the rules on re-consultation and conciliation. Finally, one should not completely dismiss Parliament's ability to exercise political control over the Commission. The vote of censure may be a "blunt weapon", but it is nonetheless available. Moreover, Parliament exercises additional control over the Commission by virtue of the latter's obligations to submit to it the annual general report on the Communities, to respond to questions from MEPs and to take note of Parliament's amendments and resolutions.

Nevertheless, the problem of the democratic deficit has to be addressed. This cannot be done by relying on the national parliaments. Their reduced role is the result of the wholesale transfer of legislative authority from the Member States to the Community, which can only be remedied by abrogating the original Treaties and the SEA. Moreover, the role of the national parliaments has been further undermined by changes in the Council's voting procedures. As long as unanimity was more or less required for the Council's decisions, as a result both of the Treaty provisions and the Luxembourg Accords, a certain control over its activities could still be exercised by national parliaments. Where all Ministers have to assent to a particular legislative act, they can be held to account by their own legislatures. The SEA, however, not only increased the number of matters requiring only a qualified majority but also broke the hold of the Luxembourg Accords. Qualified majority voting has since become the most widely-used way of enacting legislation in the Community. In such situations, where a national Minister may have opposed the legislation or agreed to it only as part of a secret deal, it becomes difficult to hold that Minister to account. As a result, any remaining measure of control that national parliaments might have exercised over the Council's legislative activity is more or less eliminated. The Commission's new commitment to consider their input when drawing up its legislative proposals is not likely to increase significantly the parliaments' influence, any more than publication of the formal votes in the Council.

This inability of the national parliaments to control the exercise of legislative power over large areas of activity thus seems to be irreversible. Yet, as the European Parliament declares with considerable panache in its Declaration of Fundamental Rights and Freedoms, the democratic principle requires that "every public authority must be directly elected or answerable to a directly elected parliament."[764] Given that neither the Council nor the Commission are directly elected, this would suggest that the democratic deficit can only be cured by giving the European Parliament the means of controlling the exercise of legislative power in the Community. This way, the power lost by the national parliaments is transferred to the European Parliament,

764. At pt. 17(2).

which, as the only directly elected Community institution, represents the agglomeration of the national electorates.

This is certainly the view of the European Parliament, which wants, at the very least, to share in the legislative authority of the Council, to appoint or confirm the Commission and to be able to exercise effective political control over it, to have a greater say in the legislative program of the Community and to end the secrecy of the Council's deliberations.[765] Its ultimate aim, building on the axiom that "democracy is not fully attained until all power is based on the people,"[766] is apparently to take over the Council's legislative authority and to acquire complete control over the Commission, including its right of legislative initiative.

This federalist solution would, however, prove unworkable as it provides no mechanism for taking account of the national interests of the Member States. Even in federal states, the regional interests of its component parts are usually represented in the legislative process. In the United States, for example, this role is played by the Senate and in Germany by the Bundesrat. A failure to provide such a mechanism inevitably places severe strains on a federal system, as Canada's recent constitutional tribulations attest.

These strains would be even greater in the European Community, and it is unlikely that they could be contained by the creation of a Senate within which the Member States would be represented. The European Community is still being constructed, and even with a central government it will still contain sovereign states. Moreover, over the coming decades, many new Member States are expected to join the Community and each will have to adapt to living with its partners. Conflicts between different national interests are likely to increase rather than decrease, and the only effective way of resolving them will continue to be through the inter-governmental deliberations of the Council.[767] To attempt otherwise would be to court disaster and cause the possible ruin of the Community. In any case, there is considerable disagreement over the composition of a Euro-Senate and its exact role, and the whole idea has been vigorously opposed by the Commission, the European Parliament and some Member States.

Leaving aside the TEU reforms for the moment, the best solution is surely to build on the strengths of the pre-Maastricht system. It not only provides for a fruitful interplay of the three Community institutions representing the Community, the national and the popular interest but, more important, recognizes the validity of each interest. The obvious shortcoming of this system is the inferior position of Parliament. Thus, the ideal solution would be to give Parliament an effective veto by making its approval a legal requirement for Community legislation. Parliament should also be able to advocate directly its amendments before the Council. This way, no legislation could be enacted in the face of Parliament's disapproval, and the chances of parliamentary amendments being incorporated into the final text would be significantly increased. Parliament's influence could be further enhanced by giv-

765. *See* its Resolutions of 17 June 1988 on the democratic deficit and of 14 March 1990 on the Intergovernmental Conference.

766. Resolution of 17 June 1988 on the democratic deficit at pt. 2.

767. This is also the view taken by Freestone and Davidson, *Institutional Framework of the European Communities* at p. 55.

ing it the right to initiate legislation, but this is not essential in order to bring about a proper balance in the legislative process of the Community. It should, however, be given effective control over the Commission.

The final text must continue to be a compromise of the three interests, albeit with increased consideration for Parliament's viewpoint. The fact that the European Parliament is directly elected should not obscure the fact that both national and Community interests also constitute valid inputs into Community legislation. The new Europe will not be built by riding roughshod over legitimate national interests any more than by ignoring the will of its collective electorate; and it will always require the Community interest to be a central concern. Nor should we be too beguiled by Parliament's clarion calls to democracy. Not only is the allocation of seats such that the electors of the various Member States are very unequally represented,[768] the European Parliament is also a peculiarly idiosyncratic body. With some exceptions, candidates for the European Parliament are all European enthusiasts so that their electors are not given a proper choice in European elections. People who do not share this enthusiasm either do not vote or vote for their preferred candidate without necessarily sharing his or her European ideals. As a result, MEPs do not always accurately represent the feelings of their electorate. This is why it is possible to have a pro-European British Conservative group at Strasbourg and a much more nationalistic party at Westminster. It also explains the discrepancy between the European Parliament's overwhelming support for European Union[769] and the more reserved attitude of the national electorates that became apparent during the ratification process of the TEU.

Thus, Parliament should no more have the right to make unilateral changes to legislation than the Council. It is also crucial that any dialogue between Parliament and the Council include the Commission as an equal partner. If indeed Parliament is given a right of initiative, this should be subject to two conditions. Firstly, the Commission's proposals should take precedence in a crowded legislative agenda in the same way as government bills do over private members' bills in the British parliamentary system. Secondly, the Commission's right to withdraw legislative proposals must extend to those initiated by Parliament; otherwise its veto power is impaired and with it the ability to protect the Community interest.

The TEU, through the Co-decision procedure and, to a lesser extent, the veto, offers a reasonable solution to the democratic deficit. Its reforms would make the European Parliament a full partner in the legislative process without giving it a predominant role that would merely create a new imbalance in its favor among the interests that must bear on the enactment of Community legislation. While Parliament's approval is required for the final text of all legislation, it cannot act unilaterally. The Council retains joint legislative authority and a direct dialogue is established between it and Parliament in order to settle differences between them.

768. *See supra* at pp. 42-43. The re-allocation of seats decided upon by the European Council at its Edinburgh meeting will largely resolve this problem.

769. *See inter alia* Resolution of 11 July 1990 on the Intergovernmental Conference at pt. 3; Resolution of 11 July 1990 on the European Parliament's guidelines for a draft constitution for the European Union at pts. A, 1; Resolution of 12 December 1990 on the constitutional basis of European Union, in Part II of *1993. The New Treaties. European Parliament's Proposals.*

The Commission participates in this dialogue. Its influence is certainly reduced, but it retains the right to amend and withdraw its proposal and is given the task of facilitating a compromise between the Parliament and the Council. The overall result is that all three institutions have an equal input into legislation and all have a right of veto. Thus, the final text continues to be a compromise of the three interests but with proper consideration for Parliament's viewpoint.

The TEU does not give the European Parliament its much-desired right of initiative, but this is not essential to achieve a proper balance between the three institutions. Instead, it will be able to request that the Commission make a proposal, which, after all, is all that the Council can do. Parliament is, however, given the right to approve the appointment of the Commission, which strengthens its political control of this body. It will also render the vote of censure a more effective weapon as Parliament must also approve the replacement Commission.

The substance of the TEU's reforms is thus correct. They cannot and do not attempt to restore the authority of the national parliaments, which could only be achieved by reconstituting or paralyzing the Community. At the same time, the Treaty resists the federalist temptation and creates instead the proper supranational balance that the Community needs at present.

This does not mean that we may not criticize some of the Treaty's details. For example, the subsidiarity principle should have been spelled out in more detail, which, of course, the European Council has now done at its Edinburgh meeting. It is also a pity that the majority required to pass a vote of censure is not lowered, as this would certainly sharpen up Parliament's most potent means of control over the Commission. Some of Parliament's suggestions for the functioning of the Co-decision Procedure might also have been followed. In particular, the TEU should not have given the Council the right to re-confirm the Common Position after failure of the conciliation process, which gives it an unnecessary advantage in the legislative process as Parliament may not always be able to muster the absolute majority of MEPs needed to reject the text again on a Third Reading.

As far as the secrecy of the Council's deliberations is concerned, which the TEU leaves untouched, this is probably needed to permit the type of horse-trading that still accompanies its decision-making process. If Parliament's suggestion were followed to the letter and the Council's meetings became entirely open to the public,[770] these negotiations would merely take place beforehand. Nevertheless, secrecy is unacceptable in a legislative body and attests the continuing inter-governmental aspect of the Council. As mentioned earlier, the European Council has now made proposals for a limited degree of openness for Council sessions, but it is not clear how effective they will be.[771]

The real weakness of the TEU's reforms is their scope, which in important aspects is far too limited. The European Parliament's joint legislative authority under Co-decision and its power of veto under the traditional procedure are both restricted in their application. The majority of EEC matters as well as all ECSC and EAEC matters are left unaffected. As a result, Parliament remains overall the junior

770. Art. 146a (EP Draft Treaty). The Conference of Parliament supported this suggestion at pt. 17. of the Proceedings of the Parliaments of the European Community.

771. *See supra* at p. 66.

partner in the legislative process. While the Commission and, to a much lesser extent, the Council prefer Parliament's cooperation, they are able in most cases ultimately to proceed without it. Maastricht is on track, but it hardly leaves the station. To this extent, it is best described as constructive but disappointing.

It is highly unlikely that the European Community will move very far towards a federal Europe in the foreseeable future. The reticence in some of the present Member States towards European Union and the difficulties of absorbing new members, most of which share this reticence, preclude such a development. For this reason, the TEU, should it be ratified, will remain the basis for future institutional development and the limit to which democracy is likely is pushed within the Community. Its reforms, to the limited extent that they apply, are a half-way but adequate solution at present to the problem of the democratic deficit.

3. A FEW WORDS ON LOBBYING

Lobbying the Community institutions in order to influence the outcome of the legislative process in the European Community is a complex task. The three institutions that are involved in the process all have different priorities and make their decision in different ways. Timing is also very important.

The Commission is the guardian of the Community interest, and, in order to make any headway in trying to influence its decisions, lobbyists must find a Community dimension to their representations. The Commission is simply not interested in favoring any particular company or nation, particularly if they are from outside the Community. The most effective way for non-European interests to lobby the Commission is thus to make common cause with Community industry or to act through a European organization. Many North American subsidiaries in Europe have become very active members of their European industrial organisations in recognition of this fact.

The best time to approach the Commission is while it is elaborating its preliminary draft proposal, as the basic thrust of the legislation is not yet settled and quite substantial changes of direction are still possible. Once the preliminary draft is finalized, the room for manoeuvre is reduced as the Commission is normally only prepared to consider refinements to the proposal or changes that relate to how its objective is to be attained. The objective itself is usually fixed by this stage.

Lobbying of the Commission requires considerably more subtlety and tact than lobbying in national capitals. Initially, it will probably center on the Division officials responsible for the proposal as it here that the proposal is elaborated rather than at the higher level of the DG or the Commissioners themselves. High-level contacts are always useful, however, and become especially important to a lobbying effort in the later stages, particularly after Parliament has passed its amendments. As a normal rule, the approach should be formal. Commission officials will sometimes accept social invitations, but they will not react positively to what are perceived as attempts to "soften them up." The best results are normally achieved through well-prepared meetings at the Commission's offices in the Rue de la Loi (Wetstraat) in Brussels.

When the legislative process shifts to the European Parliament, lobbying resumes its more normal form. MEPs are like politicians in any legislature and will respond to the same persuasions and blandishments. That being said, the lobbyist must realize that the European Parliament contains a much greater variety of people than many national parliaments and represents the complete spectrum of political opinion. Careful research is needed into which countries, regions and political groups are likely to respond the most favorably to the lobbying efforts.

At this level, too, timing is extremely important, as it is the committee that really determines the basic thrust of Parliament's reaction to a legislative proposal. It is thus important to find out which committees are going to be involved with a particular proposal and to concentrate on lobbying their members. The most important persons to contact are the Rapporteur, where there is one, and the Chairman of the responsible committee. Once the committee has presented its report for the First Reading or Opinion of Parliament, the chances of influencing the outcome of Parliament's deliberations are significantly reduced. The plenary sessions tend not to change committee reports substantially, but lobbyists neglect the general body of MEPs at the risk of seeing amendments that they have worked for at the committee stage being voted down. Where the Cooperation (or Co-decision) Procedure is being used, lobbying should be concentrated on the First Reading of Parliament as there are limitations on the amendments that Parliament will make at its Second Reading.

Lobbying the Council of Ministers as such is not possible, and the lobbyist must rely on influencing individual Member States. This can be done by going through the Permanent Representation that each nation has in Brussels and which sits on COREPER or by lobbying in the Member State itself. The latter strategy is probably the more effective as the Permanent Representatives act on the instructions of their Governments.

Clearly, it is advisable to seek out a national ally or work through a national industrial organization when lobbying a national Government, although some governments are more sympathetic to non-European concerns than others. In this context, it should always be remembered that there are twelve Member States, and lobbying efforts should be directed at all that might prove sympathetic or that share the lobbyist's interest. Indeed, no matter what voting procedure is used, the support of more than one Government member of the Council will always be needed to effect the desired changes. Non-European lobbyists should also not neglect their home governments, who can make representations directly to a Member State or States. This was done in the case of the Broadcasting Directive, for example, when American pressure on the Netherlands caused that country to withdraw its support from the Commission's Re-examined Proposal.

Depending on the Member State, lobbying of national MPs or deputies may not be an effective strategy for influencing national policy. This is true, for example, of the United Kingdom where there is often an astonishing lack of interest at Westminster about all but the most controversial pieces of proposed Community legislation. It is always open to the lobbyist, of course, to stimulate the interest in order to bring pressure on the Government. In this connection, it should be noted that the TEU urges the Member States to involve their parliaments more in the

Community legislative process by ensuring that they are properly informed about the Commission's proposals.[772]

Lobbying in order to influence the shape of Community legislation is, thus, a very complex task. It requires representations to be made at many levels, in many countries, under a variety of systems and in differing forms. Above all, it requires a good understanding of the legislative process in the European Community and the interplay of the Commission, the European Parliament and the Council.

772. **13th Declaration (TEU)**.

Table 1: TRADITIONAL PROCEDURE

(Articles and changes that are introduced by the TEU are given in bold type)

ARTICLE	SUBJECT MATTER	CO	CONSULTATIONS + *Other Comments*	PROP
	EUROPEAN (ECONOMIC) COMMUNITY/UNANIMITY			
8a(2)	Exercise of rights of movement and residence	U	Assent of EP	CM
8b(1)	Exercise of rights to vote and stand as candidate in municipal elections	U	EP	CM
8b(2)	Exercise of rights to vote and stand as candidates in European election	U	EP	CM
8e	Changes to citizenship rights	U	EP: *MSS ratify*	CM
51[773]	Social security measures	U		CM
56(2)	Coordination of public policy laws[774]	U	EP	CM
57(2)	Coordination of laws[775] on self-employed activities	U	EP	CM
70(1)[776]	Coordination of exchange policies entailing step back from liberalization	U[777]		CM

773. Under **Article 2(3) of the Social Agreement,** social security measures require consultation of EP and ECOSOC.
774. The coordination of regulations and administrative practices is carried out by the Cooperation Procedure under the EEC Treaty and the Co-decision Procedure under the EC Treaty.
775. The coordination of regulations and administrative practices is carried out by the Cooperation Procedure under the EEC Treaty and the Co-decision Procedure under the EC Treaty
776. This Article ceases to operate as from January 1, 1994 per **Article 73a (EC)**.
777. Where there is no step back from liberalization, a qualified majority suffices.

ARTICLE	SUBJECT MATTER	CO	CONSULTATIONS + *Other Comments*	PROP
	EUROPEAN (ECONOMIC) COMMUNITY/UNANIMITY			
73c(2)[778]	Measures on capital movements to and from TCC entailing step back from liberalization	U[779]		CM
75(3)	Transport policy where serious effect[780] on MS	U	EP: ECOSOC	CM
84(2)	Application of Treaty rules to air and sea transport where serious effect[781] on MS	U	EP: ECOSOC	CM
99	Harmonization of indirect taxation	U	EP: **ECOSOC**[782]	CM
100	Approximation of laws	U	**EP: ECOSOC**[783]	CM
100c(1)	Visa rules for TC nationals	U[784]	EP. *MSS may request a proposal per Art. 100c(4). CCJHA contributes to work of CO*	CM
103(2)[785]	Emergency economic measures	U		CM
103a(1)	Emergency economic measures	U	*MC* [786] *contributes to work of CO per Art. 109c(1)*	CM
104c(14)	Replacement of Protocol on excessive budget deficits	U	EP: EMI.[787] *MC contributes to work of CO*	CM

778. This Article operates as from January 1, 1994 per **Article 73a (EC)**.
779. Where there is no step back from liberalization, a qualified majority suffices.
780. Where there is no such serious effect, a qualified majority suffices under the EEC Treaty and the Cooperation Procedure is used under the EC Treaty.
781. Where there is no such serious effect, a qualified majority suffices under the EEC Treaty and the Cooperation Procedure is used under the EC Treaty.
782. Consultation of ECOSOC is required by the EC Treaty.
783. Consultation of Parliament and ECOSOC becomes a general requirement under the EC Treaty, whereas it is only necessary under the EEC Treaty where the approximation would involve the amendment of national legislation.
784. This legislation will require only a qualified majority as from January 1, 1996.
785. This Article is replaced in the EC Treaty by **Article 103a (EC)**, but the legislative procedure remains the same.
786. The MC is replaced by the EFC at the start of the third stage of Economic and Monetary Union as per **Article 109c(2) (EC)**..
787. The EMI is replaced by the ECB at the start of the third stage of Economic and Monetary Union. Prior to January 1, 1994, its consultative role is filled by the Committee of Governors. *See* **arts. 109f(8), 109l(2) (EC)**.

ARTICLE	SUBJECT MATTER	CO	CONSULTATIONS + *Other Comments*	PROP
	EUROPEAN (ECONOMIC) COMMUNITY/UNANIMITY			
106(5)	Changes to Statute of ESCB	U[788]	EMI: *Assent of EP*	CM
126(b)[789]	New tasks for European Social Fund	U	EP: ECOSOC. *This action is taken on the opinion of CM.*	NONE
130(3)	Industrial Policy	U	EP: ECOSOC	CM
130b	Regional aid outside the Structural Funds	U	EP: ECOSOC: COR.	CM
130d[790]	Reform of Structural Funds	U	EP: ECOSOC	CM
130d	Structural Funds and Cohesion Fund	U	EP: ECOSOC: COR *Assent of EP*	CM
130o	Structures for execution of Community R&D programs	U	EP: ECOSOC	CM
130q(1)[791]	Structures for execution of Community R&D programs	U	EP: ECOSOC	CM
130q(1)[792]	Adoption of multiannual R&D framework programs	U	EP: ECOSOC	CM
130s[793]	Most environmental measures	U[794]	EP: ECOSOC	CM
130s(2)[795]	Certain environmental measures	U	EP: ECOSOC	CM
138(3)	A uniform voting procedure for the EP	U	*Assent of EP. MSS ratify*	EP
145	Delegation of implementing authority to CM	U	EP	CM

788. Once the ECB is established at the start of the third stage of Economic and Monetary Union, the Council can also act by a qualified majority on a recommendation of the ECB. The Commission must be consulted and the assent of the EP is still required.
789. This Article is eliminated by the TEU.
790. This Article is replaced by **Article 130d (EC)**, but the legislative procedure remains the same.
791. This Article is replaced by **Article 130o (EC)**, but the legislative procedure remains the same.
792. This Article is replaced by **Article 130i(1) (EC)**, which provides for use of the Co-decision Procedure.
793. This Article is replaced by **Article 130s(1),(2) (EC)**, which provides for use of the Cooperation Procedure or the traditional procedure.
794. Some environmental measures are enacted by a qualified majority under the EEC Treaty.
795. The normal procedure for environmental measures under the EC Treaty is the Cooperation Procedure.

ARTICLE	SUBJECT MATTER	CO	CONSULTATIONS + *Other Comments*	PROP
	EUROPEAN (ECONOMIC) COMMUNITY/UNANIMITY			
201	System of own resources for Community	U	EP. *MSS ratify*	CM
209(a)	Financial regulations	U	EP: CA	CM
235	Residual power to attain objectives of Treaty	U	EP	CM
SA, 2(3)[796]	Social security, worker rights, TC workers, job creation	U[797]	EP: ECOSOC	CM
SA, 4(2)	Implementation of management-labor accords	U[798]		CM
	EUROPEAN (ECONOMIC) COMMUNITY/QUALIFIED MAJORITY			
28	Changes to Community tariffs	QM		CM
43(2)	Common Agricultural Policy	QM	EP. *CM must consult ECOSOC*	CM
55	Application of official authority exception to FMW	QM		CM
59	Extension of free movement of services to third-country nationals	QM		CM
63(2)	Free movement of services	QM	EP: ECOSOC	CM
69[799]	Free movement of capital	QM	*CM must consult MC*	CM
70(1)[800]	Coordination of exchange policies	QM[801]		CM
73c(2)[802]	Measures on capital movements to and from TCC	QM[803]		CM

796. The Social Agreement is contained in the **14th Protocol (TEU)**, but it is part of the EC Treaty.
797. The Council acts by the Cooperation Procedure where other social issues are involved.
798. The Council acts by unanimity where the agreement touches upon social security, workers rights, third-country workers or job creation; otherwise it acts by a qualified majority.
799. This article ceases to operate as from January 1, 1994 per **Article 73a (EC)**.
800. This article ceases to operate as from January 1, 1994 per **Article 73a (EC)**.
801. Unanimity is required when this entails a step back from liberalization.
802. This Article operates as from January 1, 1994 per **Article 73a (EC)**.
803. Unanimity is required when this entails a step back from liberalization.

ARTICLE	SUBJECT MATTER	CO	CONSULTATIONS + *Other Comments*	PROP
	EUROPEAN (ECONOMIC) COMMUNITY/QUALIFIED MAJORITY			
73f[804]	Safeguard measures re: capital movements to and from TCC	QM	EMI. *MC contributes to work of CO*	CM
75(1)[805]	Transport policy	QM[806]	EP: ECOSOC	CM
79(3)	Abolition of discriminatory rules for employment in transport sector	QM	ECOSOC	CM
84(2)[807]	Application of Treaty rules to sea and air transport	QM[808]	EP: ECOSOC	CM
87(1)	Implementing legislation for Treaty competition rules	QM	EP	CM
94	Application of Treaty rules on state aids	QM	**EP**	CM
100c(2)	Emergency visa requirements	QM	*This action is taken on recommendation of CM. CCJHA contributes to work of CO*	NONE
100c(3)	Format of visas	QM	EP. *MSS may request a proposal per Art. 100c(4). CCJHA contributes to work of CO*	CM
101	Elimination of distortions in conditions of competition	QM		CM
103(3)[809]	Implementation of emergency economic measures	QM		CM
104c(14)	Application of Protocol on excessive budget deficits	QM	EP. *MC contributes to work of CO*	CM

804. This Article operates as from January 1, 1994 per **Article 73a (EC)**.
805. This Article is replaced by **Article 75(1) (EC)**, which uses the Cooperation Procedure except where a measure would be liable to have a serious effect on a Member State.
806. The Council acts under both the EEC and EC Treaties by unanimity using the traditional procedure where a measure would be liable to have a serious effect on a Member State.
807. This Article is replaced by **Article 84(2) (EC)**, which uses the Cooperation Procedure except where a measure would be liable to have a serious effect on a Member State.
808. The Council acts under both the EEC and EC Treaties by unanimity using the traditional procedure where a measure would be liable to have a serious effect on a Member State.
809. This Article is replaced by **Article 103a (EC)**, which provides for the Council to act by unanimity.

ARTICLE	SUBJECT MATTER	CO	CONSULTATIONS + *Other Comments*	PROP
	EUROPEAN (ECONOMIC) COMMUNITY/QUALIFIED MAJORITY			
106(6)	Adoption of provisions in Statute of ESCB	QM	EP: EMI	CM[810]
112(1)	Harmonization of export aids	QM		CM
113(2),(4)	Common Commercial Policy	QM		CM
126(a)[811]	Changes to European Social Fund	QM	EP: ECOSOC. *This action is taken on the opinion of CM*	NONE
127[812]	Implementation of European Social Fund	QM	EP: ECOSOC	CM
130e[813]	Implementation of reform of European Social Fund	QM	EP: ECOSOC	CM
130e[814]	Implementation of reform of EAGGF	QM	EP	CM
130e	Implementation of reform of EAGGF	QM	EP	CM
130i(4)[815]	Specific R&D programs	QM	EP: ECOSOC.	CM
130s[816]	Some environmental measures	QM[817]	EP: ECOSOC	CM
SA, 4(2)	Implementation of management-labor accords	QM[818]		CM

810. Once the ECB is established at the start of the third stage of Economic and Monetary Union, the Council can also act by a qualified majority on a recommendation of the ECB. The Commission and the EP must be consulted in this case.
811. This Article is eliminated by the TEU.
812. This Article is replaced by **Article 125 (EC)**, which uses the Cooperation Procedure.
813. This Article is replaced by **Article 130e (EC)**, which uses the Cooperation Procedure.
814. This Article is replaced by **Article 130e (EC)**, which uses the same procedure.
815. This legislation used to be enacted by the Cooperation Procedure under the EEC Treaty.
816. This Article is replaced by **Article 130s(1),(2) (EC)**, which provides for use of the Cooperation Procedure or the traditional procedure.
817. Most environmental measures are enacted by unanimity under the EEC Treaty.
818. The Council acts by unanimity where the agreement touches upon social security, workers rights, third-country workers or job creation.

ARTICLE	SUBJECT MATTER	CO	CONSULTATIONS + *Other Comments*	PROP
	EUROPEAN (ECONOMIC) COMMUNITY/SIMPLE MAJORITY			
128[819]	Vocational training	SM	ECOSOC	CM
	There is no provision for enacting general legislation by a simple majority in the EC Treaty			
	EUROPEAN COAL AND STEEL COMMUNITY/UNANIMITY			
21(3)	A uniform voting procedure for the EP	U	*Assent of EP. MSS ratify*	EP
58(3)	Ending production quotas	U[820]	*CM must consult CC*	CM
59(2)	Consumption priorities and allocation of resources	U	CM	CM
72	Maximum and minimum tariffs	U	*MSS may request proposal*	CM
78h(a)	Financial regulations	U	EP: CA	CM
	EUROPEAN COAL AND STEEL COMMUNITY/QUALIFIED MAJORITY			
	There is no provision for enacting general legislation by a qualified majority in the ECSC Treaty			
	EUROPEAN COAL AND STEEL COMMUNITY/SIMPLE MAJORITY			
58(3)	Ending production quotas	SM[821]		MS
	EUROPEAN ATOMIC ENERGY COMMUNITY/UNANIMITY			
69	Fixing prices	U		CM
76	Changes to Treaty provisions on supply of materials	U	EP. *MSS may request proposal*	CM

819. This Article is replaced by **Article 127(4) (EC)**, which uses the Cooperation Procedure.
820. The Council acts by a simple majority when this measure is proposed by a Member State. In this case, the Consultative Committee is not consulted.
821. The Council must act by unanimity when this measure is proposed by the Commission.

ARTICLE	SUBJECT MATTER	CO	CONSULTATIONS *+ Other Comments*	PROP
	EUROPEAN ATOMIC ENERGY COMMUNITY/UNANIMITY			
85	Adapting safeguard application procedures	U	EP. *MSS may request proposal*	CM
90	Adjustments to Treaty rules on Community's right of ownership	U	EP. *MSS may request proposal*	CM
108(3)	A uniform voting procedure for the EP	U	*Assent of EP. MSS ratify*	EP
183a	Financial regulations	U	EP: CA	CM
203	Residual power to attain objectives of Treaty	U	EP	CM
	EUROPEAN ATOMIC ENERGY COMMUNITY/QUALIFIED MAJORITY			
31	Basic safety standards	QM	EP. *CM must consult STC and ECOSOC*	CM
41	Changes to list of industrial activities in Annex II	QM	*CM must consult ECOSOC*	CM
54	Statutes of Agency	QM		CM
96	Application of Treaty rules against discrimination in employment	QM	EP. *CM must consult ECOSOC*	CM
	EUROPEAN ATOMIC ENERGY COMMUNITY/SIMPLE MAJORITY			
24(1)	Security gradings	SM		CM
42	Time limit for submitting projects	SM		CM
92	Changes to lists of goods and products in Annex IV	SM		CM

Table One

ARTICLE	SUBJECT MATTER	CO	CONSULTATIONS + *Other Comments*	PROP
		EUROPEAN UNION/UNANIMITY		
K.3(2)	Home and Justice Affairs	U/QM	*The Presidency must consult with Parliament. CCJHA contributes to work of CO*	CM/MS

Table 2: COOPERATION PROCEDURE (WITH EUROPEAN PARLIAMENT)

(Articles and changes that are introduced by the TEU are given in bold type)

ARTICLE	SUBJECT MATTER	CO	OTHER CONSULTATIONS	PROP
	EUROPEAN (ECONOMIC) COMMUNITY ONLY			
7[822]	Prohibition of all discrimination	QM		CM
49[823]	Free movement of workers	QM	ECOSOC	CM
54(2)[824]	Freedom of establishment	QM	ECOSOC	CM
56(2)[825]	Coordination of public policy regulations and practices[826]	QM		CM
57(1)[827]	Mutual recognition of diplomas, certificates and other qualifications	QM		CM
57(2)[828]	Coordination of regulations and practices on self-employed activities[829]	QM		CM
75(1)[830]	Transport policy	QM	ECOSOC	CM
84(2)[831]	Application of Treaty rules to sea and air transport	QM	ECOSOC	CM

822. This Article becomes **Article 6 (EC)**, but the procedure remains the same.
823. This Article is replaced by **Article 49 (EC)**, which uses the Co-decision Procedure.
824. This Article is replaced by **Article 54(2) (EC)**, which uses the Co-decision Procedure.
825. This Article is replaced by **Article 56(2) (EC)**, which uses the Co-decision Procedure.
826. The coordination of public policy *laws* is carried out under the traditional procedure with the Council acting unanimously
827. This Article is replaced by **Article 57(1) (EC)**, which uses the Co-decision Procedure.
828. This Article is replaced by **Article 57(2) (EC)**, which uses the Co-decision Procedure.
829. The coordination of *laws* on self-employed activities is carried out under the traditional procedure with the Council acting unanimously.
830. The Council acts by unanimity using the traditional procedure where a measure would be liable to have a serious effect on a Member State.
831. The Council acts by unanimity using the traditional procedure where the extension of the rules would be liable to have a serious effect on a Member State.

ARTICLE	SUBJECT MATTER	CO	OTHER CONSULTATIONS	PROP
	EUROPEAN (ECONOMIC) COMMUNITY ONLY			
100a(1)[832]	Approximation of laws[833]	QM	ECOSOC	CM
100b(1)[834]	Mutual recognition of laws	QM	ECOSOC	CM
103(5)	Rules for multilateral surveillance of MS economic policies	QM	*MC contributes to work of CO*	CM
104a(2)	Application of Treaty rules on access to financial institutions	QM	*MC contributes to work of CO*	CM
104b(2)	Application of Treaty rules on credit facilities and public debts	QM	*MC contributes to work of CO*	CM
118a(2)	Health and safety of workers	QM	ECOSOC	CM
125	Implementation of European Social Fund	QM	ECOSOC	CM
127(4)	Vocational training	QM	ECOSOC	CM
129d	Trans-European networks	QM	ECOSOC: COR	CM
130e	Implementation of reform of ERDF	QM	ECOSOC: COR	CM
130e	Implementation of reform of European Social Fund	QM	ECOSOC	CM
130o	Implementation of multi-annual R&D framework programs	QM	ECOSOC	CM
130o	Supplementary R&D programs	QM	ECOSOC	CM
130q(2)[835]	Specific R&D programs	QM	ECOSOC	CM
130q(2)[836]	Supplementary R&D programs	QM	ECOSOC	CM

832. This Article is replaced by **Article 100a(1) (EC)**, which uses the Co-decision Procedure.
833. Article 100a (1) does not apply to fiscal provisions, the free movement of persons and the rights and interests of employed persons. These are dealt with under Articles 99 and 100 (EEC).
834. This Article is replaced by **Article 100b(1) (EC)**, which uses the Co-decision Procedure.
835. This Article is replaced by **Article 130i(4) (EC)**, under which the Council acts by a qualified majority using the traditional procedure.
836. This Article is replaced by **Article 130o**, which uses the same procedure.

ARTICLE	SUBJECT MATTER	CO	OTHER CONSULTATIONS	PROP
	EUROPEAN (ECONOMIC) COMMUNITY ONLY			
130q(2)[837]	Financial provisions for R&D programs	QM	ECOSOC	CM
130s(1)[838]	Most environmental measures	QM	ECOSOC	CM
SA, 2(2)[839]	Occupational health and safety, working conditions, equality and integration into labor market	QM	ECOSOC	CM

837. This Article is eliminated by the TEU, and the financial provisions are included in **Article 130i(1) (EC)**, which uses the Co-decision Procedure.
838. Certain measures are enacted under the traditional method by unanimity.
839. The Council acts according to the traditional procedure and by unanimity where the agreement touches upon social security, workers rights, third-country workers or job creation.

Table 3: CO-DECISION PROCEDURE (WITH EUROPEAN PARLIAMENT)

(Articles and changes that are introduced by the TEU are given in bold type)

ARTICLE	SUBJECT MATTER	CO	OTHER CONSULTATIONS	PROP
	EUROPEAN (ECONOMIC) COMMUNITY ONLY			
49	Free movement of workers	QM	ECOSOC	CM
54(2)	Freedom of establishment	QM	ECOSOC	CM
56(2)	Coordination of public policy regulations and practices[840]	QM		CM
57(1)	Mutual recognition of diplomas, certificates and other qualifications	QM		CM
57(2)	Coordination of regulations and practices on self-employed activities[841]	QM		CM
100a(1)[842]	Approximation of laws	QM	ECOSOC	CM
100b(1)	Mutual recognition of laws	QM	ECOSOC	CM
126(4)	Education (incentive measures)	QM	ECOSOC: COR	CM
128(5)	Culture (incentive measures)	U	COR	CM
129(4)	Public health (incentive measures)	QM	ECOSOC: COR	CM
129a(2)	Consumer protection	QM	ECOSOC	CM

840. The coordination of public policy *laws* is carried out under the traditional procedure with the Council acting unanimously
841. The coordination of *laws* on self-employed activities is carried out under the traditional procedure with the Council acting unanimously.
842. **Article 100a (1)** does not apply to fiscal provisions, the free movement of persons and the rights and interests of employed persons. These are dealt with under Articles 99 and 100 (EEC).

ARTICLE	SUBJECT MATTER	CO	OTHER CONSULTATIONS	PROP
	EUROPEAN (ECONOMIC) COMMUNITY ONLY			
129d	Guidelines for Trans-European networks	QM	ECOSOC: COR	CM
130i(1)	Adoption of multiannual R&D framework programs, including financing	U	ECOSOC	CM
130s(3)	General action programs for environment	QM	ECOSOC	CM

Table 4: CONSULTATIONS

(Articles and changes that are introduced by the TEU are given in bold type. In addition, Articles of the EEC Treaty that will be immediately replaced are marked with an asterisk.)

An 'x' before the Article means that there are no requirements for consultation.

	EUROPEAN (ECONOMIC) COMMUNITY		
ARTICLE	EP	ECOSOC	OTHER
6	√		
7*	√		
x8a(2)	Assent		
8b(1)	√		
8b(2)	√		
8e	√		
x28			
43(2)	√	CM consults	
49*	√	√	
49	√	√	
x51			
x55			
54(2)*	√	√	
54(2)	√	√	
56(2)*	√		
56(2)	√		
57(1)*	√		
57(1)	√		
57(2)*	√		
57(2)	√		

An 'x' before the Article means that there are no requirements for consultation.

EUROPEAN (ECONOMIC) COMMUNITY

ARTICLE	EP	ECOSOC	OTHER
x59			
63(2)	√	√	
x69			CM consults MC
x70(1)			
x73c(2)			
73f			EMI: MC contributes to CO
75(1)*	√	√	
75(1)	√	√	
75(3)	√	√	
79(3)		√	
84(2)*	√	√	
84(2)	√	√	
87(1)	√		
94	√		
99	√	√	
100[843]	√	√	
100a(1)*	√	√	
100a(1)	√	√	
100b(1)*	√	√	
100b(1)	√	√	
100c(1)	√		CCJHA contributes to CO
x100c(2)			CCJHA contributes to CO
100c(3)	√		CCJHA contributes to CO
x101			

843. *See* fn. 783.

An 'x' before the Article means that there are no requirements for consultation.

EUROPEAN (ECONOMIC) COMMUNITY

ARTICLE	EP	ECOSOC	OTHER
x103(2)*			
x103(3)*			
103(5)	√		MC contributes to CO
x103a(1)			MC contributes to CO
104a(2)	√		MC contributes to CO
104b(2)	√		MC contributes to CO
104c(14)	√		EMI:[844] MC contributes to CO
106(5)	Assent		EMI
106(6)	√		EMI
x112(1)			
x113(2),(4)			
118a(2)	√	√	
125	√	√	
126(4)	√	√	COR
126a*	√	√	
126b*	√	√	
127*	√	√	
127(4)	√	√	
128*		√	
128(5)	√		COR
129(4)	√	√	COR
129a(2)	√	√	
129d	√	√	COR
130(3)	√	√	
130b	√	√	COR

844. The EMI need not be consulted where the Protocol is being applied.

An 'x' before the Article means that there are no requirements for consultation.

EUROPEAN (ECONOMIC) COMMUNITY

ARTICLE	EP	ECOSOC	OTHER
130d*	√	√	
130d	√ + Assent	√	COR
130e*	√	√[845]	
130e	√	√[846]	COR[847]
130i(1)	√	√	
130i(4)	√	√	
130o	√	√	
130q(1)*	√	√	
130q(2)*	√	√	
130s*	√	√	
130s(1)	√	√	
130s(2)	√	√	
130s(3)	√	√	
x138(3)	Assent		
145	√		
201	√		
209a	√		CA
235	√		
SA, 2(2)	√	√	
SA, 2(3)	√	√	
xSA, 4(2)			

EUROPEAN COAL AND STEEL COMMUNITY

ARTICLE	EP	ECOSOC	OTHER
x21(3)	Assent		
x58(3)			CM consults CC[848]

845. There is no consultation of ECOSOC in connection with the EAGGF.
846. There is no consultation of ECOSOC in connection with the EAGGF.
847. Consultation of COR is only required in connection with the ERDF.
848. *See* fn. 820.

An 'x' before the Article means that there are no requirements for consultation.

EUROPEAN (ECONOMIC) COMMUNITY

ARTICLE	EP	ECOSOC	OTHER
59(2)			CM
x72			
78h(a)	√		CA

EUROPEAN ATOMIC ENERGY COMMUNITY

ARTICLE	EP	ECOSOC	OTHER
x24(1)			
31	√	CM consults	CM consults STC
x41		CM consults	
x42			
x54			
x69			
76	√		
85	√		
90	√		
x92			
96	√	CM consults	
x108(3)	Assent		
183a	√		CA
203	√		

TREATY ON EUROPEAN UNION

ARTICLE	EP	ECOSOC	OTHER
K.3(2)	√		